Illegal I...

This book updates the progress into adulthood of the cohort of fourteen-year-olds who were recruited and tracked until they were eighteen years old. *Illegal Leisure* (1998) described their adolescent journeys and lifestyles, focusing on their early regular drinking and extensive 'recreational' drug use. This new edition revisits these original chapters, providing commentaries around them to discuss current implications of the original publication, plus documenting and discussing the group at twenty-two and twenty-seven years of age.

Illegal Leisure Revisited positions the journeys of these twenty-somethings against the ever-changing backdrop of a consumption-oriented leisure society, the rapid expansion of the British night-time economy and the place of substance use in contemporary social worlds. It presents to the reader the ways in which these young people have moved into the world of work, long-term relationships and parenthood, and the resulting changes in the function and frequency of their drinking and drug-use patterns. Amid dire public health warnings about their favourite intoxicants, and with the growing criminalisation of a widening array of recreational drugs, the book revisits these young people as they continue as archetypal citizens in a risk society. The book is ideal reading for researchers and undergraduate students from a variety of fields, such as developmental and social psychology, sociology, criminology, cultural and health studies. Professionals working in criminal justice, health promotion, drugs education, harm reduction and treatment will also find this book an invaluable resource.

Judith Aldridge is Senior Lecturer in the School of Law at the University of Manchester. Her research spans aspects of drug use and dealing, including drug dealing within street gangs, and the sales of both illegal and legal psychostimulants.

Fiona Measham is Senior Lecturer in Criminology at Lancaster University. Her research focuses on drug trends, club drugs and music scenes; licensed leisure and the night time economy; participation in social media; and UK policy developments. She is a member of the Advisory Council on the Misuse of Drugs and the Independent Scientific Committee on Drugs.

Lisa Williams is Lecturer in Criminology at the Centre for Criminology and Criminal Justice, University of Manchester. For over a decade, she has researched both recreational and dependent drug use with a focus upon drug use across the life course.

Adolescence and Society
Series editor: John C. Coleman
Department of Education, University of Oxford

This series has now been running for over 20 years, and during this time has published some of the key texts in the field of adolescent studies. The series has covered a very wide range of subjects, almost all of them being of central concern to students, researchers and practitioners. A mark of the success of the series is that a number of books have gone to second and third editions, illustrating the popularity and reputation of the series.

The primary aim of the series is to make accessible to the widest possible readership important and topical evidence relating to adolescent development. Much of this material is published in relatively inaccessible professional journals, and the objective of the books in this series has been to summarise, review and place in context current work in the field, so as to interest and engage both an undergraduate and a professional audience.

The intention of the authors has always been to raise the profile of adolescent studies among professionals and in institutions of higher education. By publishing relatively short, readable books on topics of current interest to do with youth and society, the series makes people more aware of the relevance of the subject of adolescence to a wide range of social concerns.

The books do not put forward any one theoretical viewpoint. The authors outline the most prominent theories in the field and include a balanced and critical assessment of each of these. Whilst some of the books may have a clinical or applied slant, the majority concentrate on normal development.

The readership rests primarily in two major areas: the undergraduate market, particularly in the fields of psychology, sociology and education; and the professional training market, with particular emphasis on social work, clinical and educational psychology, counselling, youth work, nursing and teacher training.

Illegal Leisure Revisited

Changing patterns of alcohol
and drug use in adolescents
and young adults

**Judith Aldridge, Fiona Measham
and Lisa Williams**

Routledge
Taylor & Francis Group

LONDON AND NEW YORK

First published 2011 by Routledge
27 Church Road, Hove, East Sussex BN3 2FA

Simultaneously published in the USA and Canada
by Routledge
270 Madison Avenue, New York, NY, 10016

*Routledge is an imprint of the Taylor & Francis Group, an Informa
business*

© 2011 Psychology Press

Typeset in Times by
RefineCatch Limited, Bungay, Suffolk
Printed and bound in Great Britain by
TJ International Ltd, Padstow, Cornwall
Cover photo courtesy of Lisa Williams
Cover design by Hybert Design

This publication has been produced with paper manufactured to strict
environmental standards and with pulp derived from sustainable
forests.

British Library Cataloguing in Publication Data
A catalogue record for this book is available from the British Library

Library of Congress Cataloging in Publication Data
Illegal leisure revisited : changing patterns of alcohol and drug
use in adolescents and young adults / Judith Aldridge . . . [et al.].
  p. cm.
  Includes bibliographical references and index.
  ISBN 978–0–415–49552–3 (hbk.)—ISBN 978–0–415–49553–0 (soft cover)
  1. Youth—Drug use—Great Britain—Longitudinal studies.
  2. Youth—Alcohol use—Great Britain—Longitudinal studies.
  3. Drug abuse—Great Britain.   4. Drinking of alcoholic beverages—
  Great Britain.   5. Risk-taking (Psychology) in adolescence—Great
  Britain.   I. Aldridge, Judith, 1963–
    HV5824.Y68I45 2011
    362.29′12008350941—dc22

                                                          2010034629

ISBN: 978–0–415–49552–3 (hbk)
ISBN: 978–0–415–49553–0 (pbk)

Contents

Acknowledgements

So many people have helped and supported us since this project began in 1991. Most of all we must thank the over one thousand people who participated in this research, starting when they were 14 years old and into their adulthood. We are grateful to the schools that worked with us in the first four years of the research. The Alcohol Education and Research Council funded the first three years of the research, and the Economic and Social Research Council and the Home Office funded the subsequent research projects that allowed us to follow our cohort across the transitions of their lives. Special thanks to: Peter Ainsworth, Alex Aldridge, Bees Beesley, Kevin Brain, Jon Breeze, Chris Carey, Gemma Cox, Sarah Curruthers, Roy Egginton, Nicola Elson, Forrest Frankovitch, Bernard Gallagher, Kathleen Kendall, Dominic MacKenzie, Maria Measham, Ange McGibbon, Russell Newcombe, Anne Pearcey, Robert Ralphs, Craig Ruckledge, Eddie Scouller, Christine Shea, Jon Shorrock, Arden Smelser, Julie Trickey, Paul Wilding and Ruby Williams.

The NWELS team: Howard Parker, Russell Newcombe and Fiona Measham began the NWELS project in 1991. Russell left the team in 1992 and Judith Aldridge joined in 1993, working with Howard and Fiona on the study to 1997. In 1999 Fiona left the team and Lisa Williams joined it. Howard retired from academic life in 2003 to work in the addictions field. Lisa's PhD research (supervised by Judith) continued with the cohort through to 2008. In writing *Illegal Leisure Revisited*, Judith, Fiona and Lisa have had equal input. The authors are listed in alphabetical order.

We reserve special thanks to Howard Parker for his leading role over the many years of this research, and in particular for his contributions to and critique of the arguments put forward in this volume.

Tables and Figures

Tables

Figures

Introduction

The genuinely dramatic increases in drug trying and drug use amongst ordinary, conventional young people during the 1990s required new conceptual and theoretical approaches to explanation. Drug use prior to this was satisfactorily explained using sub-cultural theories, structural macro theories focusing on inequality and poverty, and positivist psychological theories emphasising individual developmental deficits and thus vulnerabilities to deviant behaviour including substance use. Thus 'speeding' mods and 'tripping' hippies during the 1970s were explained as sub-cultural, and thus atypical. Whilst the emergence of heroin-using populations in the social exclusion zones of England and Scotland from the 1980s required an explanatory mix of these three main theoretical perspectives, the emergence of widespread drug use in the normative youth population found the predominant social science theories wanting.

However, what now seems unremarkable – that many young Britons across all socio-economic groupings try and use substances like cannabis, ecstasy and cocaine as part of their conventional lifestyles – was wholly remarkable in the early 1990s. For social scientists studying British youth culture, a new explanatory challenge was set. *Illegal Leisure*, first published in 1998 (Parker *et al.*, 1998a), was the culmination of seven years of work trying to describe and explain this social transformation by tracking the role of alcohol and drugs in the changing life circumstances of a cohort of conventional young people in England from adolescence to adulthood.

Illegal Leisure Revisited brings the story up to date in three ways. Firstly it reports on how the cohort has negotiated transitions to adulthood and the changing role of drug and alcohol use therein. Secondly it brings the alcohol and drug consumption trends of youth and young adults in Britain up to date and summarises the salient political, policy and governmental responses across the last two decades. Thirdly it re-assesses the debate regarding the normalisation of 'sensible' recreational drug use. Most of the chapters from the first edition of *Illegal Leisure* have been reprinted here in full. Following on from these original chapters, we provide a section which updates the study since *Illegal Leisure* was first published.

Chapter 1, however, has been completely re-written. It offers a brief social history of the drug trying and use patterns of English youth from the 1990s to the end of the 2000s. The picture is of constant evolution as the popularity of different substances rises and falls. This sets the scene for summarising how public and media frenzies about young people's drug and alcohol use affect governmental responses in terms of legislation, strategies and specific programmes of intervention. The complex relationship between evidence-based policy and politicised responses is highlighted.

Chapter 2 describes the methods involved in managing a longitudinal cohort study. It updates the original chapter based on the first five years' data collection, by describing the recapture of some of the cohort at two points, when they were about 22 years and 27 years old, noting in particular the impact of changing information technology on research techniques. It discusses the impact of cohort attrition.

Chapter 3 provides an updated overview of the role of alcohol in the lives of younger Britons. Alcohol – now, as in the 1990s – remains the UK's favourite drug. This chapter charts the continuing ebbs and flows of drinking patterns, including binge drinking, both nationally and amongst the *Illegal Leisure* cohort.

Chapter 4 describes the patterns of drug trying, drug use and drug 'experiences' of the cohort across the 1990s. However, it provides an update based on the two recaptures of some of the cohort across their twenties showing how their drug consumption patterns have evolved.

Chapter 5 reaps the benefits of a longitudinal study by highlighting the drug pathways different members of the cohort have taken across their adolescence and with updates as they become adults nearing the age of 30, obliged to review their substance use and thus continue to reconsider whether to abstain from or use drugs, which ones and how often.

Chapter 6 builds on the original descriptive analyses of the cohort's adolescent drug journeys. It utilises a qualitative approach based on repeat in-depth interviews with a sub-sample of the original cohort and thus includes extensive quotations as the subjects describe their first drug use and how they felt about initial drug trying. What persuaded them to try certain drugs and not others? How did they make cost-benefit assessments in reaching their conclusions about drug taking and why did these assessments change through time? This chapter is updated using an innovative qualitative approach as our participants describe their ongoing assessments, as 20 year olds, faced with new priorities, relationships and responsibilities as employees, partners and parents.

Chapter 7 has been updated to both capture the original conclusions about the normalisation of recreational drug use and bring the debate up to date. The normalisation thesis, as a barometer of change around drug trying, cultural attitudes and changing drugs consumption trends, is re-assessed in light of the changes we have documented amongst this generation of young adults.

1 History lessons

Drug use trends amongst young Britons 1980–2010

Introduction

Illicit and illegal drug taking by young Britons began to rise at the end of the 1980s and continued to do so until the millennium. In retrospect, we now know that the 'children of the nineties', of whom the *Illegal Leisure* cohort were a part, became the most drug-involved generation of the twentieth century. Our research spanned much of the 'decade of dance' and included therefore the cultural phenomenon of dance music and clubbing that emerged alongside ecstasy. It was the various publications reporting the results of the North West England Longitudinal Study – including the first edition of *Illegal Leisure* (Parker *et al.*, 1998a) – that were pioneering in recording and explaining the unprecedented level of drug taking amongst these teenagers during the 1990s.

In 1998 when the first edition of *Illegal Leisure* was published, we did not have the luxury of good, nationally representative and annually collected data on drug use amongst young people. Prior to this time, the available evidence was patchy, or not of the same quality that we find today, making it more difficult to identify the trends in drug taking amongst young people that is our concern in the first part of this chapter.

From the late 1990s onwards, annual survey programmes that included self-reported drug taking began to appear, and two of these have become reliable trend indicators for adolescents and young adults: (1) the Smoking, Drinking and Drug Use (SDD) series of schools surveys on 11–15 year olds in England;[1] and (2) the Home Office's

---

1 These surveys are carried out for the NHS Information Centre by the National Centre for Social Research and the National Foundation for Educational Research in the UK.

British Crime Survey (BCS), which picks up at age 16.[2] As concerns
grew about the widespread use of drugs such as cannabis, amphetamines and LSD amongst mid 1990s young people, surveys like these
grew in size and detail, allowing an increasingly detailed picture to be
drawn. But even these surveys are not perfect. They exclude or under-
represent the young people most likely to be drug-involved (such as
those in young offender institutions, excluded from school or not living
in private households) and their results must be interpreted with this
limitation in mind.[3] Nevertheless, they allow us to chart the national
trends in adolescent and young adult drug taking that have occurred
since the publication of the first edition of *Illegal Leisure.*

The illicit drugs use 'peak' of the 1990s

Prior to the 1990s, government surveys on drug taking of the kind we
described above were the exception rather than the rule, and most of the
evidence we have from this period came from market research and
media polls. Newcombe (1995), in an exhaustive review of this evidence,
concluded that *lifetime prevalence*[4] of illicit drug taking amongst young
adults (typically 16–24 years) rose steadily from less than 5 per cent in
the 1960s, to around 10 per cent in the 1970s, to 15–20 per cent in the
1980s. This approximate doubling each decade documents a slow but
steady rise in drug taking by young people over the period. From the
1990s, however, drug taking began to rise much more dramatically.
Between 1990 and 1995, the proportion of young people disclosing
drug trying doubled from roughly one quarter to nearly one half of mid

2   The British Crime Survey became an annual survey from 2000. From January 2009 the
    coverage of the BCS was extended to include household members between the ages of
    11 and 15.
3   Even the capacity for these surveys accurately to identify changes is now being ques-
    tioned. See Aldridge (2008) for a discussion of some of the reasons comparability of
    these surveys over time may be declining.
4   The only statistic consistently available in research published prior to 2000 was the
    lifetime prevalence measure of drug taking. *Past year prevalence* is the preferred stat-
    istic for analysing trends because it captures use that occurs in each year; lifetime
    prevalence figures include those not taking a drug in the year prior to the survey, thus
    reducing their utility for examining year-on-year changes. *Past month prevalence* is
    often used as a simple proxy for current or regular drug use. However, it should be
    noted that past month use remains a particularly imprecise proxy for younger popula-
    tions, who may be less likely to have moved into a settled pattern of use (see Aldridge
    et al., 1999), and where up to a quarter of adolescent past month users are not regular
    users (Parker *et al.*, 1998a).

adolescents (Miller and Plant, 1996; Mott and Mirrlees-Black, 1995; Ramsay and Percy, 1996; Ramsay and Spiller, 1997; Roberts *et al.*, 1997). These sharply rising rates of youthful drug taking in Britain during the early 1990s have also been documented in other developed countries (see Bauman and Phongsavan, 1999).

The second half of the 1990s began with a small but temporary drop in drug taking (Balding, 2000; Plant and Miller, 2000). The SDD surveys captured this brief downward trend in lifetime drug use rates amongst 11–15 year olds and then noted a late decade upward trend, as did the British Crime Survey, where around half of 16–24 year olds had disclosed at least some drug use in their lifetimes by the end of the decade (Ramsay *et al.*, 2001). Overall, therefore, it appears that the 1990s were characterised by an initially steep rise that was interrupted briefly in the second half of the decade, with rates returning to their peak levels before the start of the millennium.

These historically high rates of drug trying reflected the widespread availability of many illegal substances, with increasing numbers of young people reporting having been in situations where drugs were available. Amongst those disclosing drug use, surveys during this period noted a propensity to try several substances, most often cannabis (herbal and resin) followed by amphetamines, 'poppers' and ecstasy, with LSD more often reported early in the decade and cocaine at its end (Ramsay and Percy, 1996; Ramsay *et al.*, 2001). Although we recognise the limitations of the term, the youthful drug taking observed during the 1990s in the main could be characterised as predominantly 'recreational'; that is, involving mostly weekend use of drugs in (recreational) social settings and at (recreational) leisure times. We do not suggest that 'recreational' use is exclusively unproblematic however (see Aldridge, 2008), and use the term throughout this book with care, to distinguish the use of the vast majority of adolescents and young adults from the daily, dependent and chaotic heroin and crack consumption usually characterised as 'problem drug use'.

An unprecedented feature of recreational drug taking that occurred across the 1990s was the involvement of substantial proportions of groups traditionally assumed to be 'protected' from drug taking: girls and young women, and people from a range of higher income and professional backgrounds and aspirations. Surveys of university students, particularly medical students (e.g. Newbury-Birch *et al.*, 2000), for example, confirm these diverse demographics.

Post 2000 drug use trends

The key feature of post millennium trends in youthful drug taking is gradual overall decline. As depicted in Figure 1.1, we can see that the decrease in the prevalence of past year drug taking occurs for both younger adolescents (aged 11–15) and older adolescents and young adults (aged 16–24). In 2001, 20.4 per cent of 11–15 year olds reported the past year use of a drug, compared to 15.0 per cent in 2008. Amongst the older group, we see a more pronounced drop: from 30.0 per cent in 2001/2 to 22.6 per cent in 2008/9. Similar reductions in use also occurred for more recent use, and for frequent use in older adolescents and young adults (Hoare, 2009). It appears therefore that it is the range of using styles amongst young people that is declining: one-off trying through to regular and frequent use.

This clear downward trend in drug use amongst young people seems compelling. Have the teenagers of the 1990s 'aged out' of a period of excess and settled down, to be replaced by a much more moderate generation of adolescent psychoactive consumers? This is probably at least part of the story. However, these general downward trends may

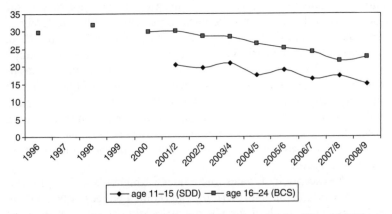

Figure 1.1 Past year prevalence (%) of 'any drug' use for 11–15 and 16–24 year olds: trends over time*

Sources: Smoking, Drinking and Drug Use Schools Surveys (Jotangia and Thompson, 2009); British Crime Survey (Hoare, 2009)

Note:
* The figure depicts connected data points where data are comparable. Although the SDD surveys were conducted in 1998, 1999 and 2000, the survey instrument used a different questionnaire format during these years resulting in past year prevalence figures of 11 per cent, 12 per cent and 14 per cent, respectively, suggesting a considerable lack of comparability with data collected from 2001 onwards.

also obscure some important evidence that sheds a somewhat different light on the close of the 'noughties'.

The first question we might ask is this: if drug taking has been declining since the new millennium, how low did it really go? The most recent data we have for the 16–24 age group (BCS 2008/9) finds levels of drug taking not very far from their earlier millennium peak, and in reality, at almost the level surveys from the early 1990s were beginning to document.[5] For example, past year use of a drug was 23 per cent[6] in 1994 (Ramsay and Percy, 1996) – almost identical to the level in 2008/9 of 22.6 per cent. This similarity between levels of use in the late noughties and in the early 1990s is also apparent for younger adolescents. For example, in 2007, 33 per cent of 14 year olds indicated having ever tried a drug in the past year (Jotangia and Thompson, 2009), a figure very near to the one we found for our *Illegal Leisure* cohort at the age of 14 (36 per cent) in 1991. It is worth noting that when we released these early 1990s findings, the figures were regarded as unprecedented, and met with disbelief coupled with scepticism that any research that included Manchester,[7] the 'rave capital of Great Britain' (Coffield and Goften, 1994: 5) could be representative of the rest of the country.

In other words, in spite of a near decade long decline in drug taking amongst young people, their rates of drug use remain not so very far from historically high levels. Perhaps more importantly, the levels of drug taking today sit at roughly the same as we found for our *Illegal Leisure* cohort in the early 1990s. In contrast to the view that today's generation of young people is disinclined to 'illegal leisure', it seems they instead share much in common with adolescents of the 1990s. We will return in the concluding chapter to the question of whether the 1990s were indeed 'special' in relation to the advent of normalisation, or whether – taking in a much broader historical perspective across the century – the 1990s represented no more than a periodic blip in always fluctuating trends.

With the exception of Wales where rates are higher, a similar profile is found in Scotland and Northern Ireland (United Kingdom Focal Point on Drugs, 2008). Each of the UK countries still sits amongst the most

---

5   Data from all administrations of the BCS are not comparable in relation to sampling strategy. Comparisons pre-2001/2 should be seen as indicative only.

6   These figures are not directly comparable: the 1994 figures aggregated by the BCS were for 16–29 year olds; the 2008/9 figures were for 16–24 year olds.

7   Although our research included a borough situated in Greater Manchester, we did not survey schools within the metropolitan borough of Manchester, but instead in a nearby borough, allowing us to include a range of socio-economic catchment areas.

drug-involved populations in the European Union and overall have the highest rates in North West Europe. For 15–16 year olds, the European Schools Survey Project, which compares substance use rates across 29 countries, continues to situate the UK in the 'Top 5' for lifetime prevalence particularly for cannabis and cocaine (EMCDDA, 2009).

The obvious counter to this observation is that the trend remains downward, and so long as this trajectory continues, young people's drug taking should soon fall below levels documented amongst their early 1990s counterparts. And perhaps this will happen. However, there are some indications (albeit early ones) to suggest that drug taking may be about to plateau, possibly even increase.

As can be observed in Figure 1.1 above, the solid downward trajectory in past year drug taking amongst 16–24 year olds has been interrupted in 2008/9, for the first time in ten years, by taking a small upward turn from 21.5 per cent to 22.6 per cent. Turning to Table 1.1 below, we can see the source of this upturn.

The increases from 2007/8 to 2008/9 in drug taking that are proportionately largest are for ketamine (from 0.1 per cent to 1.9 per cent) and cocaine powder (5.1 per cent to 6.6 per cent), as well as for any Class A drug (from 6.9 per cent to 8.1 per cent). All of these increases are statistically significant.

These small increases are not apparent across the whole of the 11–15-year-old group (Figure 1.1 and Table 1.1), but when only the oldest respondents (the 15 year olds) in this group are separated out,[8] stable or increased use for some drugs is found between 2007 and 2008. These increases occurred particularly for ketamine, the use of which doubled over the year (0.8 per cent to 1.6 per cent); with small rises for opiates (0.7 per cent to 1.3 per cent) and tranquillisers (0.6 per cent to 0.9 per cent); and stable levels of use reported for stimulants like cocaine, ecstasy and amphetamines (Jotangia and Thompson, 2009). Combined with the less pronounced rate of decline in drug taking amongst the younger adolescents over the new millennium (put another way, past year use dropped by 30 per cent amongst 16–24 year olds but only by 20 per cent amongst 11–15 year olds), these findings are indicative of the possibility that the steady decline in youthful drug taking may be coming to an end.

Amongst all young people cannabis remains dominant in drug-taking repertoires. For young adults (see Table 1.1), we find past year use of cannabis by just over one in four at the start of the decade, falling

8   The figures for 15 year olds alone are not included in the table.

Table 1.1 Past year prevalence (%) of drug taking amongst 16–24 year olds for 'any drug' and selected drugs, 2000–2008/9

	2000	2001/2	2002/3	2003/4	2004/5	2005/6	2006/7	2007/8	2008/9
Any drug	29.9	30.0	28.5	28.3	26.5	25.2	24.1	21.5	22.6
Cannabis	27.0	27.3	26.2	25.3	23.6	21.4	20.9	18.0	18.7
Cocaine powder	5.2	5.1	5.1	5.2	5.1	5.9	6.0	5.1	6.6
Ecstasy	5.6	6.8	5.8	5.5	4.9	4.3	4.8	3.9	4.4
Poppers	3.9	3.8	4.4	4.3	3.6	3.9	4.2	4.3	4.4
Amphetamines	6.2	5.0	3.8	4.0	3.2	3.3	3.5	2.4	2.6
LSD	2.5	1.2	0.9	0.9	0.5	0.9	0.8	0.7	0.8
Ketamine	–	–	–	–	–	–	0.8	0.9	1.9

Source: British Crime Survey; Hoare, 2009

to just under one in five near its close. Similarly, for younger adolescents (see Table 1.2), past year use of cannabis fell from roughly 20 per cent in 2001 to 15 per cent in 2008. This decline in cannabis use appears to be a Europe-wide phenomenon (EMCDDA, 2009). However, there are other indications that a continued orientation toward psychoactive experimentation remains evident across the noughties.

Looking at the 16–24 year olds captured by the BCS surveys (Table 1.1), we can see that, whilst use of drugs aside from cannabis takes place amongst a smaller subset, we find some interesting changes over the period in the use of these stimulant and psychostimulant drugs. Firstly, use of cannabis early in the decade represented just over 90 per cent of all substance use; but by the end of the decade, this proportion had slipped to 83 per cent. This suggests that although consumption of psychoactive substances has dropped overall, a greater proportion of these consumers are selecting from a broader repertoire of drugs aside from or in addition to cannabis. This sustained orientation toward psychoactive experimentation and polydrug use amongst the minority is evident in the stability of past year use of cocaine powder over the period, which by 2008/9 actually sits at an all-time high of 6.6 per cent – the second most popular drug in the survey. In contrast, the popularity of amphetamines and LSD have both declined substantially. Perhaps most indicative of all, past year use of ketamine doubled from 2006/7/8 levels to near 2 per cent in 2008/9, and shows sustained and then rising past year use even amongst 11–15 year olds, with 1.6 per cent of 15 year olds reporting past year use in 2008 (Jotangia and Thompson, 2009).

When we started collecting data in the early 1990s, even the most enthusiastic young drug users we encountered were scathing about the taking of cocaine – its use was considered to be beyond the pale;

Table 1.2 Past year prevalence (%) of drug taking amongst 11–15 year olds for 'any drug' and selected drugs, 2001–2008

	2001	2002	2003	2004	2005	2006	2007	2008
Any drug	20.4	19.7	21.0	17.6	19.1	16.5	17.3	15.0
Cannabis	13.4	13.2	13.3	11.3	11.7	10.1	9.4	9.0
Solvents	7.1	6.3	7.6	5.6	6.7	5.1	6.2	5.0
Poppers	3.4	4.3	4.0	3.4	3.9	4.2	4.9	2.9
Cocaine powder	1.2	1.3	1.3	1.4	1.9	1.6	1.8	1.7
Ecstasy	1.6	1.5	1.4	1.4	1.5	1.6	1.3	1.3
Amphetamines	1.1	1.2	1.2	1.3	1.2	1.2	1.0	0.9
Ketamine	–	–	–	–	0.4	0.5	0.4	0.7

Source: Smoking, Drinking and Drug Use Schools Survey; Jotangia and Thompson, 2009

hand-in-hand with heroin. In the first edition of *Illegal Leisure*, we concluded that 'hard drugs had no place in the normalisation thesis' (Parker *et al.*, 1998a: 149). What this analysis shows is how quickly perceptions about drugs can change. Amongst older adolescents and young adults (including, as we shall see in coming chapters, our cohort), cocaine emerged to become the second most popular drug behind cannabis, having even overtaken ecstasy in popularity. It seems likely that the popularity of cocaine may have peaked: 2009/10 BCS figures suggest that 2.4 per cent of adults have taken cocaine in the past year, a significant fall from 3.0 per cent in 2008/9, after having risen the year before (Hoare and Moon, 2010). Nevertheless, use of cocaine in the UK has been the highest in Europe (EMCDDA, 2009). Ketamine, a drug with widely held negative meanings amongst non-users (Moore and Measham, 2008), is increasing in popularity even amongst 15 year olds, even though levels of use remain low overall. LSD, in contrast, has now all but disappeared from the league tables of use, although early in the 1990s, this class 'A' drug was a mainstay of early adolescent experimentation.

The 1990s and 2000s have been decades of change where youthful drug use is concerned, with fluctuating levels of overall use and constantly changing popularity of individual drugs. We cannot imagine that the current configuration of the drug league tables amongst British youth will remain unchanged for very long given the pace of change in the last few decades. The most recent assessment of street drug trends by DrugScope suggests that the declining quality of illegal drugs in the UK will change patterns of use (DrugScope, 2009). The purity of street cocaine powder, for example, has more than halved over the past seven years,[9] and coupled with its decreasing availability, it is possible that annual surveys will in due course begin to chart a decline in its use. And although large-scale surveys like those reported here are only now including some of the newer 'legal highs' in their questioning, we are likely to see an increase in the popularity of a range of new synthetic drugs manufactured and sold in an attempt to evade regulatory frameworks. This is illustrated by the recent emergence of substituted cathinones such as mephedrone which were legally available to purchase on the internet and in specialist high street shops (Measham *et al.*, 2010) until banned in April 2010. An online survey conducted by the dance music magazine *Mixmag* found that before the ban mephedrone,

---

9   The average purity of police seizures has plummeted from 64 per cent to an all-time low of 22 per cent in the first quarter of 2009 (Hand and Rishiraj, 2009).

which they describe as having 'risen from nowhere', was the fourth most popular drug in their survey, with 34 per cent of more than 2,000 self-selecting respondents having taken it in the past month (Mixmag, 2010: 46). These so-called 'legal highs' – such as first generation mephedrone and second generation naphyrone (Brandt *et al.*, 2010a, 2010b) – may have a special appeal both for underage adolescents who can easily acquire them in a non-regulatory environment without age or other sales restrictions, and for the prolific and pharmacologically inquisitive young adult weekend polydrug users (Measham and Moore, 2009).

A switch to alcohol use

European comparative surveys also identify the very high rates of alcohol consumption amongst British youth compared with many other EU countries, although again downward trends and fluctuations in alcohol consumption must be tailored into our analysis. The UK has high levels of alcohol consumption, for both the adult population and also for young people. The best internationally comparable data for teenage alcohol consumption in the UK is provided by four waves of the European School Survey Project on Alcohol and Other Drugs, (hereafter ESPAD). Secondary school surveys were conducted, using randomly selected classes from a nationally representative sample, at four yearly intervals with four data collections published to date, in 1995, 1999, 2003 and 2007. The four surveys suggest that frequent drinking, binge drinking and drunkenness were more common amongst teenagers in the UK, as well as some other northern European countries such as Ireland, Belgium, Denmark and the Netherlands, compared with southern European countries. The UK scores highly on both subjective self-assessed *drunkenness* measures (such as self-reported lifetime, past year and past month drunkenness) and unit-based *heavy episodic* drinking measures,[10] as well as also reporting both more positive attitudes and less negative attitudes to alcohol (Hibell *et al.*, 2009). However, although the ESPAD surveys provide evidence that British teenage experiences of frequent drinking, heavy drinking and drunkenness remain amongst the highest in Europe, there is evidence of stability and decline in the most recently published survey. For example, self-reported lifetime and past month drunkenness, frequent drinking and

---

10   *Heavy episodic drinking* is defined as having had five or more drinks on one occasion, with a standard drink measured as 'a glass of wine (15 cl) or bottle or can of beer (50 cl), a shot glass of spirits (5 cl) or a mixed drink' (Hibell *et al.*, 2009: 406).

heavy episodic drinking remained stable or declined moderately in the 2000s. Beer drinking declined in the 2000s, but teenage girls' spirits and alcopops[11] consumption increased in the UK during the 1990s, however, suggesting that changing trends in consumption are affected by price, availability, advertising and fashion (see also Anderson *et al.*, 2009; Barnard and Forsyth, 1998).

In Chapter 3 the increases in alcohol consumption by young drinkers over this same period are discussed in detail. Although alcohol has always been British youth's (and indeed adults') favourite drug, from the early 1990s a range of factors contributed to adolescent weekly drinking doubling in quantity across the 1990s and to increased consumption by young adult women as well as young men into the new millennium. Whilst there is growing evidence that young adult consumption is decreasing in the 2000s for the generation behind our *Illegal Leisure* cohort (Measham and Østergaard, 2009), it is the men and women in their twenties and thirties who appear to be taking these higher consumption levels into middle age. Overall, the increased use of alcohol as well as illegal drugs across the two decades covered by this longitudinal study suggests that a process of (psychoactive) substance 'switching' rather than an overall reduction in substance use is occurring.

The *Illegal Leisure* cohort reached 18 and were legally able to buy alcohol in 1995, a period noted for the emergence of new alcoholic beverages such as alcopops, high strength bottled beers and ciders; a shifting emphasis towards purposeful or 'determined drunkenness' by young adult drinkers (Measham, 2004a); and the expansion of alcohol-oriented night life in towns and cities across the UK (Hadfield and Measham, 2009; Hobbs *et al.*, 2003). The late 1990s saw the emergence of '24 hour party cities' such as Manchester, Liverpool and Leeds, with urban regeneration centred on the night-time economy. A growing range of leisure venues catered for young adults, including café bars with late licences, 'pubco' national bar and nightclub chains and a shift from outdoor and unlicensed raves to commercially successful, global

---

11 Whilst the term alcopops originally was used as shorthand for Australian alcoholic lemonades such as Hooch and Two Dogs launched in the UK in 1995, the term is now used by alcohol researchers including the ESPAD study (Hibell *et al.*, 2004), as well as public sector and non-governmental organisations (eg. Alcohol Concern, 2001; Goddard, 2007), to denote a wide range of flavoured alcoholic beverages (FABs), ready-to-drink spirit mixers (RTDs) and other new alcoholic beverages which have been launched over the last 15 years. The term has been used in national statistical surveys in the UK since 1996.

branded 'superclubs' such as Sankeys in Manchester, Cream in Liverpool and Gatecrasher in Sheffield, frequented by some of our respondents (Measham *et al.*, 2001; Moore, 2010; Shapiro, 1999).

Such is the economic importance of the British night-time economy that the government's national alcohol strategy boasts that 'the alcohol leisure industry has supported a revival of city centres across England and Wales' (HM Government, 2007: 30). However, alongside a drinks industry now worth approximately £30 billion to the UK economy, with nearly one million associated jobs, the negative costs of such development have been nearly as great, with alcohol-related accident and injury, crime and disorder, violence and absenteeism from work estimated to total £20 billion (Newton and Hirschfield, 2009). The response to growing concerns expressed by police and criminal justice agencies, the press, politicians and alcohol researchers, was to fly in the face of united opposition and pass the Licensing Act 2003, implemented in November 2005. Its aim was to promote a more leisurely Mediterranean-style drinking culture rather than our prevailing British 'binge and brawl' drinking culture, by allowing increased trading hours, in the hope of staggering pub closing times and reducing tensions at disorder 'hotspots'. Critics, including the police, said it would make the problem worse, not better. Although it has not resulted in the total chaos predicted by critics, it also has not significantly decreased alcohol-related crime and disorder as claimed by the government. Instead, evaluations (e.g. Hough and Hunter, 2008; Hough *et al.*, 2008; Humphreys and Eisner, 2010) suggest that extended licences resulted in a temporal extension of disorder throughout the night and also a geographical displacement from city centres to suburbs, whilst consolidating alcohol at the heart of the urban regeneration project. Thus throughout the period of this study, alcohol has been and remains central to the British night-time economy and to British leisure.

Political and policy responses to evolving drug and alcohol consumption

Introduction

Governing a democratic society with immense public concerns about very high rates of youthful drug use and drinking inevitably involves trying to develop policies and programmes that 'work' whilst simultaneously reassuring the media and voters that their request for tough measures is embraced. Consequently, policy measures over the past 30 years often appear compromised and contradictory, without reference to existing evidence within which to base policy and practice. This section provides a summary of the main strategic responses to young people's alcohol and drug use but set on a political backcloth of media frenzies and public concern which influence the shape and content of consecutive governments' flagship policies.

Heroin, crack and crime

Although *Illegal Leisure* is primarily about 'recreational' drug use within conventional younger populations in England, political and policy responses to this population across the 1990s and to the present cannot be understood without being set against the backcloth of heroin use.

During the 1980s when heroin first arrived in the English and Scottish regional cities, there was no national drug strategy, no community drug treatment teams, no needle exchanges and no local infrastructure to plan, commission and deliver drug services. These now obligatory drug strategies and action plans only developed on the back of the 1980s heroin epidemic.

Heroin use spread rapidly during the 1980s. First located in inner cities and deprived urban estates, it spread outwards over a 15-year period until almost all British cities and towns, including some isolated 'hotspots' in Northern Ireland, hosted a small population of heroin users who most often took up heroin in early adulthood. Heroin use is primarily associated with deprivation (Carnwath and Smith, 2002; Pearson, 1987; Seddon, 2000, 2006) and the profile of the British heroin user became a 'folk devil' (Kohn, 1987; McElrath and McEvoy, 2001). Hiding in the stairwells of high-rise flats, 'smackheads' were seen as dangerous criminals constantly burgling houses, stealing from vehicles, shoplifting and bag snatching to feed their greedy habit.

In truth the first 100,000 heroin users who emerged in the UK during the 1980s, joined by a further 200,000 in the 1990s, were very often prolific offenders 'grafting' to feed their growing habits. Acquisitive crime was driven up by these problem drug users. If we add to this the emergence of the HIV/AIDS pandemic in the late 1980s and a focus on injecting heroin users, the landscape for political rhetoric and media frenzy was fertile. Consequently, and after much delay, a longstanding Conservative administration realised the need for a drugs strategy to galvanise and coordinate the responses in a period when the 'war on drugs' discourse dominated. *Tackling Drugs Together* (HM Government, 1994) was forged in a cauldron of public outrage about drugs. Although primarily a response to heroin, AIDS and crime, the new drugs strategy emerged just as concerns about young people's 'recreational' drug use and 'raves' were also hitting the headlines. Consequently, this first strategy was a striking juxtaposition of goals to tackle heroin-related crime, HIV risks to public health, and 'preventing' young people trying drugs such as cannabis in the belief that they could gravitate to heroin. The dangers of *any* drug use were thus highlighted. At this time, blaming youth, orchestrated by the then Home Secretary Michael Howard, was at a periodic peak and drug use of any sort was defined as fuel for a growing 'yob culture'. The first hoodie-with-a-spliff may as well have been a five-bags-a-day heroin injector.

New Labour's drug strategies

Although the primary focus of British drugs strategies continues to be the management of heroin/crack users, New Labour's three drugs strategies have shown growing sophistication by including a range of illicit drugs problems. In opposition, as shadow Home Secretary, Tony Blair had been developing an outline drugs strategy based on getting heroin users – and, by the late 1990s, heroin and crack users – into treatment. Blair's primary goal was radically to reduce crime by bringing and coercing heroin/crack 'Problem Drug Users' (PDUs) into treatment and onto methadone prescriptions.

However, once in government in 1997, the New Labour administration recognised the need to respond to the extensive use of cannabis and 'dance drugs' by 1990s youth. The political agenda had to address public concern that half of the youth population were trying cannabis alongside the growing popularity of rave and dance culture in the 'decade of dance' leading to a significant minority taking ecstasy, with the resulting widespread publicity for ecstasy deaths (Measham *et al.*, 2001; Release, 1997).

Furthermore, the migration of hundreds of thousands of young adults to city and town centres to bar hop, go 'clubbing' and binge drink had become a social problem with growing attention paid by the authorities to 'trouble' in the emergent night-time economy (Hobbs *et al.*, 2003). For the first time, alcohol and drugs were seen as the driver of a new kind of anti-social behaviour. The management of the night-time economy still remains a key priority (Hadfield and Measham, 2009).

So complex was the drugs agenda near the end of the 1990s that a 'Drugs Tsar' and Cabinet Office team were appointed to deliver the new strategy *Tackling Drugs Together to Build a Better Britain* (HM Government, 1998). The Drugs Tsar was sacked as government departments clashed, personal and political rivalries were fought out, and media spin machines worked against government advisors (Hellawell, 2002). The 1998 strategy was both more pragmatic and sanguine than the 1994 approach. Drugs education had failed to deliver, the 'war on drugs' discourse was gradually being undermined, and the reality that millions of young Britons who smoked cannabis and danced on ecstasy were neither dying nor turning into 'addicts', was acknowledged in some quarters. New goals were introduced to reduce the harm caused by young people's drug use and prevent them from becoming problem drug users. From this secondary prevention goal emerged FRANK, initially a 24-hour phone help line, whereby the official source of drugs information for the public was born.

The 1998 drugs strategy had the advantage of substantial ring-fenced funding for local Drug Action Teams who in turn commissioned much larger Community Drugs Teams and began to bring PDUs into treatment in far larger numbers under the auspices of the National Treatment Agency (recently abolished) from 2001. Across the 2001–2007 period there was a doubling of the drug treatment workforce and a doubling of the number of adults in treatment. A new industry was born.

In 2002 an updated drugs strategy was launched for England (HM Government, 2002) primarily as a vehicle for the Blair project of coercing PDUs into treatment via a criminal justice approach of drug testing and treatment referral – to become the Drugs Interventions Programme. This expensive programme remains in place today soaking up a disproportionate amount of the overall drugs treatment budget despite no robust evidence base for effectiveness (Best, 2004; Hunt and Stevens, 2004).

There has been little controversy about drug treatment beyond attacks on its preoccupation with methadone prescribing for PDUs at the cost of promoting abstinence and recovery for an ageing heroin/crack user population. The 2008–11 strategy *Drugs: Protecting Families and Communities* (HM Government, 2008) has continued to prioritise treating PDUs and highlighting the harm that their criminal activities cause. Two new priorities have emerged: firstly, local drug treatment agencies are increasingly expected to encourage and promote abstinence and recovery amongst their ageing heroin/crack clients; secondly, drug services are required to take the safeguarding of children living with drug-misusing parents far more seriously via more inter-agency family work. With the UK coalition government's drug strategy published as this book went to press (HM Government, 2010), this emphasis on abstinence and recovery looks set to increase.

The politics of alcohol, anti-social behaviour and disorder

The increases in alcohol consumption across the 1990s and into the 2000s amongst adolescents and young adults brought with it visible social downsides. For adolescents committed to weekend drinking, a favourite venue was 'outside': public places such as shopping centres, parks and places where young people gather in groups. These drinking gatherings became a source of much concern for local residents as well as the target of media campaigns demanding tough action against 'hoodies' and 'feral youth' and their lack of 'respect' (Bannister *et al.*, 2006; Jamieson, 2009). Whilst 'rowdy' drunken youth remain near the top of local authority quality of life surveys of residents and national assessments of fear of crime (Moon *et al.*, 2009), there has been little dialogue about either the evidence base or the effectiveness of the focus on anti-social youth in a climate of wider social change and resultant insecurities. Indeed, the last decade has witnessed 'an unprecedented period of intensive activity and regulatory reform designed to tackle anti-social behaviour that has seen the introduction of various new powers, tools and initiatives' including 'a plethora of hybrid tools of regulation that blur traditional distinctions between civil and criminal processes' (Crawford and Flint, 2009: 405). This regulation has targeted non-criminal as well as criminal behaviour, often without associated supportive interventions to address the underlying causes of the behaviour, resulting in increased marginalisation of already socially excluded youth.

The run up to the 1997 General Election featured a contest between political parties for dealing with alcohol-related anti-social behaviour. Unsurprisingly a victorious New Labour immediately produced a raft of measures to control anti-social youth via the Crime and Disorder Act 1998 and the Anti-Social Behaviour Act 2003. In the new millennium the police were given wide-ranging powers to 'disperse' under-18s, confiscate their alcohol and take them home. Recidivists were threatened with (the recently abolished) Anti Social Behaviour Orders (ASBOs). Further public drinking banning orders and a whole raft of regulatory measures have followed (Hadfield *et al.*, 2009).

The primacy of enforcement measures against younger visible drinkers is reflected in the formal alcohol strategies for England. The first alcohol strategy in 2004, *Alcohol Harm Reduction Strategy for England* (Prime Minister's Strategy Unit, 2004) formally recognised the growing harms associated with increasing alcohol use in the general population. It called for clear public health messages, better education, and communication with the public to encourage 'sensible drinking'. 'Binge' drinking was a key target. There was a goal of improving health and treatment services but, with no accompanying additional investment, this ensured little service development. A key theme of the strategy was combating alcohol-related crime and disorder to address the problems associated with weekend drinking arenas.

When the updated alcohol strategy *Safe, Sensible, Social* emerged (HM Government, 2007) the levels of alcohol harm had increased significantly in terms of alcohol-related disorder, public health and morbidity (e.g. Leon and McCambridge, 2006). The new strategy maintained the primacy of tackling alcohol-related violent crime and disorder but included a far more detailed analysis of how to address health-related harms and create local strategies to deliver formal brief interventions and treatment, moving beyond a focus on binge drinking young people in the night-time economy to recognise also the alcohol-related harms associated with more frequent drinking and home drinking including amongst middle-aged and older adults. Once again however there was no dedicated treatment funding and local Primary Care Trusts who held generic health funding failed to respond. Across England they spend only 0.6 per cent of their budgets on alcohol interventions (House of Common Public Accounts Committee, 2009). The lack of commitment to tackle the health and social harms associated with both acute and chronic drinking problems continues.

It is hard to explain why, at the end of the 'noughties', and despite alcohol harms having a much higher public focus than drug harms, alcohol interventions around health and morbidity remain the poor relative compared with illegal drugs. Sometimes the very structure and hierarchy of influence between government departments produces 'blind spots', illustrated by the divisiveness between the Home Office, Department of Health and Department for Culture, Media and Sport in the licensing deregulation in the form of the Licensing Act 2003, passed in the face of widespread opposition (Newton and Hirschfield, 2009) and with mounting evidence of the association between increased trading hours and increased alcohol-related health and social problems (Stockwell, 2006).

Recreational polydrug repertoires

Given the levels of drinking and drug use amongst younger people in England we might expect, after so many alcohol and drug strategies, that a comprehensive range of education, information and treatment services would now be in place to reduce the harm to younger drug users and their families. In fact there is no coherent platform of provision in place, particularly for the estimated about one million young adults engaging in weekend recreational polydrug repertoires (Measham and Moore, 2009). Young people's weekend recreational drug use may be *relatively* unproblematic compared to that of PDUs, but their needs must nevertheless be part of a service provision that allows them to adjust and moderate their behaviour and to reduce any consequent harms to themselves, their communities and wider society (Aldridge, 2008). In terms of information and advice, the government's FRANK website provides an information service appropriate to the internet age, with the recognition that in an era of 'googling' and social networking, young people turn to information technologies for help and information. As important are the many forums, chat rooms and websites that provide lay information and advice, including users' own experiences.[12]

A more sophisticated approach to understanding young people's drinking and use of a range of illegal drugs is to see the patterns, meanings and motivations for their consumption. The 1990s came to symbolise a generation of psychoactive consumers who rejected heroin and crack as 'dirty' drugs used by disreputable people (McElrath and McEvoy, 2001): for the clubbing minority the weekend drugs of choice in the early 1990s were ecstasy, amphetamines and LSD, sometimes consumed at raves without alcohol licences, from 1994 more often at licensed venues with minimal alcohol intake. By the late 1990s cannabis, cocaine and ecstasy alongside the growing popularity of alcohol meant four substances dominated the recreational drug scenes of that era (Williams and Parker, 2001). The use of alcohol, cannabis, cocaine and ecstasy, often consumed in combination, began to define a newly emergent population of non-opiate young treatment presenters (Parker, 2009) As the 2000s progressed, alcohol, cannabis, cocaine and ecstasy remained amongst the most popular psychoactive choices made by younger people, but an extending repertoire of weekend polydrug use began to include MDMA powder/crystal, ketamine, GHB/GBL and BZPs alongside more established recreational drugs (Measham and Moore, 2009). Low purity levels and limited access to drugs like cocaine and ecstasy also brought us into uncharted territory with the rapidly growing popularity of so-called 'legal highs' in the internet age – drugs such as substituted cathinones like mephedrone – which are cheap, easily purchased online and promptly delivered to the door (Measham *et al.*, 2010), although of variable or unknown content, purity and legal status (Brandt *et al.*, 2010b).

12 For example, the Erowid user vaults at www.erowid.org.

Within these polydrug repertoires are a range of consumption patterns by a minority of adolescents and young adults, from across a range of socio-demographic groups and social scenes, who favour varying combinations of legal and illicit substances: including the enduring popularity of ecstasy in pill and powder form for nearly half of club customers, and drinking alcohol and snorting cocaine for up to a fifth of bar customers (Measham and Moore, 2009) and the widespread use of cannabis as a social relaxant and lubricant across a range of cultural and stylistic groupings. Yet these complex and dynamic weekend recreational polydrug patterns are largely absent from alcohol and drug policy agendas and neglected by funding initiatives.

As we shall see, our *Illegal Leisure* cohort is a part of a 1990s generation who grew up with increased availability and increased usage of Class A drugs such as ecstasy in the early 1990s and cocaine in the late 1990s. As most grew into otherwise conventional, economically stable, educated and employed young adults they have, by and large, been able to regulate their substance use and fit their psychoactive 'time out' into 'work hard–play hard' intoxicated weekends (Parker and Williams, 2003). However a study of recreational drug use would be misleading if it did not recognise that some users become casualties of their drinking and drug use. This is evident in the changing profile of those who enter drug treatment services in England.

The new non-opiate substance users

Although the preoccupation with the coercive treatment of PDUs has deflected attention away from service provision for non-opiate substance users, the scale of their presentations is growing annually (Hurst *et al.*, 2009). The consecutive New Labour drug strategies supported by substantial ring-fenced funding have allowed under-18s specialist alcohol and drug services to develop from the millennium. By 2005, nearly all local areas had such a service available. These services, as part of integrated children and young people's services, receive referrals from a range of young people's agencies, particularly youth offending teams. Initially set up to capture the last waves of 1990s young heroin users, these services have in fact seen fewer and fewer young PDUs and their presentations now almost all relate to young people with alcohol, cannabis and to a lesser extent cocaine problems. In 2007–8, 24,000 young people under the age of 18 entered treatment in England. The typical 'primary' substances for which they sought treatment were alcohol and cannabis (NTA, 2009) but cocaine and other non-opiate drugs also formed part of many clients' polydrug repertoires. A similar profile of young adults is now being seen at adult services with rises in cocaine and cannabis presentations evident (Hurst *et al.*, 2009).

Importantly, a significant proportion of this growing population of younger treatment entrants is from deprived backgrounds, often troubled by minor mental health problems, unemployment, academic under-achievement and problematic family relationships. For many of these primarily 16–24 year olds, their substance problems are related to slipping from use to misuse of alcohol, cannabis and cocaine. For some, their excessive substance use represents self-medication involving high levels of alcohol intake and heavy cannabis use. Their profile is similar to those young people who took to heroin for solace in the 1980s and 1990s and for whom such drugs could be characterised as 'cocktails of oblivion' rather than 'cocktails of celebration' (Gilman, 1998). Simpson (2003) acknowledges observations like these in postulating that 'persistent drug use' may exist alongside recreational and dependent use, and that drug-use careers that slip from one to another of these characterisations have complex relationships with crime. All this is consistent with MacDonald and Marsh's (2002) observation that, particularly in areas of entrenched social exclusion, the distinction between 'recreational' and 'problematic' drug use may break down, resulting in drug-using repertoires not typically associated with recreational use.

The casualty rate for these post-heroin polydrug careers may be far higher than recent treatment numbers suggest (Parker and Egginton, 2002). After 18 years of age there are few services for young adult non-opiate drug users. Separate alcohol and drug strategies and funding streams have prevented integrated services from developing, and services remain dominated as much by a crime prevention as harm reduction agenda. The (recently abolished) National Treatment Agency continued to marginalise the development of brief interventions and treatment for non-opiate problem users, insisting they should attend adult services geared to heroin/crack users, which many do not want to do. A key challenge for future drug service provision will be to broaden the remit of the NTA beyond this ageing group of PDUs, without contracting treatment options for this or other groups. Ironically, the Drugs Interventions Programme geared for capturing heroin/crack users via drug testing of arrestees in the custody suite is now netting significant numbers of young adult offenders with non-opiate polydrug profiles who test positive for cocaine. For this growing group there are few appropriate services and most reject attempts to be coerced into traditional treatment (Duffy and Cuddy, 2008). This group is distinct from the majority of recreational drug users and clubbers who are employed, less often caught up in drug testing and less likely to present to services in significant numbers.

Young adults with alcohol problems are similarly badly served. There is a lack of adult alcohol treatment provision in general, and what does exist struggles with growing numbers of middle-aged dependent drinkers. To access such a service a young adult often needs to be a dependent drinker when in fact they are more likely to be harmful or hazardous drinkers. Furthermore, co-existent drug problems relating to polydrug use, such as combined alcohol and cocaine use, are rarely treated simultaneously in the same service (ACMD, 2010).

These problems associated with non-opiate/crack use illustrate how some substance users follow drug career trajectories that shift from their initial recreational drug use into more chaotic, dependent or daily use. The primary example of this is the growing number of cannabis casualties seeking help. This is not something we predicted a decade ago. In part this may be a result of the marketing and dominance of UK-cultivated skunk with its high THC content and absence of the anti-psychotic component CBD when compared with cannabis resin. In part it is a reminder that any psychoactive substance has the potential for misuse.

Here are the latest 'blind spots' in government strategic planning: firstly, the refusal to embrace alcohol as a 'drug'; secondly, the refusal to move on from the heroin/crack agenda and the reluctance to acknowledge that some 'recreational' polydrug use can result in problems, often associated with a wide range of other social problems including economic deprivation and social exclusion; and finally the inability to acknowledge the continued desire of young people to seek intoxication and psychoactive experience and thus provide robust information, harm-reduction advice and accessible, appropriate and flexible service provision in line with changing patterns of consumption and emergent problems.

Conclusions

This chapter has summarised the continuity and changes in the drug and alcohol consumption patterns of young people in England since the early 1990s to the present. This is the same period in which the *Illegal Leisure* cohort grew up as children of the 1990s into today's 20 and 30 year olds. As we shall see, their use of alcohol and specific drugs mirrors the macro consumption trends found in the UK.

Across this period there have been major shifts in the scale of drug trying, drug use and alcohol use. What remains constant are the comparatively high rates of alcohol and drug use in the UK compared with the rest of Europe. Consequently, there is almost constant media and public concern about one substance or another, which in turn demands political responses and shapes alcohol and drug policy, service provison and treatment interventions. Thus policy responses, whether care or control, are a strange brew of political imperatives clashing with research conclusions and evidence-based recommendations. Furthermore, we see a tension between epidemiological, public health, social science and science findings and their implications for evidence-based responses and the politics of drugs and alcohol. For governments navigating a course between research and politics, with one eye on the electorate or the media, compromises in alcohol and drug policy are unsurprising if not inevitable. This is the main history lesson to which we will return in the final chapter.

2   The North West Longitudinal Study

Overview

This chapter begins with a reproduction of the methods chapter from the first edition of *Illegal Leisure*. We follow this with an update entitled 'Evolving methods and techniques' that documents our strategies for following our original cohort into adulthood from 1999 to 2008.

Introduction

In this chapter we describe, wherever possible in a non-technical way, how we created a sample of over 700 14-year-olds (in 1991) and tracked most of them annually for up to five years. Each year we enquired about their personal and family circumstances, their disposable income, use of leisure and perspectives on personal and social relationships. We asked them in detail about their tobacco, alcohol and illicit drug use. As they matured we felt able to pursue more complex issues with them including their attitudes towards drug use and drug users, their assessment of the health education they received, and their experiences at parties and nightclubs. For those who took drugs we felt able, as they reached young adulthood, to ask them to describe their motivations for their use of individual drugs and what they experienced in so doing. We took equal care to explore the perspectives of those who had not and will not take drugs.

Five annual self-report surveys were undertaken, and 86 interviews were conducted when respondents were 17 years old. In the subsequent year a number of case studies of 'critical incidents' relating to respondents' own or others' drug use were explored (see Table 2.1). We begin this chapter by describing how this programme of research was financed and some of the things we learned in conducting the five-year study that researchers rarely have the opportunity to discuss. We

Table 2.1 Overview of the investigation

	Year 1	Year 2	Year 3	Year 4	Year 5
Mean age of participants	14 years	15 years	16 years	17 years	18 years
Questionnaire administered	In 8 schools	In 8 schools	In 3 schools and by post	In 3 schools and by post	All postal
Interviews	–	–	–	86	–
Case studies	–	–	–	–	8

explain how our samples were created and how the 'cohort' of respondents with complete data for five years was affected by attrition (the loss of research subjects over the years). We then describe the self-report questionnaire surveys. From there we discuss the way we set about interviewing a selected group of respondents in depth. Issues of validity and reliability are discussed but in an unusual way: because the research is longitudinal, it posed dilemmas not faced with one-off cross-sectional surveys, yet also unexpected opportunities to consider veracity more comprehensively. Finally, we describe how a 'pathways' analysis developed around Year 4 and how we set about systematically documenting the ways that our young respondents took distinctive pathways and journeys in respect of their attitudes to and use of illicit drugs.

Appropriate resources

Social research methods textbooks routinely implore investigators to combine quantitative and qualitative methods. Many sing the praises of longitudinal studies as, in the fullness of time, offering exceptional analytic power. What the textbooks and research training courses rarely consider seriously is just how expensive such studies are. The North-West Longitudinal Study was initially funded for three years by the Alcohol Education and Research Council, with the Economic and Social Research Council awarding funds for its fourth and fifth years. We also had an additional grant from the Home Office Drugs Prevention Initiative and some sponsorship from a commercial interest which paid for incentives (music vouchers) for the participants. The total cost of this was some £380,000. Put quite simply then, the main reason why this is the only contemporary longitudinal study of how young Britons' alcohol and drug use develops during adolescence is resources. It is extremely difficult to persuade funders to commit their limited resources to such expensive projects that must be funded for more than a couple of years. The trend towards more focused, one-off cross-sectional investigations which are relatively inexpensive, or alternatively household surveys in which a wide range of exploitable data can be collected has grown during the 1990s. Thus the biggest single obstacle to undertaking a longitudinal study is identifying and obtaining sufficient resources. Obtaining research awards in turn involves an often-mysterious combination of a stable research base, a good track record, a well-worked idea, timeliness and a hefty slab of luck.

We noted in the last chapter how politicised the issues of youth, drug use and law breaking have become during the 1990s. The politicised nature of the subject not only affected how we chose to fund the research, but also affected the implications of our choice of funding bodies upon how we have been able to report our findings. This project was funded by two Research Councils – the Alcohol and Education Research Council (AERC) and the Economic and Social Research Council (ESRC). Research Councils normally receive their monies directly from government and, to a certain extent therefore, this inevitably occurs within a political context of them constructing 'government friendly' mission statements, having government-selected chairs, and being accountable to government in terms of their 'successes' in forming public policy, making scientific discoveries, and funding students who successfully complete Ph.Ds. And yet, unlike government departments or private enterprise, both of which sometimes fund academic research, Research Councils remain relatively autonomous organisations. Even within a political context in which Research Councils operate, their purpose is to fund academic research judged solely within the relatively impartial sphere of academic peer review. Thus, each application for funding to a Research Council is sent out to other qualified academics working in the area who are asked to assess the application on its academic merits.

Although obtaining awards from Research Councils involves structuring lengthy, academically rigorous applications that meet 'political' funding criteria or 'themes', once obtained, the money is 'clean'. The Councils expect the project to be open to scrutiny and demand that all its results reach the public domain. Had this programme been funded by government departments this particular book would not have been written because the results would have been sanitised, or, in the face of resistance, delayed interminably by suspicious and nervous civil servants dedicated to not embarrassing government ministers. The war on drugs rhetoric and nature of 'media' politics would not have allowed the story we tell to be narrated via a programme funded by government. It is important therefore that any investigation which claims to tell it 'how it is' about such politically sensitive topics as young people's drug use should think carefully about the implications of obtaining funds from any particular source.

In relation to human resources, it has been very important that we have had a stable research team who have been committed to both completing the study and to the dissemination of research findings. The latter process has gone on well beyond the five years during which the project took place, and will no doubt continue to do so. Five years is a long time in anyone's research career and the investigation has benefited greatly from having had a stable core team throughout with only one early change in staffing. This has allowed a creativity to develop whereby innovations and 'experimental' and flexible approaches have flowed easily between team members who understand one another's strengths and interests.

'Experiencing' the research process

There are many things we have learned about carrying out such a large and complex piece of research that researchers rarely have the opportunity to write about, including the development of some important research skills not usually discussed in method texts.

The amount of information we compiled over the years was vast, and our methods for handling it evolved in response to our changing needs. For example, in the early years of the research we did not need or want to keep identifying information about respondents such as names or addresses, though in later years we needed to develop methods for collating this information that was accurate, efficient and accessible, yet also ethical. Methods for handling data also evolved in response to changing technology within the university setting. For example, in the fourth year of the research we moved to new premises in which all staff in our department were provided with powerful networked PCs with up-to-date software which we were no longer required to purchase ourselves from project funds.

In total, we tracked 1,125 unique individuals for one or more years, coded and processed 3,116 questionnaire returns, and now have available over 2,900 questionnaire variables and 'computed' variables. The analyses began in 1991 using SPSSX (Statistical Package for the Social Sciences) on a university mainframe computer, the only one available at the time to deal with large data sets, and progressed to SPSS for Windows, run on powerful PCs we acquired over the years. Eventually the data set became so large that we could no longer save it to floppy disk, and we were required to use our university's then newly available networking facilities and our own purchased tape streamers.

Simultaneously, we set up and managed a second database that we used to keep track of our respondents after they left school to record their voluntarily given names, addresses, phone numbers, as well as tracking our attempts to stay in touch with them through follow-up letters, second (and more) follow-up letters, Christmas cards, contacts of names of friends or relatives that respondents had given us in case they moved, as well as contacting respondents we had lost after Year 3 in a large 'recapture' of lost respondents we did over one summer. The first version of this data base was initially kept by hand when the information we needed to keep about respondents was small; in later years it was maintained through PC database software (Microsoft Access). This allowed us to combine the tasks of documenting our attempts to keep track of respondents over the years, as well as the previously separate administrative tasks of producing mailing labels, thereby halving the work involved in these related tasks.

We became quite expert at data cleaning, the process of looking through data for inconsistent responses within questionnaires or 'rogue' values. If done rigorously, data cleaning allows researchers to minimise the amount of 'error' due to miscoding or inconsistent coding, always a problem with large data sets in which teams of coders must be employed. By the end of the research we had developed a comprehensive programme of analyses which automatically identified potential candidates that may have been miscoded. We also learned through the data-cleaning process about which questions were uniformly coded by our teams of coders, and which questions tended to produce inconsistent coding or miscoding. We were able then to redesign questions in later years, therefore, not only based on how well they 'worked' with our respondents, but also to minimise coding problems. Because of the sheer size of the data sets over the years, we also had to learn how to identify appropriate temporary staff to act as questionnaire administrators and coders, to identify their always varying training needs and to meet and manage these.

The research also posed ethical dilemmas we had not predicted. One young woman's postal questionnaire in the fourth year of the research showed that she was struggling with her drug use and seemed quite unable to cope. She had included with her return a few pages of extra comments detailing her problems. She did not explicitly ask us for help, and yet it was quite apparent that she felt out of control, unable to deal with her drug use, and in need of help. Our dilemma was whether or not we should contact her; to do so was to treat her as an identifiable individual rather than as an anonymous questionnaire return – was this appropriate given that as researchers we are ostensibly uninterested in 'individuals' and only interested in 'group statistics'? After much discussion, we decided that we would contact her to offer her a listening ear and to put her in touch with services if she felt that would be useful for her. The decision turned out to be a good one; she welcomed our overture, and after meeting with her, we referred her to a carefully chosen local drug services agency. But it is entirely possible that she might have resented our intrusion, and felt her privacy invaded and our promises of confidentiality shattered. Although we already had in place a set of procedures for dealing with these kinds of problems for the 'critical incidents' part of the research, we did not anticipate encountering the problem of identifying troubled young people from their questionnaire returns. We learned therefore the need to be flexible, and the need to review our policy and procedures continuously.

The most unexpected skill we were required to develop, for which we were least well prepared and equipped, was dealing with the media. Immediately following the publication of the drug-use prevalence figures amongst 14-year-olds after the first year of the research, the media interest was intense. In that week the figures were quoted on radio and television, and in local and national newspapers, and we received 10 or 20 phone calls a day from journalists. While the interest died down in the ensuing weeks, it bubbled up again with the publication of *Drugs Futures* (Parker *et al.*, 1995).

In between the periods of intense media interest, we still received on average one phone call a week from journalists, and television and radio producers. All this meant that the more outgoing members of the team were required to develop skills in dealing with journalists, including conducting live interviews on radio and television. More than one interviewer took a frighteningly aggressive tack, seeing us as condoning drug use amongst young people and taking the opportunity to 'blame the messenger'. We learned what so many others already have: that no matter how careful you are to be clear, journalists almost inevitably misquote you. We also learned that it is easy to spend a great deal of research time in providing a basic research service for journalists eager to cover such a hot topic. In the end we had to become quite ruthless in refusing interviews and help to journalists in their research in order simply to get on with our own.

Sampling

Finite resources affected our choices of sampling techniques from the outset. The statistical ideal of the random sample was neither practical nor affordable for our research. Given that we wished to follow a sample of young people for several years it was vital to contact young people economically, and this almost inevitably means via schools and in reasonably compact geographical areas. We opted for the tried and tested schools survey procedure adopted by researchers like Wright and Pearl (1990) and Balding (1997). However, unlike Balding's survey, we decided to administer the questionnaire ourselves, without teachers present, in order to embark upon a relationship with participants both at the first administration of the survey when they could feel less worried about the possibility of being identified by teachers, and through later survey administrations where they would meet us on each occasion and be reassured through experience that their responses had not been divulged to anyone, particularly parents and teachers.

Our sample comprised eight co-educational State secondary schools in the metropolitan north-west of England, and was chosen to be as representative as possible of two of the counties therein: Merseyside and Greater Manchester. It was not possible, as with a stratified random sample, to 'structure' the sample in a proportional sense on race, class, gender and socio-economic indicators because our sampling unit was the school, rather than the pupil or respondent. In order, therefore, to choose schools in which pupils *would* be representative of the metropolitan north-west of England, we first selected a borough within each of the two metropolitan counties, that was deemed to be representative of the counties that contained them, and then selected schools within them to be representative of the boroughs. A detailed discussion of these procedures, along with evidence for the schools' representativeness at both the borough and county levels, is contained in the Appendix to *Drugs Futures* (Parker *et al.*, 1995). In summary, however, there is compelling evidence that the clustered, non-random sample we obtained is representative in many respects of the two boroughs containing the schools within the metropolitan counties as a whole. In particular, the sample at Year 1 reflected correct proportions of respondents drawn from middle- and working-class catchment areas, respondents from single-parent families, and respondents whose parents were in paid work. The proportion of males in the sample reflects their over-representation in the population for this age group. The proportion of non-white ethnic groups in Greater Manchester is only slightly higher than its population counterpart. We can be reasonably confident, then, that our sample at Year 1 (see Table 2.2) is fairly representative of the young people in the metropolitan north-west of England.

Table 2.3 identifies the change and attrition in the samples over the years. Two processes are at work. On the one hand we 'recruited' new respondents particularly at Year 2 when we returned to the schools. Given that we surveyed whole classes, we picked up new pupils as well as those who had been absent the previous year, as we did not attempt to pursue those absent on the day of the administration (though we did begin to do this after Year 3). On the other hand the loss of numbers from our original sample at Year 1 ('attrition') was also, inevitably, on-going. Furthermore, the respondents we lost numbered disproportionately among those who reported drug trying and drinking at age 14, as well as in later years (a second, but smaller group of lost respondents were Asian Muslims who numbered disproportionately among drink and drug abstainers). We cannot, therefore, consider the results in years

Table 2.2 Gender, class catchment and race of respondents at Year 1

	School catchment area			Race			
	Total	Middle class	Working class	Black	Asian	White	Other
	n %	n %	n %	n %	n %	n %	n %
Female	358	204	154	1125	304	5	
(row %)	46.3	57.0	43.0	3.2	7.2	88.1	1.4
Male	415	201	214	18	32	329	5
(row %)	53.7	48.4	51.6	4.7	8.3	85.7	1.3
Total	773	405	368	29	32	329	5
(col %)	100.0	52.3	47.6	4.0	7.8	86.8	1.4

Table 2.3 Change and attrition in the samples

	Year 1	Year 2	Year 3	Year 4	Year 5
Total respondents	776	752	523	536	529
One year only	197	129	28	8	2
Two years only	247	252	109	37	33
Three years only	92	131	146	115	117
Four years only	240	240	240	147	148
All five years	229	229	229	229	229

subsequent certainly to Year 2 as 'representative' of young people in the metropolitan north-west of England in the way that results in Year 1 were.

What do these changes and attrition rates in the sample mean for the findings we report? Primarily, they mean that the results cannot be seen as representative, in a straightforward manner, of young people in the metropolitan north-west of England. We have no basis, therefore, on which to assert that the drug use prevalence rates found in Year 5 reflect those that we would find if we were able to survey the entire population in the north-west from which our original sample was drawn, and thus we will make no attempt to make such a generalisation. Our purpose, however, is not to estimate population parameters. In the absence of a random sample, this is best done by collating the range of surveys undertaken in the UK, as we did in the last chapter. Instead we wish to describe the 'pathways' of drug abstinence and drug use for those in our sample whom we have retained. Moreover, in spite of the shift in the structure of the sample due to attrition, we still retain members of the groups with the heaviest losses (working class, male, Asian, Muslim, black, and not in A-level education at 17), though in smaller numbers.

Because the research is longitudinal in design, we are interested in not only describing statistics for the samples at each year, but also in exploring both how individual respondents change over time and, retrospectively, how the early characteristics of our respondents can be seen in the light of their later drug pathways. Thus, where we carry out analyses examining how individual respondents change over the five years of the study, we present these data for only those 229 respondents in the core cohort for whom we have complete data for five years. Chapters 3 and 4 provide results for the whole samples at each year (Year 1 = 776; Year 2 = 752; Year 3 = 523; Year 4 = 536; Year 5 = 529), but Chapter 5 presents results primarily for the core cohort with complete data (= 229). The core cohort contains *fewer* drug users than the early annual samples.

Survey procedures

Following selection of the eight schools, meetings were held with the heads and/or liaison teachers at each school to explain the aims, methods and administration of the surveys. They were reassured that no individual schools would be identified in any publication emanating from the project, and that responses of their pupils would remain confidential and anonymous. We also promised them detailed and anonymised feedback of their pupils' responses in composite tables which they have received each year. This feedback has been delivered without incident and no school has been identified publicly at any time or 'discovered' by the local media.

Administration of the surveys occurred in the autumn, avoiding the Christmas holiday season and the potential distortion of seasonal celebrations. A teacher introduced the administrators of the questionnaire to each survey group, and then left the room. The nature of the survey was explained to the group, with particular emphasis that responses would be voluntary, confidential and anonymous. After responding to pupils' questions and concerns, the questionnaires were handed out in envelopes in which they were to be sealed by the pupil when complete. Respondents took between 20 and 45 minutes to complete their returns. The issue of *confidentiality* cannot be over-emphasised. At 14 and 15 in particular our respondents were extremely concerned about who would see their questionnaire returns and needed constant reassurance that no third parties such as parents, teacher or police officers would have access to their answers. Comments on early returns reminded us lest we forgot. 'This had better be bloody confidential. If my Mum reads this she'll kill me' (Simon). 'I think it is rather personal but I hope it helps in your research and other people are cooperative for you. I also hope you keep your promise about it being totally confidential' (Debbie).

At the end of the first administration each respondent was asked to give their initials and date of birth on a separate sheet so that the following year's questionnaire could be given to them personally. If this was seen as too risky in terms of anonymity we asked them to use a nickname they would remember. Conformity was very high and after a little detective work the researchers were able successfully to tag almost every respondent. At the end of the second year administration we asked for pupils' written permission to obtain their names and addresses from their schools. This was explained as a chance to maintain contact with the sample, over half of whom would be 16 and leave school in a few months' time after GCSE exams. Again, compliance was high. Thereafter we made direct contact with school leavers using the correspondence address they gave. By Year 5 a full contact database for over 600 participants existed which was updated when someone moved. For postal returns an incentive (music voucher with a £10 value) scheme was introduced at Year 3. In Years 3 and 4 those who attended the three schools with sixth forms were surveyed in school time. In Year 5 all participants were contacted via the post.

The questionnaire

At the fifth administration, the self-report questionnaire contained four main sections: personal characteristics, general questions about drugs, questions about the last occasion of drug use and questions about alcohol. A core of questions comprising all the main 'dependent' variables (those which we are interested in explaining and predicting – such as drug offers and drug use) have remained constant across the five years of the survey. Some questions have changed, primarily for two reasons. Firstly, by the later administrations, we had benefited enormously from respondent feedback in the previous years. Many questions had been refined in some way, resulting in improved layout, better instructions and significantly reduced proportions of missing data.

In addition to modifying questions based on feedback from respondents, we also refined and elaborated on some topics, and shortened or eliminated others. In Years 4 and 5, for example, we expanded the section on drug use, limited questions on alcohol use to core questions only, and, much to the annoyance of the respondents, removed questions from previous years on sexual experiences. In designing questions for the survey, we initially drew upon questions for which evidence of reliability and validity had been demonstrated by other researchers (e.g. Balding, 1997; Plant *et al.*, 1985), as well as including new questions for which there were fewer useful precedents. By the last two years administration of the survey, we had pioneered some innovative questions to explore areas such as subjective experiences of drug use, which we felt able to ask once the sample moved into their later teens.

The main drugs-related variables in the fifth administration of the survey included:

1   attitudes toward drug taking in general;
2   for 13 individual listed drugs: ease of access, having been in offer situations, drugs tried (including recency and frequency measures), and future use intentions;
3   the last occasion of drug use;
4   for cannabis, LSD, amphetamines, ecstasy, and cocaine/crack: questions on the last occasion of use, reasons for use, experiences during and after, and typicality of the occasion;
5   poly drug use;
6   measures of drug-related harm.

We used four question formats within the questionnaire. The first was of the 'tick box' variety in which categories were mutually exclusive (i.e.

only one box to be ticked), and included examples such as race (in which respondents indicated their racial backgrounds based on categories used by the Equal Opportunities Commission), attitudinal statements in which responses could range on a five-point scale from 'agree strongly' to 'disagree strongly', and the drug offers, use/recency and future use intentions for the 13 listed drugs. The second type of question was also of the 'tick box' variety, but in which categories of responses were not mutually exclusive; in other words, respondents could tick as many boxes as applied. This question format was used, for example, for respondents to indicate all drugs taken on the last occasion of drug use; as well as for reasons, experiences during and experiences after the last occasion of use of each of five specific drugs. The third question format was of the fill-in-the-blank variety, and was used for questions asking number of cigarettes smoked yesterday, income, frequency of specific drug use within the past month, amount spent on drugs and alcohol, and number of containers (pints, cans, bottles, glasses, etc.) of alcohol consumed on last occasion and in the past week. The fourth and final type of question format was of the open-ended variety, in which respondents were free to expand on their views with regard to drugs education, drug-use experiences, and future intentions for alcohol use/non-use. There was additionally a section in which respondents could comment on any of the subjects covered in the questionnaire. All open-ended questions were optional.

In-depth interviews

Although we received a lot of commentary on the questionnaires from our sample and met all our respondents in their schools in the early years, it was not until Year 4 that we were adequately resourced to undertake in-depth interviews. We were able to interview 86 volunteer subjects when they were 17 years old. These interviews went extremely well and allowed young people, who normally only discuss drug taking with friends, to provide us with often highly sophisticated perspectives about their drug taking or abstention. Many implied that they felt able to be so open with us because of their ongoing relationship with the research team and evidence that their views were taken seriously and held in complete confidence. Indeed many subjects chastised us for being so slow to undertake interviews. One male subject, when asked if our project had got to the central issues of drug use amongst young people, compared the interview and survey approaches and was in no doubt about the supremacy of the interview.

I think it helps, it's a lot more . . . at the back of this one here [questionnaire] it asks if you've got any comments, please write them in . . . . I read this questionnaire and one of my mates had a look at it, and it's just not in depth enough. The interview can get it across more easily. [You don't think we're getting to the heart . . .?] Not with the questionnaire, the interview's a lot better. You can just pick this up [questionnaire] and you don't know what the person's like, you don't know nothing about them, whereas if you meet somebody and get to know them a bit . . . it's much better. There's a question there somewhere, it's got four questions, either I do take drugs or I don't, and it doesn't give you the option to expand, it's like tick one box and that puts you in a category. This is a bit more flexible.

(Tom, 17 years)

The interviews had several purposes. Firstly, they allowed us to explore in far more detail the key issues thrown up by the survey findings of the first three years and in particular to seek more extensive and 'open' answers to 'why' and 'how' questions about drug use. Secondly, the interviews allowed us to seek respondents' views on the efficacy of the questionnaires. We were able to ask whether respondents had filled them in accurately, whether they thought classmates had been honest and so on. We also asked interviewees some of the questions we had posed them in their fourth-year questionnaire and independently compared answers. Thirdly, the interviews, by allowing respondents to place drinking and drug use in the wider context of their everyday lives, gave us far more insight into how they spent their leisure time, how they created 'time out' from work, domesticity, study or unemployment. Finally, part of the interview explored future expectations. Did interviewees expect to begin or cease to take drugs or change their regularity of use? What were the factors which they felt would affect prospective drinking and drug use?

All the interviews were voluntary. They were undertaken by fully trained 'young' interviewers, most of whom were brought up in the same regions as the respondents. The interviews were taped using a compact, battery-run tape recorder. They were later all transcribed. Most interviews took place in the respondent's home and the remainder in a quiet area of a leisure centre, library or public house. All interviews were one-to-one and conducted out of earshot of any third party. Respondents received a £10 music voucher for participating in these interviews which lasted between 45 and 90 minutes, and on average about an hour.

There were 46 female and 40 male interviewees of whom 82 were white. All of the original eight school populations were well represented and respondents came from the full range of socio-economic backgrounds.

In terms of their drugs status, 26 of the sample had never tried an illicit drug and 60 had. There were 25 current users and seven were ex-users, having taken a drug but not expecting to do so again. The remainder were, at the time, reflecting on and reviewing their drugs status.

Most of the interview data will be presented in Chapters 4, 5 and 6, but in the next section we will illustrate what interviewees said about their experiences of filling in the annual questionnaire returns as we discuss validity and reliability.

Validity and reliability

In our view a well-conducted self-report survey, if it can demonstrate confidentiality and can present itself to young people (over the age of 13) as competent and 'streetwise', *is* the most cost-effective way of measuring alcohol and drugs prevalence and describing related behaviours. Ideally, however, these surveys should be set alongside interviews or focus groups which are more effective at teasing out subtleties, complexities and, more importantly, *contradictions*. A five-year longitudinal study throws up far more untidy data because it is obliged to measure people's ability to recall events over time and is also measuring, in this case, the impact of maturation in adolescence. Eighteen-year-olds often think 18 is an appropriate age to allow young people to drink in pubs but the same respondents in our research at the age of 16 nominated 16 as the right age. Thus if we compare the answers to this question for the same people over time we get quite different responses. We are not identifying a lack of validity in method here, or respondents lying, but a change of mind. So in this section we deliberately focus on anomalies and briefly discuss how we explain them, or not, in respect of validity and reliability.

Firstly, we always applied the standard internal tests which have been discussed in detail elsewhere (Parker *et al.*, 1995). In Year 5, as in previous years, we employed two main methods for assessing possible under- and over-reporting of drug use. To assess under-reporting, we asked all respondents who did not report any drug taking whether, if they had tried an illegal drug, they would have admitted doing so in the questionnaire. In the complete Year 5 sample who had valid responses to this question, four respondents (1.8 per cent) indicated that they would not admit to drug use, and in the cohort with complete data for all five years 11 (2.1 per cent) indicated they would not admit to drug use. These figures are indicative of a high level of honest reporting.

To assess possible over-reporting, we included a (changing) 'dummy drug' item (e.g. 'nadropax' and 'penamine'), which only one respondent in the Year 4 sample (0.2 per cent) and two respondents in the Year 5 sample (0.4 per cent) claimed to have used. Thus, nearly all respondents distinguished between this dummy drug and all other listed drugs, a finding that is suggestive of honest reporting.

In Year 1 we had to disqualify as spoiled four returns where close scrutiny showed the respondents, one called David Bowie, were simply not taking the exercise seriously. There have been no spoiled returns since. However, having processed over 3,000 returns from nearly a thousand individuals we have inevitably identified anomalies. The most important ones refer to situations where an individual says in one year he or she took a drug but in a subsequent year or years contradicts this. One-off snapshot surveys do not have to deal with this process. We believe there were three main causes for anomalies in our study. Firstly, certainly in Year 1, there was some fabrication and over-reporting which later honest reporting contradicted. This was not only evident from analysing the survey data set but in the interviews respondents agreed that at 14 the first survey did capture some bravado.

> The first time we had this questionnaire, I thought it was a bit of a laugh. That's my memory of it, I can't remember if I answered it truthfully or not. I've got a feeling I did answer it truthfully, but I'm not sure. I've got a feeling I answered it seriously. It had a list of drugs and some of them I'd never heard of, and just the names just cracked me up.
>
> [Has your attitude changed as it's going on?] Yes. I think it's just the level of maturity. [Did you have any doubts about the confidentiality of the answers you gave?] Yes. I still do. I'm not too bothered about it and I know that it wouldn't get back to my parents and that's the main thing, but the thing is, you can still get in touch with me now – you've still got my name and my phone number. [Interviewer reassured] I know that it wouldn't get back to my parents, that's not the problem at all, I'd just like to know how you're swinging it.
>
> (Tom, 17 years)

The second reason for anomalous reporting is related to inaccurate reporting due to the level of commitment and concentration of the completer. If the questionnaire is too demanding, too boring, too long or if the respondent has not been given the appropriate introduction to and significance of a question, then young people may well treat it lightly. The most obvious sign of this is missing data. Levels of missing data declined dramatically from Year 1 to Year 5. In our research, missing data was initially most problematic with our attempts to measure *exactly* how much people drank in a drinking session:

> [Looking back, were there any questions you might have answered dishonestly?] Only the ones about drink because I couldn't remember about the last time or how much, but I didn't do it on purpose, I just couldn't remember, so I just took it from the last time I remembered.
>
> [Did you underestimate?] I couldn't remember the quantity, so I just took it from the time I remember how much. [Underestimate it?] No probably not, because in school it [drinking pattern] was all the same, exactly the same every week.
>
> (Anne, 18 years)

The third cause of anomalous reporting, which is specifically a feature of longitudinal research, is the redefinition or reconstruction of past events through time. For instance a single puff of cannabis reported at 14 is, a couple of years later, disregarded as an actual drug-taking episode, particularly by a subsequent 'expert' regular user. The strongest evidence that this reconstruction process is widespread comes from the interviewees whom we actually confronted with some examples and which they often explained and 'understood' in this way. When we look at the survey data we find that 27.2 per cent of the anomalous reporting we identified in relation to reported drug use between the first and fourth years of the survey were related to solvent (and gas) use – the archetypal ambiguous 'drug' used almost exclusively as an experimental substance in early adolescence. It is a classic experience to review and redefine in later years such use as 'kids' stuff'. Thus an early quick sniff of glue at the age of 14 may be reinterpreted as a non-event in light of later knowledge of others' more 'sophisticated' and purposive solvent use involving inhalation through bags or tubes. It was also notable that ex-users at the age of 17 (who had reported trying a drug at 14 or 15 but were now abstainers) produced a disproportionate number of anomalies. Again this is highly suggestive of a process also identified by Plant and colleagues (1985) and Fillmore (1988) of rescripting one's earlier (often embarrassing) adolescence to diminish cognitive dissonance as one settles for a particular personal identity upon entering young adulthood. Reforming biographies is a topic close to the heart of researchers using longitudinal-survey techniques (Collins *et al.*, 1985).

In conclusion, although we have identified some anomalous reporting, it may be less significant in terms of issues of reliability and validity and more significant as an opportunity for us to engage in creative understanding of the meaning that young people bring to both their drug use and to their opportunities to document that use in a questionnaire return. Some contradictions emanated from early misreporting, some from imprecision or confusion and some from personal 'reconstruction'. Even though we identified these three possible reasons for anomalous reporting through exploring the data, they simultaneously resonate with common-sense explanations of why young people might occasionally misreport on sensitive issues.

Summary

The North-West Longitudinal Study involved following several hundred young people from Year 1 when they were 14 years old for five years until they were 18. The overall aim of this study was to assess how 'ordinary' young people, growing up in England in the 1990s, developed attitudes and behaviours in relation to the unprecedented ready availability of drugs alongside other consumption options such as alcohol and tobacco. Their drugs status was to be situated in a broader analysis of their leisure 'time out' pursuits, and equally importantly within their maturation during adolescence.

This investigation involved the use of both quantitative and qualitative methods. The primary technique was a self-report questionnaire administered personally by the researchers to several hundred young people initially within eight State secondary schools (and then by post) in two, non-inner-city, boroughs of metropolitan north-west England. In Year 1, the sample was representative of those areas by gender, socio-economic status and ethnicity. However, attrition partly reduced this over time with the disproportionate loss of some 'working-class' participants and some respondents from Asian and Muslim backgrounds. However, there are strong indications that the 'core cohort' which has been with the project throughout the five years is very similar to the larger annual samples particularly in Years 4 and 5.

A longitudinal study is able to address issues of validity and reliability far more extensively than one-off snapshot surveys but in turn must also explain 'anomalous' or inconsistent reporting that occurs over the years. Although we believe that 'misreporting' was not a major problem there is good evidence that most anomalies were created as the participants became more honest and reliable each year, feeling able to trust the research team whom they saw annually and without any negative consequences such as a breach of confidentiality.

During Year 4, 86 respondents were interviewed in depth. The transcribed interviews were a particularly rich source of data through which we were able to place the use and non-use of drugs in the broader backcloth of everyday young lives in which education, training, work, leisure, friendships, courtships, domestic relationships and enjoying 'time out' at weekends were all explored. The interviews also acted as a validation technique for the surveys and a stimulus for the pathways analysis. Alongside these, but during Year 5, a small number of case studies of 'critical incidents' related to drugs were undertaken, prompted by respondents reporting significant events to the researchers.

Basically by Year 4 we identified four distinctive drugs pathways which proved to be robust conceptual tools. These pathway groups were regular *current drug users*, *abstainers* who had never used nor intended to use illicit drugs, *ex-triers* who had experimented with drugs but did not intend to do so again and a large group *in transition*. Those in transition may or may not have used an illicit drug but believed it possible or likely that they would do so in the future.

This pathway analysis provides a far more sophisticated conceptualisation of how young people develop attitudes and behaviours through time. In particular it distinguishes between drug experimenters, regular drug users and those who have never tried an illicit drug, whilst showing how these behaviours are both dynamic yet remain linked to many other attitudes and attributes as will be seen in subsequent chapters.

We turn now to an updated discussion of our strategies for following our sample into adulthood from 1999 to 2008.

Evolving methods and techniques (1999–2008)

Signs of the times

In updating this methods chapter we are particularly struck by how dramatic the changes in our use of information technology have been over the two decades since the research first began. We refer on page 29 to our early use of 'mainframe' computers – large, centrally located machines stored in climate controlled rooms, to which data analysis jobs were 'sent' from remote terminals across the university campus. It was only after our research began that we were able to make what then seemed like an exciting move to desktop PCs powerful enough for analysing large datasets using programs like SPSS/PC and SPSS for Windows. Mainframe computing such as we used back then will be alien to most social researchers today. We also refer to eschewing 'floppy disks' in favour of 'tape streamers' to back up our increasingly large dataset; this too dates us in information technology terms. These days, a cheap USB memory stick that can be held in the palm of the hand has space for 100 or more times the data than we were able to hold on the hard drive of a typical desktop computer in the early 1990s, and the recent move towards 'cloud computing' often means that data and even software can be stored via virtual servers over the internet. It is not only in relation to the large datasets generated by our surveys that we witness change, however. Our first in-depth interviews were recorded on what now seem to be clunky and cumbersome cassette tape recorders. Interviewers had to remember to turn the tapes over before the allotted time on one side had run out (45 minutes, or on the extra long ones, 60 minutes). These days, cheap digital voice recorders are the norm, and by the time of the final data collection in 2005, these were used for recording interviews. Their sound quality is excellent and their battery life long. Even basic models can store tens or even hundreds of interviews directly on the recorder itself in the form of MP3 files: no more cassette tapes to carry around, damage or lose. The digital world today brings its own problems for qualitative researchers, particularly in relation to data security as researchers deal with the proliferation of versions and copies of data that result when voice recordings and their text transcriptions multiply over the course of a research project (Aldridge *et al.*, 2010). In the early days of our research, data security was a simple matter of using a lockable filing cabinet.

Another change we implemented during the project involved revising the format of our drugs questions in the questionnaire. Starting in the sixth survey administration for the NWELS project in 1999 (when members of the cohort were 22 years old), we used a new method for asking questions about drug taking that we had innovated and tested as part of a different research project on adolescent drug taking (see Aldridge *et al.*, 1999). We sought to compare this new approach to the one we (and others) had been using up to this time, in which one question (e.g. about drug offers) was asked in relation to a long list of drugs before moving on to the next question (e.g. about use). Using our new approach, all of the questions we were interested in (in relation to recognition, offers, ease of availability, use, frequency of use, and future use intentions) were asked for one drug, before moving on to ask each question again for the next drug. Over the years, the number of questions we wanted answers to in relation to each drug was growing – and so too, therefore, was the questionnaire's complexity and the level of missing/inconsistent data generated in each survey administration. We anticipated that our new approach would result in less missing data and fewer inconsistent responses. This is exactly what we found in our pilot research comparing the standard method to our new approach. Moreover, in the cognitive testing we did, we found that respondents preferred our new approach. This change has now been taken up in the annual English schools surveys 'Smoking, Drinking and Drug Use', whose cognitive testing replicated our own (see Boreham and Shaw, 2002).

When *Illegal Leisure* was published, the North West England Longitudinal Survey was one of the few longitudinal studies of its kind. Even today, most surveys of drug taking are repeated cross-sectional surveys: apt for working out whether drug taking is rising or falling over time in the population, and much less resource intensive than longitudinal surveys. What these repeated surveys cannot do, however, is determine how *individuals* change over time – when they start taking drugs, slow down or stop, and maybe step-up again or switch substances. Two notable research undertakings that have included a focus on alcohol and drug use are exceptions. The *Belfast Youth Development Study* began tracking almost 4,000 young people annually from 2000 to 2005, and again in 2007 and 2010 (McCrystal, 2009). The *Edinburgh Study of Youth Transitions and Crime* (McVie and Bradshaw, 2005) began with a single-aged cohort (11/12 years) of over 4,000 young people who started secondary education in 1998 and followed them annually until 2003 at the age of 17/18, with a further follow-up currently underway at age 21/22.[1] Both projects benefit from large samples, and the Edinburgh study in particular from very high response rates. The North West England Longitudinal Research Study, on which *Illegal Leisure* is based, therefore, may no longer be unique in its ability to map the drug-taking journeys of individuals over time, but its coverage, so far spanning 14 years in the lives of the cohort, alongside its early beginnings as far back as 1991, characterise its unique place amongst studies of its kind.

Indeed, over the many years of conducting such a lengthy piece of longitudinal research, one of the skills we needed to develop was dealing with the public interest generated from the publication of our

---

1   Although the longitudinal Home Office 'Offending Crime and Justice Survey' collects data on drug taking amongst young people, the only longitudinal analyses involving drug use have treated drug use as one amongst a number of forms of offending (see Hales *et al.*, 2009).

findings. Whilst dealing with the press was something the team had not initially anticipated or been trained in, as publicly funded academics employed on a publicly funded research project, we were committed to the public dissemination of our findings. As the study progressed and became increasingly high profile, the team developed a public dissemin- ation strategy that included annual press releases to coincide with key publications, carefully constructed with the help of the university press office. Our aim was to move beyond the 'shock, horror' headline stat- istics on the scale of contemporary drug use; to help foster a public discussion of broader issues relating to the role of drugs in young people's lives, how users weigh up the benefits as well as the costs when making drug-related decisions, and distancing 1990s recreational drug use from the prevailing media representations of drugs, disease, death and crime. Perhaps unsurprisingly, and with a few notable exceptions (Guardian, 1998), the press coverage focused on the headline preva- lence figures and rarely went beyond this to the measured and in-depth discussion of drugs issues that we hoped for (as also recognised by Blackman, 2004). This can be illustrated by the press coverage for the *Drugs Futures* report (Parker *et al.*, 1995). In recognition of the fact that lifetime prevalence rates were increasing towards the halfway point for young people's recreational experimentation, the report ended with what at the time could be interpreted as a potentially controversial phrase: 'Over the next few years, and certainly in urban areas, non-drug trying adolescents will be a minority group. In one sense they will be the deviants' (1995: 26). BCS prevalence figures revealed that young adults' drug trying did indeed reach the 50 per cent level soon after this pre- diction. When trying to discuss the 1990s increase in recreational drug use to unprecedented levels, issues of normalisation and non-problem drug use, one member of the team was interviewed by the Daily Express newspaper (and only once). The resulting article could not have been further from our dissemination aim: a full-page feature headlined 'You don't take drugs? You're a deviant!' with a large illustration of a hypodermic syringe alongside the article (Daily Express, 1995).

From 18 to 22 and 27/28 years old

Our research over the first five years described earlier in this chapter incorporated a qualitative element in the form of some one-off face-to- face interviews conducted when members of the cohort were 17 years old. Back then, it was primarily through the repeated surveys we undertook annually that we gained a longitudinal understanding of individual drugs careers.

After the members of our cohort entered adulthood, however, we shifted our research focus to trying to understand more precisely the dynamics of how people make decisions about their drug taking over time – and how these decisions are connected to the big events of early adulthood such as accessing further and higher education, getting jobs, settling into relationships and having children, as well as, for some, coping with unemployment, the breakdown of relationships and bereavement. We decided that these questions could best be answered by talking at length with members of the cohort; by listening to the stories of their lives in their own words, rather than forcing them into the more restrictive 'tick box' or short-answer style of replies we could obtain from a questionnaire alone. We therefore shifted the balance of our research strategy from the primarily quantitative survey approach we'd used in for the first five years of the research, to one in which the in-depth qualitative interview was perhaps more central to our attempts to understand how drug decisions evolve from adolescence to adulthood.

Two further data collection attempts resulted: one when the cohort was 22 years old, and another at the age of 27/28. The first was funded by the ESRC, and data collection took place in 1999 and 2000, eight years after our first contact with the cohort in 1991. We collected the usual questionnaire data from 465 members of the cohort – representing a 71 per cent response rate – and spent considerable time and resources to achieve this, which we considered to be critical since four years had elapsed since we'd last had contact with the sample. The strategies we used are described in detail elsewhere (Parker *et al.*, 2002), but we summarise these briefly here. Prior to administering the postal questionnaire, we sent a Christmas card in 1998 to all for whom we had contact details and asked them to confirm their address and consent to take part in the study again. This was followed by a postcard in the summer of 1999 to those who had not responded. The Electoral Register was also checked to confirm addresses where possible. In autumn 1999, we sent our questionnaire to all confirmed and non-confirmed addresses, followed by a reminder after about a month, and then again a month later, the second time enclosing an additional questionnaire. We made one last follow-up attempt by phone. A £10 music voucher was promised and provided for all returned questionnaires. Taken together, these strategies helped us to reduce attrition and achieve the response rate we did. Although there was attrition from the sample we'd last captured four years previously (n = 529), our new sample at age 22 was reasonably similar to the sample at age 18.

In 2000, we also interviewed 86 members of this sample. These interviews had more depth and breadth than those we did at the age of 17. The issues we covered included education, work and housing history, leisure time, friendships and intimate relationships, offending activity, friends' drugs experiences, interviewees' own use of alcohol, tobacco and other drugs and, of course, their own drugs experiences. Interviewees were selected 'purposively': to include individuals who had a range of drug-taking experiences, including having started and stopped taking drugs and lifelong abstainers, and as well as representing as far as possible the key demographic characteristics of gender, ethnicity and socio-economic school catchment area.

The final phase of data collection occurred over a period of two years: a survey sweep in 2004 when the cohort was 27 followed a year later by in-depth interviews in 2005 when the cohort was 28 years old. Table 2.4 describes the data collected over the entirety of the North West England Longitudinal Research Study.

The seventh and final data collection sweep was carried out solely by Lisa Williams as part of her doctoral studies, and funded by a competitively awarded ESRC studentship. Although a questionnaire was again sent out to all past respondents we had ever held postal address contact information for during the research (765 in total), only 217 returned questionnaires. This represented just under half (47 per cent)[2] of the sample of 465 at age 22 and 28 per cent of the original sample at

Table 2.4 Summary of data collection 1991–2005

Data collection sweep	Year	Modal age of cohort	Survey returns	Interviews
1	1991	14	776	
2	1992	15	752	
3	1993	16	523	
4	1994	17	536	86
5	1995	18	529	
6	1999	22	465	86
7	2004	27	217	–
	2005	28	–	19

2   This return rate followed only one questionnaire posting, with no follow-up attempts at contact. In previous years, efforts to increase returns included follow-up letters, phone calls and checking the Electoral Register for updated information. Indeed, that so many returned a questionnaire after only one attempt to contact them following a five-year hiatus is suggestive of considerable trust and commitment to the research amongst members of the cohort.

the very start of the study. This level of attrition is not at all surprising, given the many transitions faced by young adults in their twenties, including changes in accommodation; employment; training, retraining and continuing education; moving into, and sometimes out of, longer-term intimate relationships; having children; and, for some, leaving the country. Given finite resources, a decision was made not to attempt to boost the questionnaire returns further due to the disproportionate time and effort required to track down more members of the original cohort. The research priority, instead, was to focus on conducting interviews in even greater depth than we had at the age of 22, and involving, as far as was possible, those individuals that had also been interviewed at 17 or 22. The 19 interviews conducted involved the use of techniques that were both 'cutting edge' (asking interviewees to read and reflect on the transcripts of their interviews from six years before, and more generally on their involvement in our research over 13 years of their lives) and 'traditional' in qualitative research terms (e.g. life history, story-telling approaches). These interviews were much longer, with the bulk lasting between one and a half and two hours (a few were less than this, and a few were longer, with the longest lasting three hours). The result was incredibly rich qualitative data on drug taking at two points in time, five years apart (Williams, 2007).

Given all these considerations, Lisa made the decision to use the questionnaire data primarily as a means to inform her sampling decisions for the qualitative interviews. She was able, therefore, to implement the qualitative research ideal of employing 'theoretical sampling' – selecting individuals for interview based on the detailed data respondents provided in their questionnaires. The resulting understanding generated from the first few interviews can thus be refined and tested by selecting useful test cases for later interview. This approach to qualitative research demonstrates a finesse we were unable to achieve with our previous interviews. The drawback, of course, was that the questionnaire sample size of 217 when members of the cohort were 27 years old was substantially impoverished in size and analytic utility.

Representativeness of samples

It is surprising therefore, given the response rate of 47 per cent, that the samples at age 22 and at age 27 are as comparable as they are, containing similar proportions of males (about 4 in 10), those from middle-class school catchment areas (about 7 in 10), and those from ethnic minorities (about 1 in 20) at both survey administrations (see Table 2.5 for descriptive statistics for the sample at age 27). As we discuss in the first edition of this chapter, it seems that the problem of attrition had its most marked effect on the make-up of the cohort in the interval between survey administrations at 16 and 17 years old – with the age of 16 in Britain representing the end of compulsory education back in the 1990s. It was from that point that our subsequent data collections were no longer broadly representative of earlier ones – much more substantially under-representing males, those from working-class school catchment areas, and those from ethnic minorities – and, most importantly of all, those who had up to that point been more drug involved. Our later 'recapture' efforts were fruitful, but never managed to reverse the effects of uneven losses across the cohort when they turned 16.

Table 2.5 also shows that the majority of respondents in the sample at the age of 27 were gainfully employed either full time (almost 8 in 10) or part time (about 1 in 10). Only a small number (1.4 per cent) were unemployed. The majority no longer lived with their parents (8 in 10), and just over half lived in a home they owned rather than rented. Most

Table 2.5 Characteristics* of the sample at 27 years of age (%)

	Age 27 (n = 217)
Female	59.4
Secondary school was in a:	
working class catchment area	28.1
middle class catchment area	71.9
Ethnicity	
white	95.4
Employed full time	77.3
Employed part time	11.6
In education or training	11.6
Looking after children or relative full time	10.6
Unemployed	1.4
Living:	
in own home	51.2
with parents	20.3
in rented accommodation	19.4
Relationship status:	
Living with partner	38.2
Married	26.7
Seeing someone	18.9
Single	17.5
Divorced/separated	1.4

* Note that not all categories for the variables are listed; therefore not all add to 100.

(65 per cent) were married or living with a partner, and fewer than one in five described themselves as 'single'.

Anomalous reporting of drug use or 'recanting' amongst young adults

Earlier in the original element of this chapter we discussed a methodological artefact unique to longitudinal research – what we referred to as 'anomalous' reporting: respondents not disclosing drug use that had been disclosed in previous survey administrations. This has since been taken up and referred to in the literature as 'recanting' (e.g. Fendrich and Rosenbaum, 2003). Our analysis suggested that recanting may result from (1) over-reporting in the earlier years (exaggeration, having a 'laugh' in questionnaire responses); (2) genuine errors (diminished concentration, ticking the wrong box by mistake, forgetting); (3) the redefinition or reconstruction of events over time, such that the second 'recanted' report is viewed by the respondent as an accurate representation of their experiences; and (4) some misidentification of respondents between the first and second years of the survey due to concerns about confidentiality amongst pupils the very first time we entered their schools, resulting in some mismatch between data from the first and second survey sweeps, particularly at a couple of the schools.

We think it likely that the reasons for recanting amongst young adults may have shifted somewhat from the reasons for adolescent recanting. By the time of the last full survey in 2004, those members of the cohort who remained with us have shown a remarkable commitment to the project over the 13 years since we first met them at the age of 14. It is unlikely that these 27 year olds will be engaging in the same level of over-reporting and exaggeration that we documented instances of early in the research. It is also likely that genuine errors, whilst not disappearing entirely, will have dwindled as our cohort matured intellectually. Indeed, their longstanding commitment to the research may mean that respondents take greater care when filling in questionnaires as adults.

Still, the phenomenon of recanting remains even in adulthood amongst our cohort – although at somewhat reduced levels – and in Chapters 4 and 5 we note this occurring between the ages of 18 and 22. We expect that recanting may for adults still involve the biographical reconstruction we noted amongst adolescent recanters, as respondents reinterpret and recast previously reported experiences. This possibility is consistent with our updated finding that initiation into drug taking occurred throughout the late teens and twenties. In other words, 'novice' experiences are not unique to adolescents. More intentional reasons for under-reporting may also play a role in explaining anomalous reporting. In spite of the undoubted trust in the research process we have earned amongst our respondents through survey returns over 13 years, contingencies in the lives of individual respondents cannot be ruled out as reasons for non-disclosure, especially where illegal activities are concerned. As we shall see in the Chapter 5 update, recanting amongst young adults was highest amongst ex-users (17 per cent) and opportunistic users (9 per cent). Both these groups, by definition, involve drug use amongst those most ambivalent about defining themselves as drug users. It may not be surprising, therefore, that recanting occurs amongst individuals who may be less 'settled' – more ambivalent – about their drug taking to begin with.

Final remarks

In the chapters that follow, we update the drugs journeys of our cohort as they enter and negotiate their twenties, and in doing so we use the surveys and interview data we collected at 22 and 27/28[3] years of age. We recognise, for the reasons discussed above, the limitations of the survey data. *We are very clear that our findings presented here under-represent the more drug-involved.* Nevertheless, it is also clear that we have managed to retain a sufficient number of these that we are able to document ongoing and sustained recreational drug taking amongst the cohort, even as they head toward their thirties. And as we shall see, the overall 'settling down' in regularity of recreational drug taking that we observe masks a surprising willingness to continue to engage in recreational drug taking, alongside continually revised drug decisions throughout adulthood – regular chopping and changing of drug status, even amongst some of the most steadfast 'abstainers'. Our data do not allow us to estimate population parameters, and are not therefore representative of young adults across Britain. We do, however, feel confident that our data capture the variety and the complexity in the drug journeys taken by the adolescents of the nineties who became the young adults of the noughties. Our research is, indeed, unique in this regard.

We would, finally, like to draw the reader's attention to a limitation to the longitudinal analysis of the qualitative data, between the ages of 14

---

3   The final data collection period spanned more than one year, and included a sample of questionnaire returns when the cohort were mostly 27 years old, and in-depth interviews when they were mostly 28 years old. In the coming chapters, we refer to the age of respondents as 27 where we report analyses of survey data, and 28 where we report analyses of interview data.

and 18 on the one hand, and from age 22 up on the other. The reason for this is that were unable to use the same pseudonyms that we used for the first edition of the book, when referring to quotations from respondents' interviews as we revisit our cohort in adulthood. Whatever original document that linked the pseudonyms we used at that time to ID numbers was long ago misplaced as those staffing the project came and went over the years (our best guess is that this will have been shredded in the purge of original questionnaires that was forced upon us in 2005 when storage space was restricted in our university premises). Our strategy as we update our chapters has been to provide the gender and age of the respondent when interviewed, in addition to the unique ID number; this will allow interested readers to identify different quotes for individual adult respondents.

3   Alcohol

'Our favourite drug'

Overview

This chapter begins with a reproduction of the chapter on alcohol from the first edition of *Illegal Leisure*. We follow this with an update entitled '1999 to 2005: Alcohol – still our favourite drug' that follows our cohort into young adulthood.

Introduction

We start our story about young people and drugs by focusing on their favourite drug, alcohol. This is because alcohol is usually the first and the most widely consumed psychoactive drug by young people in the UK and in fact its consumption is legal for young people over the age of five. It is also one type of drug use which British youth share with their elders. Indeed, we can see that drinking is already normalised: it is the most widely practised form of recreational drug use in the UK (Royal College of Psychiatrists, 1986).

In this chapter we look at the stability in levels of adolescent drinking documented in the 1970s and 1980s before identifying important changes which have been occurring in the 1990s. We then turn our attention to our own respondents' drinking profiles and patterns and discuss the numerous ways in which the young people in this study mirror these national changes. When we look at the products young people drink, how often, how much and where, it appears that our sample is fairly typical of contemporary youth. Alongside these patterns of alcohol consumption we will attempt to illustrate the meaning and significance attached to drinking alcohol, going to pubs, socialising with friends, having 'good times' and 'bad times', and alcohol's role in young people's leisure-time experiences.

Whatever pathway status young people take, whether they drink or not, whether they take illicit drugs or not, they almost invariably talk about the importance of 'time out' from everyday life, of socialising with their friends, having a good time, having a laugh and relaxing from the stresses and worries they feel. For most young people alcohol is a key component of this 'time out' and it is this centrality to their leisure which makes alcohol the 'favourite drug' for our respondents. Within the range of approaches to drinking evident in this study there is a spectrum from abstainer to heavy drinker, from occasional celebratory drinking with families to regular polydrug use of a wide repertoire of legal and illicit drugs in pubs, clubs and parties. Whilst some young people express concern about their own or their friends' or relatives' drinking, most by and large see their bad experiences, hangovers and drink-related problems as a necessary downside to alcohol consumption.

Patterns, past and present

An overview of recent research regarding trends in young people's drinking across Britain over the last three decades will provide us with the backdrop upon which to situate the drinking patterns of our respondents as they move through adolescence.

By looking at how much young people drink, how often, which drinks are consumed, where, from what age and with whom, we are able to build up a profile of adolescent drinking. In general, the 1970s and 1980s have been characterised as decades of apparent stability in young people's drinking (Duffy, 1991; May, 1992), although periods of public concern occurred within them. There were moral panics around issues of under-age drinking both in and away from licensed premises, drink-related disorder, the emergence of 'lager louts' in the Home Counties and 'champagne charlies' in the City, public drinking, the role of alcohol in football 'hooliganism', and the scale of young people's drinking on continental holidays (Marsh and Fox Kibby, 1992; Marsh *et al.*, 1978; Tuck, 1989).

The 1990s, by comparison, have been characterised by signs of change in young people's alcohol consumption. Three areas of apparent change include frequency of drinking, quantities of alcohol consumed and types of alcoholic drinks favoured by young people, with the introduction of designer drinks, high-strength bottled lagers and ciders, fortified wines, 'alcopops' and mixer drinks aimed at the youth market (Brain and Parker, 1997; Measham, 1996).

Given the problematic nature of comparisons of the findings of alcohol research, there are clear limitations to an attempt at the identification of patterns of continuity and change in young people's drinking behaviour. The complexities, limitations and lack of comparability of research looking at alcohol consumption by adults are increased when looking at young people and particularly for what is such a widespread, regular, legal and socially acceptable activity. The two main methodological types of alcohol research, the quantitative and the qualitative, each have their own limitations. School-based quantitative surveys are affected by whether administrators are teachers or external researchers, smartly or casually dressed and so on. Household-based quantitative surveys of young people face problems of privacy when conducted in the parental household and issues of sample representativeness and the exclusion of non-household-based teenagers such as those living in local authority care, in hostels or homeless. Qualitative studies of young people's drinking are rarer, less well funded, less generalisable by definition and currently no longer *en vogue*. Both qualitative and quantitative alcohol studies face problems of lack of comparability relating to under-reporting, over-reporting, faulty recall, reinterpretation of previous events and experiences over a period of time, and methodological issues regarding alcohol-consumption measures in general and the standardisation of units of measurement in particular, especially in self-reported drinking (Lemmens, 1994; Miller *et al.*, 1991; Turner, 1990). Nevertheless, given its legality and availability, information can be more easily gathered on alcohol than on illicit drugs. Thus a third source of information on drinking is 'official' statistics on the manufacture, sale and consumption of alcohol collated by drinks manufacturers, the marketing industry and associated trade organisations, some of which will be of relevance to young people's drinking.

The 1970s and 1980s

With little large-scale alcohol research conducted before the 1970s and even fewer studies which included young people, our first impressions of youthful drinking date from the 1970s and increased with more detailed surveys being administered during the 1980s. The first national survey focusing on young people's alcohol consumption was *Adolescent Drinking*, conducted in 1984 (Marsh *et al.*, 1986). Further quantitative studies by academic researchers, the Health Education Authority, the Department of Health and the OPCS added to the picture of youthful drinking in the late 1980s.

Despite the problems of comparability raised earlier, it is worth noting the consensus on some of the broad patterns in adolescent behaviour and attitudes surrounding alcohol found in the research of the 1970s and 1980s. From primary school age when young children developed negative and 'moralistic' attitudes to alcohol (Fossey, 1992; Jahoda and Cramond, 1972) they began to change their perceptions of drinking at around secondary school age and started linking alcohol with images of adulthood, sociability and excitement (Aitken, 1978). The average age young people had their first alcoholic drink was at about 10 for boys and 12 for girls. At around the age of 13 occasional drinking developed, most usually at home supervised by parents during family celebrations and holidays. By the age of 14–15 young people's drinking increased from occasional to more regularly, with about four or five in ten at this age having had an alcoholic drink within the week prior to the research. A considerable number of young people by this age had moved away from parentally supervised home-based drinking to obtaining alcohol from off-licence premises, either directly or indirectly, and consuming it with peers in streets, parks and private parties. At this point in the development of youthful drinking, the consumption of cheap ciders, beers and fortified wines for maximum levels of intoxication may have been favoured. By the age of 16–17 only a very small percentage of young people had not had an alcoholic drink and growing numbers were drinking in licensed premises with friends on an occasional or regular basis (e.g. Hawker, 1978; Marsh *et al.*, 1986; Plant *et al.*, 1985, 1990). The frequency and quantity of alcohol consumed increased throughout the teens to a peak of nearly eight in ten women having had a drink in the past week at 18 and nearly nine in ten men having had a drink in the past week at 20, linked to marital status, children, disposable income and opportunities for drinking (Goddard, 1991; Goddard and Ikin, 1988).

Although national alcohol consumption figures remained fairly stable throughout the 1970s and 1980s, there were substantial variations in drinking patterns when looking at population groups differentiated by gender, race, religion, age, social class, marital status, geographic region and so on. The north and north-west of England, for example, had the highest levels of male and female weekly alcohol consumption (Plant and Plant, 1992).

The 1990s onwards

Against this historic backcloth of overall stability in the patterns of youthful alcohol consumption there have been several changes in young people's, leisure and drinking styles during the 1990s. There are indications of changes in relation to sessional consumption, light/occasional drinking, the manufacture and marketing of alcoholic drinks, the development of licensed premises, the rise of illicit and polydrug use, and the dynamic impact of gender and race on young people's drinking behaviour and attitudes.

One of the key changes of the 1990s has been in the arena of young people's leisure-time pursuits and opportunities. The emergence of the 'rave' dance music scene in the late 1980s and its continuation in a strong dance club culture throughout the 1990s (Collin, 1997) has led to a club-based leisure industry with an increase in the availability and consumption of recreational 'dance drugs' such as ecstasy and amphetamines, combined with a rise in the purchase of soft drinks at the expense of alcohol sales (Measham *et al.*, 1998). The Henley Centre for Forecasting estimated that attendance at 'rave' events was over 50 million a year in Britain in 1993, with each person spending an average of £35 per evening on admission charges, soft drinks and 'dance drugs'. In the same year, the value of the 'rave' market as a whole was calculated to be £1.8 billion (Thornton, 1995: 15).

Alongside the booming dance club culture other leisure facilities have attracted young customers including the growing number of public and private gyms, sports centres, multi-screen cinemas, restaurants and electronic games arcades. These new youth leisure facilities, combined with a switch from licensed to off-licence sales (with the increase in home drinking, home entertainments, the emergence of satellite and cable television and home video viewing) have all resulted in decreased spending in pubs by young people.

The identification of a reduction in on-licence sales of alcohol by the drinks manufacture and marketing industries, and less spending by young people in pubs in particular, led to attempts to revitalise the youth drinks market in three main ways. Firstly, drinking venues were updated and refurbished for the youth market and set up in competition with the leisure-time alternatives for young people. This is evident in the introduction of a range of licensed premises including 'fun' pubs, themed pubs, wine bars, speciality beer pubs, continental-style cafe bars and pub entertainments such as satellite sports television, personality DJs, live music, comedy, karaoke, quiz nights and so on. The drinks companies became increasingly sophisticated in their targeting and marketing of pubs to specific sections of the population such as town teenagers, students, 'twentysomethings', older traditional drinkers, young families and so on, using the location of pubs, their decor, ambience and the range of food, drinks and entertainments on offer to carve out a niche for their chain.

Secondly, the drinks industry introduced new alcoholic drinks whose distinct designs and marketing were aimed at the youth market. In the early 1990s strong bottled white ciders and premium lagers were directed at young drinkers along with fortified wines and aperitifs. These were followed by the alcoholic lemonades and colas after 1995 now known as 'alcopops', and 'ice' lagers and ciders whose strength was increased through the manufacturing process. The lucrative dance club market was tapped through the introduction of updated soft drinks: isotonic drinks, mineral waters, and high caffeine and 'energy' drinks for those young people who preferred not to drink alcohol at dance events. The drinks industry pushed further into the dance club market with the introduction of sophisticated club cocktails, aperitifs, wine and spirit mixers and alcoholic 'energy' drinks with added herbal extracts such as guarana, combined with the sponsorship of dance club events and alcohol promotion nights (Measham *et al.*, 1998). Such was public concern over their popularity with young people that some licensed premises stopped selling the new 'alcopops' and the drinks industry reluctantly introduced a voluntary code regulating the packaging and advertising imagery used in the marketing of 'alcopops' (Brain and Parker, 1997).

Thirdly, alongside the manufacture and marketing of new alcoholic and soft drinks for young people there has been an across-the-board increase in the average alcohol by volume strength of drinks sold in the 1990s. Studies of young people's drinking since the mid 1990s have confirmed the growing popularity of this new generation of stronger alcoholic beverages such as bottled white ciders, premium and 'ice' lagers, fortified wines and aperitifs aimed at the youth market (e.g. Health Education Authority, 1996; Hughes *et al.*, 1997; McKeganey *et al.*, 1996; Measham, 1996; Scottish Council on Alcohol, 1996).

Young people's drinking and drug use are not mutually exclusive, however, with evidence of some young people combining alcohol with illicit recreational drugs during their leisure time. Such combined drug use is in part dependent on the social situation and desired effects of use. So, for example, alcohol and cannabis may be favoured combination drugs in relaxed home settings whereas alcohol and amphetamines or 'poppers' are reportedly used together in a range of club settings.

Research has shown evidence of some emerging patterns in relation to youthful drinking which are only in part the result of changes in the marketing of pubs and alcohol. There appears to be a polarisation of drinking behaviour with numbers of occasional and light drinkers increasing alongside consumption levels by heavy drinkers. For example, an increase in light/occasional drinking and in the numbers of non-drinkers has been identified by Balding and Regis (1996) for both girls and boys in the 11–15-year-old age group.

Amongst more frequent drinkers, the proportion of young people who drink on at least a weekly basis does not appear to be rising during the 1990s. However, weekly drinkers do appear to be drinking more alcohol per week. Balding and Regis (1996) found an increase in the number of standard alcohol units per week consumed by weekly drinkers in 1990–94 and this was confirmed by Goddard (1996) and Miller and Plant (1996). Whilst acknowledging the critical issue of accuracy of measurement, research suggests that changing drink preferences alongside changing attitudes to intoxication are leading to increased sessional consumption by weekly drinkers (Measham, 1996). Amongst these weekly drinkers are a minority of heavy, regular and problematic young drinkers who routinely drink up to and indeed beyond the current 'sensible' drinking guidelines and have been identified as more likely to engage in various sorts of risk taking or 'deviant' behaviour. The links between alcohol, smoking, under-age sexual intercourse, illicit drug use, violence, disorder and criminal behaviour have been discussed more fully elsewhere (Newcombe *et al.*, 1994; Plant and Plant, 1992). It should be noted here, however, that not all heavy end alcohol use and 'abuse' can be linked to socio-economic and psychological problems. There is increasing evidence that young 'risk takers' are predominantly 'normal' in their psychological assessment scores and are more curious, outgoing, sociable and pleasure-seeking than their risk-avoiding peers. Not only do these 'risk takers' question rules and authority, not surprisingly, they also have impressive educational attainments, and are increasingly likely to be females and from middle-class backgrounds too (Leitner *et al.*, 1993) than previously was supposed (Plant *et al.*, 1985).

Finally in this section we consider the changing nature of the impact of gender and ethnicity on drinking behaviour amongst young people in Britain. There is some evidence to suggest that young women in the 1990s are closing the teenage gender gap in drinking during the early and mid teens with few significant differences in frequency and quantity of consumption at this age. Young women have a greater disposable income and there is evidence that they are adopting working and behavioural patterns such as drinking and smoking which were traditionally seen as more male-oriented (Rowlands *et al.*, 1997). Choice of drink remains highly gendered, however, illustrating how drinking alcohol is linked with self-image, identity and consumer marketing for young people. Women and men also discuss their drinking in different terms, with themes such as self-control versus disinhibition suggesting that gendered attitudes to drinking continue. The gender gap in frequency and quantity of consumption re-emerges during early adulthood, however, with young women's drinking peaking at around 18 then declining thereafter. Men's drinking continues to increase and peaks later at around 20 then stabilises rather than declines during the mid twenties (Goddard and Ikin, 1988), although we should not be surprised if these patterns are redefining at the end of the millennium.

Ethnicity and religion both exert significant influences on youthful drinking behaviour in Britain in the 1990s. In representative surveys of young people which include minority ethnic respondents in their sample, ethnic, religious and cultural factors amongst certain specific groups appear to delay the onset of regular drinking and of pub-based socialising. Muslims, for example, are significantly more likely to be abstainers than young people of other religious groups or those who hold no religious beliefs. The differences between white and Afro-Caribbean young people's self-reported drinking, however, are less significant (James *et al.*, 1997; Newcombe *et al.*, 1994).

From our consideration of general trends in adolescent drinking in the 1990s, we now turn to the present research to see how the respondents in this study compare. Our sample of young people was asked various questions on alcohol consumption both in their five annual questionnaires and also in the in-depth interviews. The following section discusses some of the key findings in relation to onset of drinking, frequency, quantity, types of drink, location, reasons for drinking, positive and negative experiences after drinking, and typical and ideal leisure-time scenarios, obtained by using these quantitative and qualitative methods.

The North-West Study: Alcohol through adolescence

Onset of drinking

In the first year of the study, at the age of 14–15, nine in ten respondents reported having tried an alcoholic drink at least once in their lives. The average age of their first drink was 11, with a slight gender difference: boys tried their first drink at approximately 10.7 years old and girls tried their first drink at approximately 11.9 years old. As Table 3.1 illustrates, over the course of the five years of the study almost all respondents came to have tried an alcoholic drink: at the age of 14, 90.2 per cent of young people had tried alcohol and this rose to 96.8 per cent by the age of 18. A core 3.2 per cent of our sample continued to totally abstain from alcohol at the age of 19.

Table 3.1 Respondents ever having tried an alcoholic drink (%)

	Year 1 n = 776	Year 2 n = 752	Year 3a n = 523	Year 4 n = 536	Year 5 n = 529
No	9.8	7.4	5.0	4.7	3.2
Yes	90.2	92.6	95.0	95.3	96.8
Total (n)	776	752	521	536	529
(%)	(100)	(100)	(100)	(100)	(100)

Drinking frequency

Throughout the five years of the study, frequency of alcohol consumption was assessed by asking respondents to estimate how often they *usually* drink alcohol. Methodological issues relating to the usefulness of the usual drinking frequency question with youthful respondents are discussed in detail elsewhere (Aldridge and Measham, 1997). Respondents' self-reported usual drinking frequency from the age of 14 to 19 is shown in Table 3.2. Answers were grouped together in five categories of response: weekly, monthly and occasional drinkers, those who had tried an alcoholic drink but no longer drank alcohol and those who had never tried alcohol. Our findings show how, over the course of the teenage years covered by this study, young people move from an occasional alcoholic drink to much more frequent drinking, with the majority of respondents developing into weekly drinkers by the time they reach the age of 18. Thus 29.9 per cent of the young people in our sample considered themselves to usually drink alcohol at least weekly at the age of 14 but this rose to 80.2 per cent by the age of 18. Monthly drinkers who reported that they usually drank alcohol less than once a week but once a month or more fell from nearly a quarter of the sample at the age of

Table 3.2 Usual drinking frequency (%)

	Year 1 n = 776	Year 2 n = 752	Year 3 n = 523	Year 4 n = 536	Year 5 n = 529
Weekly	29.9	40.7	56.6	72.1	80.2
Monthly	23.9	26.4	24.2	15.1	10.8
Occasional	32.4	22.8	12.1	6.2	4.6
Ex-drinker	3.9	2.7	2.1	1.9	1.1
Abstainer	9.9	7.5	5	4.7	3.2
Total (n)	769	747	521	535	526
(%)	(100)	(100)	(100)	(100)	(100)

14 to 10.8 per cent by the age of 18. Occasional drinkers (who drank less than once a month) fell from almost one-third of young people at the age of 14 to under 5 per cent by the age of 18. Non-drinkers (including both those who had tried alcohol at least once and those who had never tried it) fell from 13.8 per cent at the age of 14 to 4.4 per cent of the sample at 18.

Figure 3.1 shows the five years' trend towards more frequent drinking in graphic form. The rising peak frequency of consumption across the five years of the study is clear, with most young people drinking two or three times a week by the age of 18, usually on Friday and Saturday nights.

Each group identified by their reported usual drinking frequency had significantly different profiles, with the differences between abstainers and drinkers being the greatest. Weekly drinkers were more likely to try their first alcoholic drink at an earlier age and consumed greater quantities of alcohol on their last drinking occasion. They drank with their friends in public places, streets, nightclubs and at their own and friends' houses and were less likely to drink alcohol with their parents. Weekly drinkers reported both more positive and more negative experiences after drinking than their less frequently drinking peers. More frequent drinking was also linked to various indicators of 'deviance' including lifetime prevalence of illicit drug use, drink-related sexual experiences and contact with the police. Abstainers were more likely to be Asian and Muslim.

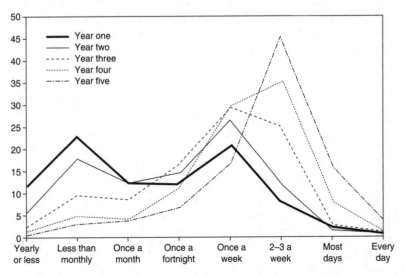

Figure 3.1 Changes in usual drinking frequency over five years (%)

Quantity of alcohol consumed

Alongside frequency of drinking, a second key measure of alcohol consumption is the amount consumed. Given the methodological difficulties in structuring such a question, the format was refined throughout the course of the study to reflect the widening choice of alcoholic drinks available to young people in the early to mid 1990s, allowing us to calculate as accurately as possible the total number of standard units of alcohol each respondent had consumed the last time they had a drink (using the equation based on one unit of alcohol equalling eight millilitres of absolute alcohol.) All respondents who had ever tried alcohol were asked to specify the number and type of alcoholic drinks they had consumed on their last drinking occasion, whenever that was, and also in later years of the survey, how much alcohol they had consumed during the previous week. Respondents were asked to include as many details as possible about their choice of drinks including brand names and sizes of bottles and glasses used for drinking. The complexity of this question format increased over the five years of the study, resulting in a three-page table of drink types by Year 5 in order to maximise accuracy of response. Table 3.3 shows changes in quantity of alcohol consumed over the course of the five years with answers grouped together into ranges of standard alcohol units.

Figure 3.2 shows the trend towards heavier sessional consumption between Years 1 and 5 of the study in graphic form. The rising peak of medium and heavy consumption of over five units of alcohol on last drinking occasion clearly contrasts with the decline in light sessional drinking of under five units.

Table 3.3 Quantity of alcohol consumed on last drinking occasion (%)

	Year 1	Year 2	Year 3	Year 4	Year 5
Units of alcohol					
1–2	29.2	21.9	17.5	14.1	13.9
3–4	18.4	15.4	16.6	20.1	12.7
5–6	9.2	9.5	12.3	11.9	14.9
7–10	16.8	20.5	21.6	20.3	22.3
11–20	13.1	23.4	24.4	27.2	23.9
21–28	6.0	5.1	4.5	4.2	8.4
29–40	3.0	2.7	2.9	1.2	2.8
41+	4.4	1.5	0.2	1.0	1.0
Overall mean units	10.1	9.5	9.1	9.3	10.6
Overall modal units	2	2	1	4	2

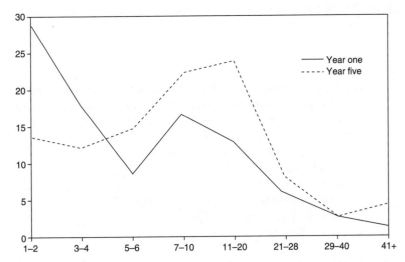

Figure 3.2 Changes in quantity of alcohol consumed on last occasion over five
years (%)

There was little change in the overall mean level of alcohol consumption on last occasion reported by young people throughout their teens.
Throughout the five years of the study respondents reported drinking
an average of about nine or ten units the last time they had a drink. At
each stage the modal (most frequent) response was between one and
four units of alcohol. The low mean and mode in Year 3 may reflect the
loss of heavy end drinkers in the sample due to attrition (see Chapter 2).
Increases in Years 4 and 5 reflect more conservative young people
remaining in the sample after Year 3 who increased their drinking after
the age of 16, coupled with a move to drinking in licensed premises. If
we look in more detail at the table and group the results into light,
medium and heavy sessional consumption, the proportion of the sample at each year who were light sessional drinkers decreased whilst
medium and heavy sessional drinking increased over the five years.
Light sessional drinking of one to four units decreased from 48 per cent
at the age of 14 to 27 per cent by the age of 18. Medium sessional
drinking of five to ten units increased from 26 per cent at 14 to 37 per
cent at 18 and heavy sessional drinking of 11 to 40 units increased from
22 per cent to 35 per cent respectively. Responses of over 40 units of
alcohol consumed during last drinking occasion are suspicious and may
represent over-reporting; these were negligible after the first year.
    Indeed if researchers and readers are sceptical of the large quantities

of alcohol young people report that they consume, the respondents themselves are sometimes incredulous. One 18-year-old interviewed for the qualitative component of the longitudinal study was surprised at his own consumption levels on occasion.

> [Do you ever estimate the amount of alcohol you have consumed in terms of standard units of alcohol?] In a situation where I've got unfeasibly drunk and I've worked out how many units I've had. There was one instance when I was in the lower sixth so I would have been seventeen. We hired this place for our sixth form Christmas do and I worked out that I'd had something like three weeks alcohol in one day. I thought I should be drunk – this was the day after, at lunch time when I was at the chippy – I thought I should still be drunk. That's why I worked it out.
>
> (John)

By the age of 18 over one-third of the sample were classified as heavy sessional drinkers; that is, they had consumed 11 units of alcohol or more on their last drinking occasion. The profile of this group of heavy drinkers suggests that they were significantly more likely than light sessional drinkers to be male, to drink alcohol once a week or more frequently, to have tried illicit drugs and to be pupils at the schools located in working-class catchment areas. At the age of 18, 80 per cent of male drinkers and 80 per cent of female drinkers reported drinking more than the current 'sensible' sessional drinking guidelines of four and three units of alcohol respectively on their last drinking occasion.

Turning now to past week consumption for 18 year olds, the average number of standard units of alcohol consumed by this age group in the previous week was 25, with a mode of five units. Of those who drank alcohol in the week prior to completion of their Year 5 questionnaires, one in ten drank no more than four units, four in ten drank five to 20 units, three in ten drank 21 to 40 units and a staggering 18 per cent reported drinking over 40 units of alcohol during the previous week. Of male drinkers at the age of 18, 50 per cent reported drinking more than the current 'sensible' weekly drinking guidelines of 28 units of alcohol during the previous week. Of female drinkers at the age of 18, 36 per cent reported drinking more than the current 'sensible' weekly drinking guidelines of 21 units of alcohol during the previous week.

Do young people themselves consider their drinking in terms of measuring the quantity of alcohol consumed in general, and counting standard units of alcohol in particular? Eighty-six respondents were interviewed on a one-to-one basis at around the age of 17. Whilst over nine in ten young people interviewed had heard of the term standard units of alcohol, only 17 respondents (22.5 per cent) ever applied this to themselves and attempted to estimate the amount they drank in terms of standard units. Of these, only four respondents ever set limits on their own drinking in terms of the number of standard units of alcohol they would consume. Two of these did so for driving purposes. One heavy-drinking young man who was interviewed was asked if he had heard of standard units of alcohol:

> Yes. What is it . . . one unit or something per pint or something? Measuring like driving and stuff. I haven't passed my test so it doesn't matter. I can just walk home or stagger, or someone else will carry me home. I know how many I've had because I'm on the floor.
>
> (Michael)

Given the longitudinal nature of this study we are able to consider whether those individuals who reported more frequent and heavier drinking in earlier years are the same individuals as those who report more frequent and heavier drinking in Year 5. Several earlier studies of adolescent drinking have shown low correlations between younger heavy drinkers and later heavy drinkers (Plant *et al.*, 1985). Looking firstly at the relationship between frequent drinking (twice a week or more often) in the early and later teens, over three-quarters (76.5 per cent) of more frequent drinkers at the age of 15 were also frequent drinkers at the age of 18. Turning then to heavy consumption (11 units of alcohol or more on last drinking occasion) the relationship is less clear with under half (41.4 per cent) of heavy sessional drinkers at the age of 15 being also heavy sessional drinkers at the age of 18.

Types of drinks

The North-West Study found that the choice of drinks consumed by young people in this study reflects national findings regarding the prevalence of beer, lager and cider consumption, and in particular the popularity of strong bottled lagers and ciders.

Respondents were asked which alcoholic drinks they usually drank, which ones they consumed on their last drinking occasion and which were their three favourite drinks. Throughout the study between one-quarter and one-third of young people reported usually drinking cider, with slightly lower numbers reporting usually drinking lager. When respondents were asked which were their favourite alcoholic drinks, the majority of current drinkers were brand-name specific when considering their favourite drink. At the age of 15 for example, 18 per cent of respondents gave brand names of cider as their favourite drink and a further 8 per cent mentioned cider in general without specifying any brand names. Specific brands of lager were reported as their favourite drinks by 15 per cent and a further 8 per cent mentioned lager in general. After cider and lager, brand-named aperitifs and liqueurs were the third most popular group of drinks for 13 per cent of current drinkers although none mentioned them in general. The fourth most popular group of drinks was spirits, with 10 per cent mentioning specific brand names and a further 8 per cent mentioning spirits in general. Of all alcoholic drinks, both brand name and generic, the most popular drink was a brand of bottled strong white cider, with a strength of over 8 per cent alcohol by volume (Measham, 1996).

Table 3.4 shows the percentages of young people drinking each type of drink in their late teens, along with the average amount of alcohol consumed on the last occasion for each of these types of drink. Looking at drink choice on last drinking occasion at the age of 18, we can see that beers, lagers and ciders are significantly more popular than other alcoholic drinks with this age group. Over eight in ten young people report drinking beer, lager or cider the last time they had a drink and over a third had spirits. Over a quarter had at least one aperitif or glass of wine the last time they had a drink. 'Alcopops' are reportedly the *least* most likely alcoholic drink for 18 year olds with only one in five having consumed alcoholic lemonade or cola on their last drinking occasion. Research by Brain and Parker (1997) confirms the popularity of ciders and lagers over and above 'alcopops', even two years later when a wider variety of 'alcopops' were manufactured and marketed. The picture which emerges refutes the recent demonisation of 'alcopops' by some sections of the media and public. Not only are 'alcopops'

Table 3.4 Type of alcoholic drink consumed on last drinking occasion and mean number of standard units of alcohol imbibed for each type of drink, for all current drinkers at age 18

	% n = 502	Mean standard alcohol units
Ciders/lagers/beers	81.7	8.6
Spirits	37.8	4.7
Aperitifs	29.7	3.7
Wine	27.5	5.2
'Alcopops'	19.9	3.7
Total	100	10.6

the least popular drink with this age group, they are also linked with the lowest levels of consumption by those who do choose to drink them. Lagers and ciders are the preferred drink for heavy sessional drinkers, with an average of nearly nine units of lager or cider consumed on the last occasion for the eight in ten drinkers who had those drinks. An average of five units of wine and spirits were consumed on last drinking occasion by those who drank wine and spirits. Under four units of aperitifs and 'alcopops' were consumed on last occasion by the two or three in ten young people who drank them.

Drinking locations

Regarding the location of youthful drinking episodes, previous alcohol research has identified a shift during the mid to late teens from home-based drinking supervised by parents to pub-based drinking with friends. This study included several questions relating to where our respondents drank alcohol and with whom. In the first three years of the study respondents were asked a general question regarding where they usually drink alcohol. In the latter two years of the study the question format was changed from a general to a specific question which asked respondents where they were the last time they drank alcohol. Whilst the general and specific questions are not directly comparable, Table 3.5 illustrates some of the changes in answers to these two questions over the five years of the study by looking at a selection of five key locations featured within the more extensive list of items in the questionnaire.

At the ages of 14 and 15 young people reported that their own home, followed by friends' houses, were the main places where they drank alcohol. The third most usual drinking location for young people at 14 and 15 was outside in the streets, parks and other public places. By the age of 16 there was a considerable increase in the numbers of young people drinking in licensed premises such as public houses and

Table 3.5 Changes in selected places where alcohol is consumed (%)

	Year 1	Year 2	Year 3	Year 4	Year 5
Home	77.5	83.7	87.2	20.4	18.2
Friends' houses	66.8	79.9	82.4	12.4	9.7
Outside/streets/parks	65.0	70.6	45.6	0.8	0.6
Clubs/discos	51.9	47.0	74.2	24.2	17.6
Pubs	46.3	69.1	86.7	49.5	59.9

nightclubs alongside continued drinking at home and in friends' houses. The increase in public-house drinking occurs at around the same age as the decrease in public street drinking, most probably related to some young people's ability to gain entry to licensed premises from the age of 16 and to obtain alcohol either directly from bar staff or via older-looking friends. This suggests that by the age of 16 young people prefer drinking in pubs to outside on the streets, but that they will drink on the streets when unable to gain access to pubs and unwilling or unable to drink at home.

By the age of 17 most young people are able to obtain alcohol in pubs and clubs, whether directly or indirectly. Nearly three-quarters of 17-year-old drinkers consumed their last alcoholic drink on licensed premises: half of young people had their last drink in a pub or bar and a quarter of them last drank alcohol in a nightclub. Another third of 17 year olds had their last drink in either their own home or a friend's house, leaving less than 1 per cent of drinkers having had their last drink outside on the streets. This trend continues up to 18 so that by the time young people can legally purchase alcohol in licensed premises six in ten had their last drink in a pub, whereas under three in ten had their last drink in their own or their friends' homes. Negligible numbers drank outside.

Reasons for drinking

Drinking location illustrates how young people's drinking develops in the mid teens as a part of both their celebrations with family and their leisure-time socialising with friends. Although aware of the limitations and subjectivity of attempts at ascertaining reasons for drinking through the use of self-report questionnaires, we attempted to identify some of the reasons young people themselves give for why they drink alcohol. During the first three years of the study respondents were given a check list of various reasons for drinking alcohol compiled from answers given during piloting of the questionnaire with young people of a similar age. Table 3.6 summarises the main reasons given by 14–16 year olds for drinking.

The importance of light/occasional, home-based, parentally super-vised drinking is reflected at the ages of 14 and 15. The main reason for drinking given by two-thirds of drinkers was to celebrate special occasions including birthdays, weddings and seasonal festivals. The positive and sociable aspects of drinking were also given as reasons by between a quarter and half of young drinkers in their early teens: they say they drink because they find it fun, their friends drink alcohol, it makes them

Table 3.6 Reasons for drinking alcohol (%)

	Year 1	Year 2	Year 3
Special occasions	67.6	65.6	59.7
It's fun	44.1	49.5	44.6
Makes me less shy	40.1	44.6	38.5
Friends drink	33.1	28.9	21.9
Like being drunk	26.4	32.9	28.4
Boredom	20.0	22.3	14.4
Helps 'chat up' people	19.0	22.1	19.1
Like pubs and clubs	16.9	34.0	66.7
Alcohol is kept at home	7.1	5.8	5.5

less shy and it helps them 'chat up' potential partners. We suggest that they enjoy the sociability of *who* they drink with rather than *where* they drink at this age, with understandably only 16.9 per cent of 14 year olds seeing their enjoyment of the atmosphere in pubs and clubs as a reason for drinking. Of some concern, however, is the consideration that over a quarter of 14 year olds reported that they like being drunk and one-fifth of them are drinking to relieve boredom.

By the age of 16, whilst the celebration of special occasions is still given as a key reason for drinking, the importance of the role of pubs and clubs in young people's social lives has surpassed this as a reason for drinking. The percentage of young people who report drinking alcohol because they like pubs and clubs increased from 16.9 per cent of drinkers at the age of 14 to 66.7 per cent by the age of 16. This mirrors pubs changing from one of the least usual to most usual specified drinking locations over the course of the teens in Table 3.5.

By way of comparison, the qualitative interviews with 17-year-old respondents also asked about reasons for drinking alcohol. The seven main reasons given to this open-ended question were: to socialise (58.3 per cent), for enjoyment (28.6 per cent), liking the taste (26.2 per cent), to relax (25 per cent), to get merry/drunk (22.6 per cent), to have a good time (16.7 per cent) and to increase confidence/reduce inhibitions (13.1 per cent). One 17-year-old young woman summed it up; 'It's a social thing, a friend thing. It makes you relax. I suppose it helps you have a good time as well, or a better time if you're having a crap time' (Sarah).

Alcohol, pubs, clubs and 'time out'

Despite declining brewery profits and sales in the on-licence trade and the closure of hundreds of pubs across Britain every year, licensed premises remain a central leisure-time location for young people in the mid 1990s, and as we have seen, the attraction of pubs and clubs is reportedly a key reason for drinking in the late teens. Turning our attention to the ways in which pubs, clubs and 'time out' are discussed alongside reasons for drinking in the qualitative data, one 17-year-old respondent summed up why he drank as 'basically I like it. I just like drinking. I like being drunk as well, but I just like sitting in a pub and drinking.' A heavy-drinking male respondent who drinks nearly every day said he drinks alcohol: 'When I'm socialising, I go out for a pint with my mates. It gets me out of the house. And I have a laugh while I'm having a drink, go for a game of darts or something' (Steven). One young woman interviewed who drinks pints of cider at her local pub links the taste, the effects and the pub itself as reasons for her drinking:

> I like getting drunk. I like the taste. Well, I used to like the taste of cider. I'm getting a bit sick of it now.
>   [Why do you like getting drunk?] It makes me more outgoing.
>   [Could you imagine going to the pub and not drinking alcohol?] Yes. Sometimes I just go and get a coke if I don't feel like drinking. But more often than not I do start drinking because you just go, order your pint and you sit down.... It's quite strange because before I was eighteen it was the only pub that didn't ask for ID because they don't expect young people to go in there because it's not a fashionable pub. ... I get really loud when I'm drunk and it's not very nice really but they're all right about it.
>
> (Marie)

Public houses have been a central leisure location in Britain for 150 years, at least for working-class men, and alcohol has traditionally been the main focus of spare-time socialising within them (Harrison, 1971). Since the mid nineteenth century 'within the sphere of commercialized leisure . . . the pub played a central role' in Greater Manchester (Davies, 1992: 169). In the late twentieth century, despite changes in young people's lives and in the leisure industry, by and large the consumption of alcohol in pubs remains an integral part of British leisure as illustrated by this study, with adolescents developing into weekend pub drinkers during their mid teens, drinking alcohol in some form in pubs of some sort or other. With the extension of adolescence, the expansion of higher education, delayed entry into the labour market and later moving out of the parental home, the desire for a social space away from parents and siblings is heightened. Respondents in this study mentioned the possibility of open-air venues for socialising in summer (the beach was a regular spot for some of our sample in their mid teens), but pubs were one of the few alternatives to their own home on cold, dark and wet winter nights. Thus the continuing importance of pubs and bars in young people's lives reflects not only their historic attractions but also the lack of attractive, affordable local alternatives.

When discussing their reasons for drinking, some respondents interviewed illustrated the movement between the legal and illicit drugs markets in their selection of leisure time drug(s). In a world of increasing availability of illicit drugs, as we shall see in later chapters, decisions surrounding their drinking become entwined with decisions surrounding their use of other psychoactive drugs. Described elsewhere as a pick 'n' mix approach to recreational drug use (Parker and Measham, 1994), alcohol is only one of a range of possible drugs in young people's repertoires, although favoured by many because it is relatively cheap, legal, tolerated (and even facilitated) by many of their peers and elders, and is associated with youthful socialising and celebrating centring on pubs and clubs. For example, one young man said that his main reason for drinking was because 'it's a change ... have a drink instead of having a smoke [of cannabis]', although he qualified this by saying that he prefers to smoke cannabis than drink alcohol if he has to drive, adding that 'I just don't really want to go out and get drunk on it [alcohol] all the time' (Martin).

Although not essential to it for all young people and certainly recognised as problematic to a greater or lesser extent by many, alcohol is part of the overall (p)leisure package embraced in modern youth culture. These 'good times' with alcohol do not come cheap, however. Amongst our interviewees who reported having a drink in the previous week, young women spent an average of £12 in the past week on alcohol and young men spent an average of £21.

Alcohol is a thread throughout young people's leisure times, the good and the bad. Hence it is no surprise that alcohol was the most popular drug amongst the young people interviewed. Of these 86 young people, those who had tried illicit drugs (69.8 per cent, n = 60) were asked whether they had a 'favourite drug' and if so, which one(s). One-third of interviewees who had tried drugs (33.3 per cent, n = 20) said that their favourite drug was (still) alcohol. Cannabis was their second favourite drug, chosen by one-sixth of interview respondents (16.7 per cent, n = 10), and tobacco and ecstasy were joint third choice as favourite drugs (8.3 per cent each, n = 5). One person said amphetamines were her favourite drug. No other drugs were mentioned. It is interesting to note the proportion of young people who considered legal as well as illicit drugs in their replies when asked to name their 'favourite drug', with 41.7 per cent (n = 25) nominating alcohol or tobacco. Our respondents explain the reasons for their preference for alcohol below. For example, when asked which was his favourite drug one regular drug user said:

> Alcohol. Saying that, I'm not addicted to alcohol like I'm addicted to cigarettes. I really enjoy going out and getting legless. Because it's so social. You can go out and you can have a really good time. That's very ambiguous but say I saw someone I didn't like and I was drunk, I'd go up to them and say 'All right? How are you doing?' It's very cheap for a start.
>
> [Availability?] Availability's brilliant. That's another thing. There's places set aside for you to drink – pubs – rather than like a smoking room so that's a bonus. I can do it with my family, because I'm very close to my family.
>
> [Where do you prefer to have it?] Pub. Especially when you've got a local.
>
> (John)

Alongside access, availability and legality, young people also expressed a preference for alcohol because of its predictability regarding its quality, strength and effects. One young woman explained how 'I know there's not going to be anything wrong with it and I know what sort of state I'll be in if I drink too much' (Tracy).

Furthermore, alcohol fits into a larger drug repertoire. Two-thirds of drug users in the interview sample had used more than one drug at the same time (n = 40) and almost all of these mentioned using a combination of drugs which included alcohol. Three-quarters of interviewees who reported having a 'favourite combination of drugs' described a combination repertoire which included alcohol. Thus, not all young people drink alcohol exclusively nor do they substitute illicit drugs for alcohol in their late teens; for some they develop polydrug repertoires in which alcohol is consumed alongside, before or after other drugs. During one-to-one interviews, 52 different combinations of drugs were mentioned which included alcohol and at least one other drug: including cannabis (n = 18), tobacco (n = 11), amphetamines (n = 6), ecstasy (n = 4), LSD (n = 1) and poppers (n = 1). Forty-one of the 52 specified combinations involving alcohol combined with illicit drug use. Such alcohol/poly drug use may be actively sought for specific effects by some respondents. However, there were also some young people included in this group of alcohol and illicit drug users for whom alcohol acted as a disinhibitor leading to unplanned and potentially more dangerous poldrug use. This is illustrated in the comments of one female drug user who said the main thing which helped her make up her own mind about taking drugs was that 'I was drunk at the time as well and I think that made a hell of a difference, because when you're sober you've just got a different perspective on it totally' (Zoe).

This acknowledgement from young people that they themselves see alcohol and tobacco as drugs may be in part an indication of the success of health education in schools on this subject and also in part result from their perspectives on their parents and elders' preference for legal rather than illicit drugs. Their discussion of legal and illicit drugs in relation to their perspectives on 'time out' suggests an interchangeability for many, depending on their circumstances, situation and mood. The importance of 'time out' is evident in many of the answers given by young people who were interviewed who were asked about their spare time, their ideal weekend and their ideal leisure location. Most young people's ideal weekend included several features from a general programme whose similarity is evident in the following five quotes from a variety of young women and men interviewed: 'going out clubbing Friday night. Spending Saturday morning in bed. Go into town clothes shopping Saturday afternoon. Probably going to the pictures Saturday night. And then sleeping Sunday and then going out somewhere for the afternoon' (Sandra). Or 'going out to clubs. All nighters. A lot to drink. Drink on one night, drugs on the other night and then a mellow Sunday, just chill out Sunday' (Kate). Or 'go to the pub on the Friday night. Go to a football match on the Saturday and Saturday night go to a club. [Sunday?] Sleep' (Laura). Or 'just going out to a club, getting drunk, having a laugh. I just like going out. I like going out with the girls. I like going out, getting drunk and everything, acting the fool' (Jenny). Or:

> Friday – I reckon go to the pub on the Friday, bit of a piss up and then probably go back to someone's house, sit around. Then sleep all day Saturday and do nothing and just eat, and then go out to town and have a good night out, and then not work on Sunday which is what I normally do. Just relax really.
>
> (Louise)

A similar formula was in evidence when we asked young people about their ideal leisure location. Whilst there were some interesting and unusual answers which would challenge any leisure company (such as synthesised, Ibiza-style, tropical holiday resorts), the most usual response was an appeal for some sort of integral entertainments site available under one roof and open up to 24 hours a day, which we have called the 'pleasure dome'. Within this 'pleasure dome' young people requested a wide range of entertainments, services, sports and leisure facilities including multi-screen cinemas, a variety of cafes, bars and pubs, fast food chains, upmarket restaurants, pizza parlours, one or more night clubs, bowling alley, electronic games arcade, quaser, shops, sports centre, swimming pool and so forth. Young people favoured the town/city centre rather than out of town for their multi-complex dream leisure location, well served by public transport facilities and trust-worthy security staff. Whilst tolerating the possibility of families and young children in their 'pleasure dome' in the day time, many were explicit in their preference for a venue specifically oriented towards young adults in the evening. A few went further in their fantasies and included the sale of certain 'soft' drugs which they considered accept-able in specific venues, reminiscent of Amsterdam-style cannabis cafes. 'Not allowing people over forty in' would bring a new twist to proof-of-age cards currently promoted by adult worlds.

Having considered the social context for young people's drinking we now discuss their own assessment of alcohol, and its positive and negative effects.

Positive effects of drinking

Some quantitative details were obtained regarding young drinkers' views about the effects of drinking alcohol, both positive and negative. Alongside reasons for drinking, detailed questions on how young people felt after they had been drinking were included in the first three years of the questionnaire, although it is recognised that reasons for drinking and effects of drinking clearly overlap. (These questions were omitted in the last two years of the study for reasons of space, due to the changing focus of the questions.) Tables 3.7 and 3.8 contain details of the self-reported positive and negative effects of alcohol for 14–16 year olds. It is clear that even at the age of 14 the majority of young

Table 3.7 Self-reported positive experiences after drinking (%)

	Year 1	Year 2	Year 3
Felt happy	87.6	92.2	95.7
Had a good time	82.1	90.1	93.8
At ease with friends	77.8	84.3	88.2
At ease with strangers	53.9	65.4	78.7

drinkers enjoy having a drink: over eight in ten feel happy and have a good time after drinking. Over three-quarters of them feel more at ease with their friends after drinking and, perhaps of more concern, over half of them also feel more at ease with strangers. Whilst feeling more at ease with strangers is included here with positive effects of alcohol consumption, the negative impact of an effect such as this is clear. Respondents may consider such a quality as positive in that it facilitates meeting and mixing with their peers but it also raises issues of personal safety and vulnerability for young people under the influence of alcohol at the age of 14, particularly in public drinking locations where they are not supervised by older relatives or friends.

By the age of 16, almost all young people report enjoying alcohol at least sometimes when they drink. Around nine in ten drinkers feel happy, more at ease with friends and have a good time after drinking alcohol. Nearly eight in ten report also feeling more at ease with strangers. This is hardly surprising, given the way alcohol acts primarily as a depressant drug, slowing the rate of activity of the central nervous system, hence resulting in feelings of relaxation, disinhibition, confidence and enjoyment in social situations for drinkers.

Negative effects of drinking

In general fewer young people report negative than positive experiences after drinking alcohol. Table 3.8 shows the percentages of 14–16 year olds for the ten highest reported negative experiences from a list of items included in the questionnaire, a list which included effects which could be considered negative in some way either physically or emotionally. Over a third of drinkers had experienced eight of the

Table 3.8 Self-reported negative experiences after drinking (%)

	Year 1	Year 2	Year 3
Unable to remember things	58.3	58.3	58.9
Had headache	54.6	55.2	55.4
Been sick	40.6	43.6	52.4
Felt guilty	48.0	46.6	51.8
Had hangover	40.2	42.8	47.5
Felt unhappy	38.4	41.4	47.3
Fell over	52.6	50.7	45.0
Worried about sexual encounter	32.4	34.9	32.9
Had argument	28.0	24.7	25.6
Had drinking criticised	19.2	18.3	21.1

listed negative experiences at least sometimes when they had a drink. The most frequently reported negative repercussion of drinking was that young people were unable to remember some aspect of their drinking occasion the next day. From the age of 14 approximately six in ten drinkers sometimes forgot things after drinking. Around four or five young drinkers reported negative physical effects which might indicate a considerable quantity of alcohol was consumed: they had a headache, vomited, had a 'hangover' and had fallen over after drinking. About half of young people in their early to mid teens felt guilty after drinking and about a third were worried about some sort of sexual experience or encounter they had had after drinking. One-quarter of young people had argued either with friends or relatives after drinking and about one-fifth had had their own drinking criticised by others for some reason. Four in ten 14 year olds and five in ten 16 year olds reported feeling unhappy at least sometimes after drinking.

The qualitative interviews with respondents when they were aged 17 to 18 provided an opportunity for them to elaborate on the sorts of experiences they had had after drinking, providing the details and the context for their experiences, along with their own perspective and understanding of these events. One young woman reflected on the sorts of arguments she had with her boyfriend and her parents about her drinking, the former also illustrating the gendered nature of constraints on young people's drink-related behaviour:

> We were absolutely ratted, stinking drunk, me and my friend and we were with my boyfriend and a couple of his friends. And we started being sick. We made a total show of ourselves and my boyfriend screamed at me the next day and told me to control myself. . . . It caused an argument. Once there was a time when my mum and dad caught me drinking. I told them I was staying for the weekend at a friend's but instead we camped out in the park. She found me in the park, drunk. I got grounded. . . . Sometimes if an argument has started I can sometimes get out of hand, I can take it a bit too far, when really you should just let it go. I tend to do more of that when I've had a drink.
>
> (Vicky)

Another young woman who is a heavy sessional drinker hinted at the link between drinking and 'casual' sexual relationships, with alcohol acting as a disinhibitor for her:

I've gone completely all the way because I do know what I'm doing but you're drunk and you want to when you're drunk.

[Do you regret it afterwards?] Sometimes yes. 'What have I done, who's he?' . . . It's just like at a club on holiday last year I was going out with my boyfriend and I got up to no good. I told him three months later. You can't help it when you're on holiday.

(Jenny)

For young drinkers in general and young women in particular, control emerged as an important theme. Issues of self-control, personal safety, vulnerability and risk were linked with both their own and others' intoxication. Whilst some young people wanted to lose control through their drinking and drug use, describing it in terms of 'losing it' or 'getting out of it', others clearly liked to feel intoxicated without crossing the threshold to total loss of control. For example, one polydrug user whose favourite drug is alcohol described how she had regulated her drinking on her last drinking occasion: 'Not overly [drunk]. We were drunk but more giggly. We weren't to the point where we didn't know what we were doing' (Sandra). Another respondent discussed drink-related casual sexual relationships, socialising with strangers and perceptions of risk during her interview:

You know when you're out and that and you're bladdered. And you think 'oh that person's gorgeous' and then you come home and you don't remember a thing. And then when you're out the next week people say 'that's the fella you got off with'. And you're just like 'oh I never'. That's happened a few times. I went back to some house once. I completely sobered up. I was on my own. I completely sobered up and I just shot off. I was out another time and I met these lads from Newcastle. And you know when you feel that someone's all right. And I went back to their hotel but they let me have one of their rooms on my own. They were dead sound. But a lot of my mates thought I was AWOL. Like when I came in they said 'oh they could have done anything to you, raped you or murdered you' and that. They never. I was lucky.

(Karen)

During the qualitative interviews three 17-year-olds, all female, revealed that they had consulted their doctors for problems which were in some way either directly or indirectly related to their drinking. One was generally 'run down', one had kidney problems which she thought were related to her use of ecstasy as well as alcohol, and the third young woman reported some sort of blood poisoning related to her alcohol consumption. 'I used to get bruises everywhere and it was from the drink. They thought I was anaemic but it turned out it was because I was drinking too much. It's something to do with the blood' (Sharon).

Tables 3.6, 3.7 and 3.8 illustrate how adolescents begin to assess the effects of drinking alcohol in terms of their positive and negative experiences. Most people in Britain, adults as well as teenagers, see moderate drinking as an acceptable, enjoyable and legitimate part of their leisure time and, indeed, young people's drinking cannot be understood without a consideration of adult society's use (and mis-use) of alcohol. When young people start drinking in their early teens and they begin to learn how to drink, they experience the positive and sociable effects of the drug and balance these against the physical and emotional consequences of drinking too much. For the young people in this study, alcohol was associated with relaxation, enjoyment and disinhibition in social situations. These were balanced against the expense of alcohol, the hangovers, sickness and memory loss linked with over-indulgence, and also drink-related problems with friends, relatives and strangers. They learned, both directly and through friends, relatives and elder siblings' experiences, *how* to drink alcohol and the optimum levels of consumption for the desired degree of intoxication. This process of learning how to drink and how much to drink was evident when young people talked about their drinking in more detail in one-to-one interviews. For example, one 17-year-old interviewed who was asked what sorts of limits she put on her drinking said:

> I don't put any limit on in terms of units. I kind of know my limit, of how many wines or how many vodkas I've had. It's just a feeling really. Unless I've got to work the next morning or whatever and I know that I don't want to get drunk. I'd count them then.
>
> [In general what sort of limit would you put on your drinking?] Just until I don't want any more. I don't let it get to the sickness stage, I don't like that.

(Elaine)

One 17-year-old male respondent explained how he decided how much alcohol to have on a drinking occasion:

> What I do is like I'll drink and drink and drink, and then when I feel a bit ill I think well I think I should stop now. I'm not really

conscious about how much I've drunk. It's just suddenly . . . hang on I'm drunk here or I'm going to be sick, so I stop drinking.

(John)

Similarly, a young woman explained the sorts of limits she put on her drinking in terms of gauging how she felt during the course of the drinking session rather than counting the numbers of drinks she consumed. 'I normally drink until I feel drunk and then I'll stop because once I feel drunk I don't particularly like to drink any more' (Vicky).

Young people's cost-benefit assessment evident here in their use of alcohol occurs for most young people well before their first experimentation with illicit drugs and, however uncomfortable this makes adult worlds feel, it is this approach to legal drugs which provides a framework for later decisions surrounding experimentation, continuation or cessation of illicit drugs made by the young people we interviewed.

Non-drinkers

And what of the small minority of young people who did not drink alcohol throughout their teens? At the age of 16, for example, 26 respondents had never had a whole alcoholic drink. When asked why they never drank alcohol, religion was the main reason given. Fifty-two per cent of 16-year-old abstainers said that it was because their religion forbids it. All except one were Muslim. Four in ten abstainers said alcohol is bad for one's health and four in ten said they did not agree with drinking alcohol for general reasons. Both parents and friends were influential on non-drinkers' decisions, with one-third (mainly Muslim) saying they did not drink alcohol because their parents disapproved and one-third saying they did not drink because their friends abstained too. Practical and legal considerations were less often stated reasons for not drinking: one-quarter did not like the taste of alcohol and 16 per cent of abstainers said they did not drink alcohol because they believed that it was against the law. By the age of 18, 15 of the 17 abstainers remaining in the sample were Muslims.

Smoking

The final section of this chapter concludes with details of survey results for tobacco, the second 'favourite' legal drug with our respondents. Tobacco use has been falling in Britain in all age groups from about half of the adult population over 16 in the 1970s to about one-third of over-16s in the mid 1990s. Research in the late 1990s, however, is suggesting young people's smoking rates are beginning to rise again, particularly amongst young women (Rowlands *et al.*, 1997). As with alcohol, the north and north-west of England have some of the highest levels of cigarette smoking, along with Scotland (Plant and Plant, 1992). Table 3.9 provides details of current smokers across the five years of this study. By the age of 18 one in four men and one in three women smoke cigarettes, despite the considerable health risks involved. In each year of the study, young women are significantly more likely to smoke than young men.

Conclusion

The North-West Study provides evidence to reinforce and elaborate on earlier studies of adolescent drinking. In general, young people start drinking alcohol in their early teens and most drink alcohol on a regular basis by their mid teens. During the adolescent years covered by this study we see evidence of the transition from home-based, parentally supervised, moderate and 'special occasions' drinking to experimental drinking in public places, parks and streets with friends, to socialising in licensed premises in the mid to late teens. From celebrating with relatives to socialising with friends, alcohol is an integral part of young people's leisure and pleasure in Britain in the mid 1990s. Considerable quantities of alcohol are consumed, with eight in ten of the respondents in this study drinking alcohol once a week or more by the age of 18 and with an average of nearly 11 units of alcohol being consumed per drinking occasion.

This study mirrors the trends identified in other studies of young

Table 3.9 Five years' data on smoking cigarettes by gender (%)

		Current smoker	*Non-smoker*
Year 1	F	37.6	62.4
	M	22.2	77.8
Year 2	F	39.4	60.6
	M	25.1	74.9
Year 3	F	37.0	63.0
	M	27.9	72.1
Year 4	F	33.2	66.8
	M	30.6	69.4
Year 5	F	37.4	62.6
	M	29.5	70.5

people's drinking in the 1990s covered earlier in this chapter regarding increased sessional consumption, the popularity of high-strength ciders and lagers, and so on, suggesting our respondents are not untypical of young people in Britain in the mid 1990s. The fragmentation and diversification of the licensed trade, in part a response to declining business due to home drinking, eating out, dance club culture and alternative entertainments, has led to the development of a range of premises such as continental-style cafes; bars, family-friendly pub restaurants, theme pubs, 'fun' pubs, live music pubs and traditional pubs in the late 1990s. As the results of this study testify, although the form changes, the pub stays with us and remains a desirable place for modern youth to spend their 'time out' with their favourite drug.

From their early teens young people decide how much to drink and indeed whether or not to drink using a cost-benefit calculation which is part of their wider risk assessment regarding the repertoire of psychoactive substances to which they have access. Young people's cost-benefit calculations, whether conscious or not, involve weighing up alcohol (and possibly illicit drugs) and deciding whether the positive effects outweigh the negatives. By the age of 16 over nine in ten drinkers report having a good time and feeling happy after drinking. Conversely, at the same age about half of drinkers reported feeling unhappy after drinking, having had a 'hangover', been sick, and had a headache.

A decade after the Royal College of Psychiatrists' report (1986) alcohol remains 'our favourite drug', although in the mid 1990s it is complemented by or replaced by illicit drugs, such as cannabis in quieter social settings and the stimulant dance drugs like amphetamines and ecstasy in club settings, by growing numbers of young people. This study, as we shall see, confirms the links between heavier drinking and the use of tobacco, illicit drugs and other risk-taking behaviour. There is evidence from our interviews with young people of a blurring of the legal and illicit in their 'pick and mix' psychoactive culture, with alcohol and tobacco acting as possible gateway drugs through to the illicit range, in a literal sense in that they usually precede experimentation with illicit drugs but more particularly because of the relationship between heavy and frequent drinking and drug use. Also of relevance to alcohol's possible gateway role is its physiological effect as a depressant or disinhibitor affecting or excusing young people's judgement, leading to alcohol being considered to be a cause of unplanned drug use for some of our respondents when they were intoxicated with alcohol. There is also evidence that some young people switch between psychoactive substances depending on desired effects, price, availability, social setting and so on, a subject we will scrutinise in later chapters.

As we have seen in this chapter, most young people learn to drink throughout their teens and it is an established part of their leisure-time socialising by the time they are old enough to drink legally in pubs and clubs. Neither victims nor delinquents, most young people drink because it is an enjoyable and acceptable part of their 'time out' from the stresses and pressures of their lives, a rational choice after weighing up the 'good times' and the 'bad times', a part of their celebrations with the family and their socialising with friends. Most young people enjoy their drinking but for a minority the frequency and severity of the negative effects associated with their drinking is, however, cause for concern.

We turn now to an updated analysis of our alcohol-related findings in relation to our cohort as they progress through their early adult years.

1999 to 2005: Alcohol – Still our favourite drug

Introduction

Alcohol is central to the leisure and lifestyles of our sample from the age of 14 up to 28. In line with national alcohol consumption patterns, we see our cohort progress from their first alcoholic drink in their early teens through to a range of drinking patterns which are established in adulthood. These patterns of consumption reflect typical pathways through life: from single, school pupils and then college students, based at the parental home; through to employed, romantically attached and home-owning adults. Such changes in late adolescent and young adult drinking can be mapped against significant changes in the UK during the course of this study from 1991 to 2005. This chapter update considers the role of alcohol in the lives of our respondents from the age of 18, when legally allowed to purchase alcohol, through to 28, in the period from 1995 to 2005 which can be characterised by the rise and fall of the British 'binge drinker'. It should be noted, however, that the later years of the longitudinal study increasingly focused on drug use rather than drinking, and so our data on alcohol consumption in adulthood is more limited than in the earlier adolescent years.

Legal drinking – the pull of the pub

By the age of 18 our sample contained a high proportion of social drinkers and recreational drug users (discussed further in forthcoming chapters) who valued going out with friends during their leisure time. Perhaps because so many were still living in the parental home and with limited privacy in early adulthood, we should not be surprised that they spent so many evenings 'out' socialising, combining both the 'pull' factors of the burgeoning British night-time economy of the late 1990s (discussed in Chapter 1) with the 'push' factors out of the parental home. At the age of 22 we asked our respondents how often they go out, for instance, to visit friends, play sport, attend evening classes or go to the pub. We found that two-thirds of young adults spent more nights out in any given week than staying in at home, with males being more likely to go out or stay out after work or study, and unsurprisingly, alcohol remains central to these nights out. The pub remains the number one leisure venue for British young adults to socialise in, and alcohol consumption (usually) comes with it:

> The majority of the people I socialise with will all be down the pub on any, you know, it's the sort of situation where I can go down to my local on any given night and there will be at least four or five people who I know in there who I can go and sit with and chat to so, it is purely to socialise really. There's no other reason why. I don't, I don't really drink to get drunk anymore unless, you know, it's just something that happens. If you are there in the pub for long enough it will happen. But I never go out with the purpose right I am going to get absolutely smashed tonight. So it is just to socialise.
>
> (43X05, male, age 22)

The main reason given for drinking by our young adults was to socialise, followed by relaxation. Indeed, socialising took increasing pre-eminence in discussions on alcohol as respondents grew older. For example, when interviewed at the age of 22, the key difference noted by respondents in their drinking between their teen years and their twenties was in terms of increasingly drinking to socialise rather than drinking to get drunk. For example, in discussing how their drinking had changed from 18 and earlier:

> When I was 18 it was just to get pissed, and now it's just like a social event I suppose. (33661, female, age 22)

> Probably drink like half a bottle, no, a bottle of vodka or something when I was erm 18, but now like I'll go out and I'll drink sort of glasses of wine and you know ... because ... when I was 18 I was going out to get drunk, whereas now I'm just going out to socialise. (43369, female, age 22)

> Well, then it was like to go out and get drunk for the sake of it, and if you didn't get caught, and things like that but now, it's more, it's just part of your lifestyle now. It's something that is expected of you and you expect to do, I think. (63474, female, age 22)

When you're 18 you had to drink to get drunk, or maybe that was younger? But yeh, it was kind of drinking to get drunk. Now it's, I suppose you still drink to get, I don't know, it's more social now it's more, just the way it is.

(13109, female, age 22)

Some respondents also recognise the ability to go out socialising, even go to pubs, and not feel obliged to drink alcohol. One respondent noted that at 18:

I think, I did, I wouldn't say I drank for the sake of drinking, but, towards that side of it whereas now, I'd quite happily go to a pub and not drink at all, or go out . . . to a party not drinking, take the car instead. (33661, female, age 22)

Probably because when you are 18 it's a case of like erm, you have to go out, you have to get drunk and everybody else is doing it and plus, when you're 18 you are not quite as confident to walk into a pub especially like me, you look about fifteen and it's a case of, you know, am I going to get served and all that kind of thing. So no, now it's just more for enjoyment you know.

(83X26, female, age 22)

Another respondent considered that her drinking is 'a social thing but then again I can go out and sit in a pub and just have a coke and just have a good time and have a laugh' (83839, female, age 22).

There was a notable and unsurprising shift amongst the cohort once drinking became legal in pubs and bars: for some, moving from the pursuit of clandestine drunkenness towards sociable drinking. For others, however, getting drunk remained the primary aim of drinking and being drunk was a pleasure in itself. Indeed, one respondent, when asked what was the most important part of his social life, answered 'booze', adding frankly that 'if there was no booze I don't think I'd really go out, to be honest with you' (53375, male, age 22). One woman noted that she drank more now she was in her current job and went drinking with work colleagues:

It's more to do with who I'm hanging around with at work, because they tend to drink so I just go out with them and get drunk basically. I think it's a bit of a giggle. Most of the time I go out I don't intend to get drunk or anything like that. It just happens [laughs].

(83X40, female, age 22)

Others, when asked why they drink alcohol, also mentioned the pleasures of drunkenness. For example, a young man said 'I enjoy it, I like being drunk, er, makes me socialise a lot easier, better, I feel more confident' (23194, male, age 22). Similarly a young woman said she drank 'mmm, to get drunk and [laughs], dunno, just to get drunk, to have a good time' (23174, female, age 22). For many, however, adulthood brought an increasing distinction between extreme drunkenness and more moderate intoxication, in order for them to achieve a desired level of intoxication which would not result in a hangover. One young man explained this further:

> We used to just go out and get blotto and now, my mates still say 'oh let's go and get blotto' but I don't. I say 'let's go out and get blotto, but not get absolutely hammered'. [Laughs] And sort of, they've changed in terms of, and I like to just have a bottle of wine or something. In fact, I prefer just that. I prefer to stay in and have a bottle of wine rather than go out and get absolutely blotto cos I can be pretty drunk after half a bottle of wine, but feel relaxed and feel better in the morning. That's why I, one of the main problems as well as, the morning, if I have too much to drink I feel like crap.
>
> (83911, male, age 22)

Further discussion of reasons for drinking and their relationship to consumption patterns is explored in Parker and Williams (2003).

Drinking frequency, quantity and last drinking occasion

Alcohol consumption remains at a consistently high rate from ages 18 to 27 (Table 3.10). Eight in ten of the sample were weekly drinkers at 18 and 22, falling slightly to seven in ten by their late twenties, with many of these regularly drinking alcohol several times a week. Heavy

Table 3.10 Drinking frequency in adulthood (%)

	18 years	22 years	28 years
Weekly	80%	83%	72%
Monthly	11%	8%	13%
Occasional (less than monthly)	5%	4%	9%
Non-drinkers (abstainers and ex drinkers)	4%	5%	6%
Smokers	34%	36%	36%

NB Samples are not directly comparable between years due to changing composition of samples.

sessional consumption remains a feature of drinking patterns through-out the study. Two-thirds of respondents aged 22 reported that their last drinking occasion was a typical one. Men remain both more frequent and heavier drinkers throughout their twenties: on their last drinking occasion spending £13.32 at the age of 22 compared with £9.36 for women. By the age of 27, the average amount spent by respondents on their last drinking occasion had increased substantially (and above the rate of inflation in the intervening years) to £16.93.

At 22, respondents drank an average of ten units of alcohol on their last drinking occasion, with 70 per cent of females and 55 per cent of males reporting consumption consistent with binge drinking levels (Department of Health, 1995). These findings support other surveys of young adult drinkers in the north-west of England in terms of heavy sessional drinking (Measham and Brain, 2005) and, for this cohort reaching adulthood in the late 1990s, an associated 'normalisation of determined drunkenness' (Measham, 2004a: 321). The impact of this consumption in terms of acute alcohol-related problems is also clear: 13 per cent of our 22 year olds had been to accident and emergency hospital outpatient facilities and 3 per cent to their GP for an alcohol-related problem.

Drinking locations, drinking motivations and drinking groups

A key influence on our respondents' drinking was their ability to enter pubs and purchase alcohol legally once they reached the age of 18. This is reflected in the shifting location of alcohol consumption from the late teens onwards. For example, reporting on their last drinking occasion at the age of 22, over half (53 per cent) were in a pub or bar the last time they drank alcohol, over a quarter (28 per cent) were at home, another 14 per cent were in a club and 13 per cent were in a friend's house. Six in ten (60 per cent) were drinking with their friends, one third (37 per cent) with their boyfriend, girlfriend or partner and one in ten (11 per cent) were with their parents. Furthermore, for young women, they felt that, alongside reaching the legal age to purchase alcohol, there had also been a growing acceptance of women's presence in pubs in the 1990s. This was reflected in one young woman's reason for drinking alcohol: 'I think the biggest one is because it is a lot more socially acceptable for women to be in pubs, for me to be in a pub and I like it [laughs]' (33661, female, age 22).

For another, she drinks:

Erm, to unwind I suppose, just to relax a little, socialise. It's a social thing, you go out to the pub, you have a drink. Erm at the end of a week at work you just, quite, you quite enjoy sitting down with a glass of wine you just, you think 'ah, that's another week over with', so, so just that.

(43X28, female, age 22)

By their early twenties, the respondents were settling into leisure/life-style patterns which in turn both reflected and reinforced their decisions around alcohol and drug use. There was still a considerable amount of social mixing at this age, though. So, for example, one young woman noted how:

I have a group of friends who are [cannabis] smokers and a group of friends which are drinkers and I've got friends which are clubbers . . . It's just nice to have different types of friends who do different things.

(83819, female, age 22)

This social mixing on a night out was echoed in a growing pharmaco-logical mixing. Ecstasy, for example, had been the archetypal 'club drug' throughout the 'decade of dance', with its use associated with raves and dance club venues (Measham *et al.*, 2001; Shapiro, 1999) and more often drinking bottled water rather than alcohol. By the end of the 1990s, however, our respondents reported drinking alcohol when out clubbing and also reported that they might take a 'cheeky pill' on a night out drinking, in part due to the widespread availability and plummeting prices of ecstasy pills at the millennium (Measham, 2004a). When asked in what situations he took ecstasy, one respondent who was a regular clubber at Cream and other dance events said:

If we are out round the bars in town or if we are going clubbing yeah. Um. I've had them round town just like, someone says do you want them so I said yeah. There's a couple of my mates that have always got them on them at the weekends. I know someone that sells them so he's always got them and he's like 'do you want one?' Sometimes I say yeah if I am leathered anyway. I'll have gone out thinking I'm not going to have any but when I'm drunk and some-one offers me one I'll say yeah.

(23145, male, age 22)

Types of alcoholic beverages

As our respondents matured, so their preferences regarding alcoholic beverages also matured. Gender also remained highly significant to alcoholic beverage choice throughout the teens and twenties, with men aged 22 far more likely to drink beer, lager and cider (80.3 per cent) than women (22.7 per cent), who preferred spirits, wine and spirit mixers. One young woman noted that in her teens:

> I used to go out and just drink anything, whereas now I seem to have acquired more of a taste for drink, and you know I'll choose what I'm drinking instead of just pouring it down my throat.
>
> (83X43, female, age 22)

One female drinker exemplifies the typical drinking 'career' of our respondents in terms of moving from the cheap and sweet British teen-age favourites of cider and alcopops to vodka and wine once in her twenties. This mirrors national trends in female alcohol consumption and in favoured drinks in the late 1990s and 2000s, with increased wine consumption by women across all age categories (Measham and Østergaard, 2009):

> I used to drink cider, Scrumpy Jack or whatever I used to drink, and I used to drink Blastaway (Diamond White and Castaway). But then I actually used to, one thing was lager and lime, I started to drink, and I still drink that now . . . I used to drink Taboo as well and now I've changed and I drink vodka quite a lot and I don't, I didn't really drink wine then. Then I started to drink white wine and I can't drink white wine anymore, I drink red wine. I think I stopped drinking pints of things really because of a bloatedness, it makes me bloated. And the Taboo just, I still drink it a bit now, but that's very rarely as it's too sweet, my taste's just changed . . . But also it's whether you tend to drink what everybody else around you is, and you find you say 'Oh get me that as well' and a lot of my friends drink vodka, so it's one of those things.
>
> (83U04, female, age 22)

For both men and women, they felt that their tastes had matured, they had become more discerning, and for a considerable number, that included wine:

> When I was 18 I drank because of my friends, but now I actually

enjoy drinking and I like the taste of it. I like trying different wines and things. Although I'm not that hung up on it!

(83857, female, age 22)

Non-drinkers

Whilst alcohol is central to the social lives of most of our sample, it should also be noted that some respondents stopped drinking in their twenties. Although only a small number, they are indicative of a wider trend of growing numbers of abstainers in the UK, for reasons which have not yet been fully explored (Measham, 2008). Ethnicity, religion and gender are not insignificant here, with seven in ten non-drinkers in our sample of non-drinkers at the age of 22 being Asian Muslim, and also seven in ten being female. At the age of 28, six respondents who report never having drunk alcohol remain in the sample, three of whom are Asian Muslims who report not drinking primarily for religious reasons.

Alongside the small number who had never had an alcoholic drink, there was a small but growing number of respondents in their twenties who had not had an alcoholic drink for over a year, who drank very occasionally or had decided to stop drinking alcohol altogether. Reasons given for this included health issues, disliking the taste or side effects, and for some, like the following respondent, a combination of factors:

I don't particularly like it and I suppose cos I don't go to pubs. But I think even if I did, I probably wouldn't either. And my friends, they do drink but, you know, not in excessive amounts or anything. So yeah, it's partly religious beliefs but not that that, you know, dictates that you can't drink at all. It's just maybe not in excessive amounts like other people. I probably just don't see the need for it . . . After a wedding, if there's champagne or you know, wine at the table, I'll have a bit but even then, I don't like to have more than one glass.

(83X39, female, age 22)

Tobacco use

Tobacco use changed little through the teens and twenties. Just over one third of the cohort remained current smokers throughout the study, with 36 per cent reporting smoking at the age of 22 and 27, nearly all of whom have been smoking since their mid teens. At the age of 22, smokers reported having smoked an average of nine cigarettes on the day prior to interview.[1] Gender remained statistically significant throughout the study with young women significantly more likely to be smokers throughout their teens and twenties reflecting the function of nicotine as stimulant and appetite suppressant, alongside the influence of gender on drug use linked to issues of identity formation, body image and gender stereotyping in contemporary Western society (Denscombe, 2001; Ettorre, 2007; Wearing *et al.*, 1994).

Whilst the overall percentage of smokers changed little once past their mid teens, interviews revealed that the ways in which young people smoke have changed, reflecting the impact of work and home on their smoking habits. Also, although the study was conducted before smoking in public places was banned and before the minimum purchase age was raised to 18, the growing restrictions on smoking introduced in the early 2000s (before legislation was passed) influenced smoking patterns and contexts. For example, one young woman who became a nurse described how although still a smoker, she tended to smoke in short, heavy sessions when not working at the hospital rather than on a daily basis:

> I did used to be, not a really heavy smoker, but a fairly heavy smoker. But you can't smoke in the hospital so I have to do like 10 hour shifts without, going without a cigarette at all, so I've found now I can quite easily go for three or four days without having one. So I'm more of like a social smoker. It's when I'm out drinking I'll smoke a pack of twenty in one night ... It's disgusting [laughs], I don't know why I do it ... You smell, it costs a fortune, it's awful.
>
> (23174, female, age 22)

When asked if anything would make her stop smoking, she downplayed the quantity of cigarettes smoked on a night out, replying 'Erm, no, probably not. The health risk scares me but it doesn't really bother me cos I just think to myself "well I only have one every now and again so it won't affect you".'

One young woman who still smoked at the age of 22 had stopped when pregnant and then resumed again after the birth. She noted how much 'I always love to have a fag when the baby has gone to bed', adding:

---

1   This question was not asked at 27.

But I don't smoke a lot any more. I used to smoke 30–40 a day.
Probably, I go through between 5 and 10 now. That's it. I think they
are really expensive now as well – £4-something for a packet of
bloody 20 and you go in to pubs and for 16 they are £4.50. So no,
no, but probably about 5 or 10 I smoke.

(23125, female, age 22)

For this woman, as noted in the body of research by Graham and
colleagues (e.g. Graham, 1989, 1994; Graham and Blackburn, 1998),
cigarettes are a small, affordable treat used as 'time out' from the chores
in a mother's busy day. When asked what she liked about smoking she
noted:

I do enjoy you know, having a cup of tea and a fag, you can't beat
it. You know in the morning and after a meal. But I don't know. I
think it is just the hand isn't it, it's nice to . . . I don't know. I'll have
to think about that one next time I have a cigarette, think what do I
like about this? . . . It's your time isn't it? You know? But because I
don't really, I don't drink hardly anything anymore, it's my, you
now, it's my treat, are my fags. Rather than alcohol.

(23125, female, age 22)

By the age of 22, our smokers no longer saw themselves as eternally
youthful, although in their twenties their concerns about smoking
related more to the potentially ageing effects on the skin rather than a
future risk to their health or the even more abstract concept of
mortality. This was evident in the young mother's investment in a
premium anti-ageing product in order to facilitate her continued
smoking:

I don't think I will always smoke actually. I don't know, now I
know what it does to the skin. But then I was at the training I did in
Manchester a couple of weeks ago, and she said 'this bottle you
know it stops all ageing, premature ageing'. So I said 'well if I am
using this day and night, religiously, I could smoke and smoke and
smoke couldn't I?' She went, she looked at me and went 'well, er, I
suppose so then, yes'. 'Right I'll use it, give me a bottle now for
day and night'.

(23125, female, age 22)

When asked under what circumstances she might envisage stopping
smoking in the future, she said:

Pregnancy definitely. Definitely pregnancy. Um. And I don't know. I think I am too young to have like, you know, for them to say 'stop smoking now or you are going to drop dead'. It usually tends to be when they are older doesn't it? So, but it'd probably just be pregnancy.

(23125, female, age 22)

For other smokers in their early twenties, the longer-term health risks were starting to weigh on their minds and make them consider giving up smoking at some point in the future:

I like to think I would give up because when you see old people and they can hardly walk cos they can't breathe properly and I think aah, I should give up. But I don't know, you try. Maybe for a couple of days . . . I do get really ratty. And maybe I'm okay until I have a drink and I think 'aah, I'll just have another drink' and then something happens and the next thing you do is light a cigarette up.

(23191, female, age 22)

Summary

The majority of our cohort continue to drink alcohol on a weekly basis into their twenties, although a very small number have reduced or stopped consuming alcohol, or never started drinking, for a range of health, religious and personal reasons. Alcohol is seen as central to most young adults' social lives, although preferences in types of alcoholic beverages change, mostly from the cheap and sweet drinks of their teenage years to drinks that they increasingly acquire a taste for, such as wine. In interview, respondents also reveal a subtle shift in emphasis, in terms of their motivations for drinking, away from clandestine drunkenness in parks or friends' homes vacated by parents for the evening, towards a less pressurised and more sociable leisure time spent with friends in pubs or at each other's houses. Heavy sessional consumption continues to be a feature for many young adults and drunkenness remains a goal for some. Although smoking rates have changed little, with one third of young people remaining smokers throughout their teens and twenties, some of them are starting to express concerns about its impact on their health and appearance, and to make periodic attempts to stop smoking.

4 Patterns

An overview of drug offers, trying, use and drugs experiences across adolescence

Overview

This chapter begins with a reproduction of the 'Patterns' chapter from the first edition of *Illegal Leisure*. We follow this with an update entitled 'Patterns: An update from 18 to 27 years of age', which documents the changes in drug-taking patterns that occurred for our cohort in adulthood.

Introduction

In this short chapter we provide an overview of the drug-related behaviour of our samples over the five years they were tracked from early adolescence into the beginnings of young adulthood. Essentially the findings, as laid out here, are typical of the way facts and figures about adolescent drug use in the UK are presented and published. Thus tables of drug offers, lifetime trying and more recent or regular use are presented. Nearly all the studies mentioned in Chapter 1, for instance, use this format and presentation style. The only obvious difference is that we are, uniquely, describing the situation based on the evidence of a five-year study which allows us to spot trends and see developmental change through time.

Drug offers and availability

Each year the young people in our samples were asked about whether they had been in situations where illicit drugs were available for free or to purchase. Even in Year 1 when our respondents were only 14 almost six in ten had been in such situations rising annually to over nine in ten in Year 5. Cannabis, as we can see from Table 4.1, is the drug most likely to be 'offered' or available, followed by amphetamines,

Table 4.1 Drug offers (age 14–18 inclusive)

	Year 1 (n = 776) %	Year 2 (n = 752) %	Year 3 (n = 523) %	Year 4 (n = 536) %	Year 5 (n = 529) %
Amphetamines	29.6	40.6	47.9	600	67.0
Amyl nitrite	24.1	37.3	41.7	51.4	58.9
Cannabis	54.6	61.6	72.7	77.4	83.9
Cocaine	8.0	12.7	12.4	19.4	23.7
Heroin	5.4	8.2	5.4	6.6	5.4
LSD	40.4	55.0	56.1	65.3	65.6
Magic mushrooms	24.5	32.5	29.2	26.9	26.2
Ecstasy	21.4	32.9	36.3	49.7	62.3
Solvents	25.6	27.2	23.1	33.7	27.3
Tranquillisers	4.3	11.4	7.1	12.8	14.4
At least one	59.1	70.9	76.5	87.5	91.1

LSD and, in later adolescence, ecstasy. Heroin and, to a lesser extent, tranquillisers and cocaine, remain the least accessible or available drugs for this particular generational cohort though this patterning seems likely to change amongst younger cohorts behind them (Parker *et al.*, 1998c).

Ever tried a drug

The statistic which inevitably becomes the headline figure when a survey of youthful drug use is published is the 'ever used' or lifetime prevalence rate. Table 4.2 describes these rates for our samples.

We can see that self-reported drug trying rose from over one-third at the age of 14 through to almost two-thirds by the age of 18 years. This is a remarkably steep upward climb and is an important indicator of the degree of penetration of illicit drug trying amongst 1990s' adolescents. The most important epidemiological trend in this table involves 'incidence', that is first-time trying reports each year. As we can see, in

Table 4.2 Lifetime prevalence of illicit drug taking

	Year 1 (n = 776) %	Year 2 (n = 752) %	Year 3 (n = 523) %	Year 4 (n = 536) %	Year 5 (n = 529) %
At least one drug	36.3	47.3	50.7	57.3	64.3

late adolescence the incidence rate is actually picking up, a finding inconsistent with the notion of drug use as adolescent rebellion and thus slowing down, with maturation, by young adulthood.

We should remember, however, that lifetime trying rates are primarily generated by annual re-reporting. Whilst two-thirds of the Year 5 sample had tried a drug, a vitally important finding, we must be very careful to emphasise that this figure will include those who tried a drug once or twice in early adolescence and those who have used drugs but have no intention of doing so again.

Ever tried, by specific drug

In Table 4.3 we redraw these lifetime rates by each of the main available illicit drugs. We can see quite clearly that cannabis dominates the drug trying of these young people, whereby the lifetime trying of cannabis is only slightly behind the overall 'at least one drug' lifetime trying rates. This said, we can also see how by mid adolescence LSD and amphetamines will have been tried by over a quarter of the samples, closely followed by amyl nitrite 'poppers'. In late adolescence ecstasy trying also climbs rapidly whereby one in five will have imbibed their first tablet. Tranquillisers and heroin and, to a lesser extent, cocaine remain 'marginal' drugs with solvents and magic mushrooms, as early experimentation drugs, showing no incidence and indeed, as discussed in Chapter 2, suffering from redefinition and under-reporting by Year 5.

Table 4.3 Lifetime prevalence of illicit drug taking (age 14–18 inclusive) by individual drug

	Year 1 (n = 776) %	Year 2 (n = 752) %	Year 3 (n = 523) %	Year 4 (n = 536) %	Year 5 (n = 529) %
Amphetamines	9.5	16.1	18.4	25.2	32.9
Amyl nitrite	14.2	22.1	23.5	31.3	35.3
Cannabis	31.7	41.5	45.3	53.7	59.0
Cocaine	1.4	4.0	2.5	4.5	5.9
Heroin	0.4	2.5	0.6	0.6	6.0
LSD	13.3	25.3	24.5	26.7	28.0
Magic mushrooms	9.9	12.4	9.8	9.5	8.5
Ecstasy	5.8	7.4	5.4	12.9	19.8
Solvents	11.9	13.2	9.9	10.3	9.5
Tranquillisers	1.2	4.7	1.5	3.9	4.5
At least one	36.3	47.3	50.7	57.3	64.3

First-time trying, by drug

At every stage of the study cannabis was the key drug tried by 'initiates': respondents who at each stage of the research were trying drugs for the first time. In early adolescence, perhaps because of their ease of availability, solvents, primarily gases and aerosols, were used and, as we can see, firmly rejected by older initiates. Nitrites (poppers) being illicit rather than illegal in the early 1990s, and fairly easily obtained, are, unsurprisingly, important for initiation. On the other hand LSD, a 'strong' Class A drug, is also a common first-experience drug. The very low cost of LSD as acid blotters or 'trips' and their ready availability will be relevant here. Ecstasy was not easily available to this sample's age group in the early 1990s and, as we shall see, ecstasy initiation is clearly age related in respect of access to dance clubs. The use of tranquillisers, heroin and cocaine as first-time drugs are for this age cohort fairly rare.

Recency of drug trying and drug use

It is vitally important to distinguish between those young people who have used one drug once or a few times only and those who become regular users of one or more drugs. We will make far more of these distinctions in the following chapter but in terms of a 'rough guide', Table 4.4 provides an initial overview.

Asking young people when they last tried particular drugs is one way of identifying not just recency of drug use but also current, possibly regular drug use. Thus, respondents who indicate recent drug trying will include virtually all current regular users, as well as one-off triers, experimenters and initiators. Thus, while we do require more sophisticated measures than presented here properly to define current regular drug use, measures we work towards in Chapter 5, recency

Table 4.4 Prevalence of lifetime and more recent illicit drug taking (age 14–18 inclusive)

	Year 1 (n = 776) %	Year 2 (n = 752) %	Year 3 (n = 523) %	Year 4 (n = 536) %	Year 5 (n = 529) %
Lifetime	36.3	47.3	50.7	57.3	64.3
Past year	30.9	40.6	40.5	46.1	52.9
Past month	20.4	26.2	27.7	34.1	35.2
Past week	–	–	–	20.1	23.4

of use does provide one rough indication of current and regular drug use.

Nevertheless, we can see that over half of the sample at Year 5 and over 40 per cent in the previous three years had taken a drug in the year prior to each survey. Whilst some of these will be 'initiates' most will not and here again is another indicator of the scale of the drug use amongst 1990s adolescents.

Past week use, a measure we introduced once our respondents were over 16 years, suggests that regular drug users make up between 20 and 25 per cent of our samples in late adolescence. We will concentrate on these drug *users* in later chapters.

The impact of gender, social class and race

In Table 4.5 we look at how gender, social class and race correlate with the basic measures of drug offers and drug trying. Remembering the caveats about the attrition of some working-class 'risk takers' and Asian abstainers, by Year 3 we can identify some significant changes in the profile of today's adolescent drug triers when compared with previous generations.

In keeping with the general trends identified in Chapter 1, we can see the closure of the gender gap in relation to drug trying. Whilst in the 1970s and 1980s we would find at least twice as many young men as young women trying drugs there are, in this study, few statistically significant differences. In line with their earlier maturation and 'older' friendship groups, young women were actually more likely to be in drug-offer and drug-trying situations in Year 1. This situation slowly reverses through mid adolescence and by the age of 17 we can see that young men are slightly more likely to be trying drugs and by Year 5 are more likely to be recent, possibly regular, users. This said, the key point to make is that well over half of the young women in this study have had illicit drugs and a significant minority take drugs repeatedly.

In respect of social class, we can see that early 'risk takers' who had tried a drug by the age of 14 were far more likely to come from 'working-class' catchment areas. This class difference slowly disperses with age and in late adolescence there is a strong sense of middle-class young people 'catching up'. Several other studies have produced similar findings in relation to social class. Again the key point to make is that social background is no longer a predictor or protector. Young people from all social backgrounds are now, broadly speaking, likely to try drugs during their adolescence.

As we explained in Chapter 2 the attrition in our sample after Year 1

Table 4.5 Gender, class and race by offer and use statistics for at least one drug

		Gender		Class		Race			
	Total %	Females %	Males %	Middle %	Working %	Black %	Asian %	White %	Other %
Year 1 (n)	(776)	(358)	(415)	(406)	(370)	(29)	(57)	(634)	(10)
Offer	59.1	64.5	54.2	55.4	63.2	72.4	26.3	61.0	60.0
Lifetime	36.3	37.7	35.2	30.8	42.4	44.8	14.0	37.5	40.0
Past year	30.9	32.7	29.4	25.1	37.3	41.4	7.0	32.0	40.0
Past month	20.4	21.8	19.3	15.3	25.9	31.0	3.5	21.0	40.0
Year 2 (n)	(752)	(362)	(384)	(426)	(326)	(27)	(50)	(636)	(8)
Offer	70.9	71.5	70.1	71.4	70.2	88.9	32.0	73.1	62.5
Lifetime	47.3	47.5	46.4	45.1	50.3	70.4	14.0	47.6	50.0
Past year	40.6	40.9	39.3	37.6	44.5	63.0	10.0	40.7	37.5
Past month	26.2	24.6	27.6	22.1	31.6	40.7	6.0	26.3	37.5
Year 3 (n)	(523)	(298)	(225)	(357)	(163)	(12)	(24)	(478)	(7)
Offer	76.5	76.2	76.9	75.6	79.1	75.0	54.2	77.8	71.4
Lifetime	50.7	49.3	52.4	47.9	57.1	75.0	16.7	51.7	57.1
Past year	40.5	38.3	43.6	38.7	44.8	66.7	4.2	41.6	57.1
Past mnth	27.7	24.5	32.0	24.9	33.7	66.7	4.2	27.8	42.9
Year 4 (n)	(536)	(302)	(233)	(364)	(172)	(9)	(30)	(491)	(5)
Offer	87.5	86.4	89.3	88.5	85.5	100.0	63.3	89.0	80.0
Lifetime	57.3	54.3	61.4	57.1	57.6	66.7	23.3	59.5	40.0
Past year	46.1	43.0	50.2	48.9	40.1	55.6	20.0	47.7	40.0
Past month	34.1	31.8	37.3	36.8	28.5	44.4	10.0	35.4	40.0
Year 5 (n)	(529)	(305)	(224)	(365)	(163)	(14)	(26)	(485)	(2)
Offer	91.1	90.8	91.5	91.8	89.6	100.0	73.1	91.8	100.0
Lifetime	64.3	62.0	67.4	64.1	64.4	71.4	38.5	65.4	50.0
Past year	52.9	49.2	58.0	54.0	50.3	57.1	26.9	54.2	50.0
Past month	35.2	28.2	44.6	36.2	32.5	42.9	15.4	36.1	0.0

has unfortunately made any statistical analysis of the impact of race unsafe after Year 3 (see Parker *et al.*, 1995). Up to that point we were able to show that Asians were considerably less likely to have ever had a drug than either young white or black respondents, but that there were no differences in rates of drug trying between black and white respondents. Whilst this statistically significant difference remained at Year 5, we reached this conclusion with only 26 Asian and 14 black respondents in the sample (of 527) and little store should thus be put on this measure.

Experiences of drug trying

In Tables 4.6 and 4.7, although still concerned with overall patterns, we begin to demonstrate how a longitudinal study gives opportunities for more adventurous questioning and analysis. In Year 5 we felt able to ask fairly sophisticated questions about actual drug-taking experiences knowing they would be relevant to over half our sample and acceptable to the abstainers who had loyally stayed with the project. We concentrated on the most used drugs of cannabis, LSD, amphetamines and ecstasy.

Table 4.6 shows that feeling relaxed, friendly, happy and carefree were the most quoted positive experiences. Amphetamines and ecstasy

Table 4.6 Respondents who reported positive experiences on last occasion of use for cannabis, LSD, amphetamines and ecstasy

	Cannabis (n = 294) %	LSD (n = 135) %	Amphetamines (n = 140) %	Ecstasy (n = 102) %
Last time I had [. . .] I felt . . .				
part of a group	14.3	16.3	12.9	19.6
energetic	4.8	34.8	75.7	62.7
excited	6.5	34.1	42.1	47.1
friendly	43.2	31.9	45.7	58.8
carefree	33.0	28.1	25.7	35.3
relaxed	61.9	13.3	17.1	36.3
had fun	37.4	40.7	46.4	51.0
confident	12.2	14.1	28.6	42.2
loving/caring	12.2	3.7	15.0	33.3
sexy	4.4	5.2	12.9	38.2
strong	1.0	7.4	13.6	17.6
happy	33.7	34.8	35.0	51.0
in control	22.1	17.0	22.9	25.5
outgoing	13.9	18.5	23.6	29.4
The last time I had [. . .] as the effects were wearing off I felt . . .				
	(n = 292)	(n = 135)	(n = 141)	(n = 102)
relaxed	31.5	11.9	12.1	17.6
loving/caring	3.1	1.5	2.1	8.8
like having more	13.4	9.6	9.2	10.8
no problem	27.1	13.3	11.3	14.7
outgoing	1.7	1.5	0.0	3.9
sad it was over	4.8	15.6	14.9	19.6
friendly	7.2	10.4	6.4	7.8
happy	12.7	11.9	7.1	10.8
proud	0.7	1.5	0.7	0.0

scored highly in providing self confidence and particularly feeling excited, energetic, sexy and loving or caring. Cannabis was seen as the ideal drug to relax with.

Turning to the negative experiences reported on last occasion of drug use in Table 4.7, the primary finding is that overall very few negative experiences are reported, and this is particularly striking when compared with positive outcomes. Aside from headaches after any drug use and more significantly a sense of depression particularly after imbibing amphetamines and ecstasy, the rates of negative experiences were very low, routinely affecting less than one drug taker in ten.

Table 4.7 Respondents who reported negative experiences on last occasion of use for cannabis, LSD, amphetamines and ecstasy

	Cannabis (n = 294) %	LSD (n = 135) %	Amphetamines (n = 140) %	Ecstasy (n = 102) %
Last time I had [. . .] I felt . . .				
angry	1.0	2.2	0.7	1.0
out of control	1.4	14.8	4.3	9.8
worried about drug content	2.0	7.4	2.1	5.9
foolish	6.8	14.1	5.0	6.9
sad	1.4	2.2	1.4	1.0
lonely	0.7	3.7	2.9	0.0
anxious	2.4	19.3	7.1	7.8
scared	1.0	14.1	4.3	4.9
queasy	8.5	1.5	2.9	3.9
frustrated	2.0	5.2	2.1	1.0
paranoid	5.1	31.1	7.1	5.9
The last time I had [. . .] as the effects were wearing off I felt . . .				
	(n = 292)	(n = 135)	(n = 141)	(n = 102)
depressed	5.8	21.5	29.8	23.5
headache	13.4	19.3	19.9	18.6
lonely	1.7	5.9	5.7	8.8
worried about drug content	1.4	3.0	2.8	5.9
afraid	1.0	1.5	5.0	2.0
disappointed	4.8	7.4	7.8	10.8
pain	0.7	0.7	3.5	1.0
worried	1.4	8.1	5.0	3.9
guilty	3.8	5.2	5.0	8.8
foolish	5.5	4.4	4.3	5.9
sick	9.6	6.7	17.0	13.7
glad it was over	4.5	16.3	2.8	6.9
paranoid	2.7	12.6	5.7	8.8

LSD shows up as the least predictable drug and the one most likely to trigger feelings of paranoia and anxiety whereby a minority of users were glad when the experience was over. Although relatively rare, 'bad trips' do, as we shall see in Chapter 6, have an important role to play, via drugs stories, in the cost-benefit assessment young drug contemplators usually make before deciding whether to try or retry a certain drug.

Conclusion

Whilst not nationally representative, the range of drug-use statistics presented in this chapter suggest that recreational drug use, dominated by cannabis and supported by LSD, poppers, amphetamines and, in late adolescence, ecstasy, has become widespread amongst ordinary British youth. Entering young adulthood, by the age of 18, almost all the young people in this study had been in drug-offer situations and over six in ten had tried an illicit drug. These early 1990s' rates, which are now being replicated in many other recent studies (e.g. Barnard *et al.*, 1996; Miller and Plant, 1996) are quite unprecedented. This level of penetration into youth culture has only been possible because of the increased propensity of young women and young people from all social backgrounds to try a drug. Being a female, middle-class, A-level student is no longer a protective drug-free profile. Once we ask recency-of-use questions it becomes clear that a significant minority of the sample, between one in four or five, probably use drugs fairly regularly, although, as we shall see, there are better ways of assessing this. This again is an unprecedented rate but clearly we are a long way off from saying that the majority of young people are illicit drug *users*.

On the other hand the increases in new triers, the rate of drug-trying incidence, shows no sign of slowing as this generational cohort moves into young adulthood. This epidemiological process combined with the fact that reported positive experiences of drug use far outweigh negative outcomes suggest drug trying and drug use are not transitory nor closely tied to the period of adolescence. These are all powerful indicators to be stored and assessed in the final chapter when we formally consider the notion of normalisation.

We turn now to an updated discussion of findings from our cohort in relation to their drug-taking patterns in adulthood.

Patterns: An update from 18 to 27 years of age

Introduction

Results from the first five years of the study revealed increasing experience with illicit drugs across adolescence. Cannabis was dominant in terms of offers and use throughout adolescence. In the early years, LSD, amyl nitrite and amphetamines were key, and in later adolescence ecstasy began to penetrate the drug-using repertoires of members of our cohort. A majority of the young people surveyed had been in offer situations by the age of 18 (more than nine in ten) and went on to try a drug (just over two-thirds). A small minority became recent or regular users (around one quarter). When analysed by key socio-demographic variables (gender and class) none of the differences in drug taking that we identified were statistically significant. This should not be read as suggesting that that these larger structural variables are not, however, important; indeed, the qualitative results we discuss in Chapters 5 and 6 reveal a nuanced relationship between drug use and structural factors.

Moving now onto an update of the cohort's patterns of drug use, this update presents quantitative data collected from the sample at the ages of 22 and 27 exploring drug use prevalence and patterns in young adulthood. We compare this new data collected in adulthood to the findings reported earlier in this chapter in relation to respondents' adolescence. We focus particularly upon continuity and change from the age of 18.

It is important to note that none of the results reported in this update is longitudinal. Instead, we present results for the different samples generated at each survey sweep (529 at age 18; 465 at 22; and 217 at 27). What may appear to be anomalous reporting (see Chapter 2) from one year to the next (for example, reporting having ever tried a drug in one questionnaire, but not in a subsequent return) may simply reflect differences amongst the subsets of individuals included in each sweep, and resulting from sample attrition. We cannot here, therefore, disentangle time trends from sample differences and anomalous reporting. We present results as we have in order to provide consistency of presentation with the first five years of the research, but we are careful not to read too much into time trends, and especially small changes from one sweep to the next.

Drug offers and availability

We continued to monitor illicit drug offers when the cohort was 22 years old (see Table 4.8). Situations of drug availability rose for the first

Table 4.8 Comparison of drug offers at age 18 and 22

	Year 5 (n = 529) %	Year 9 (n = 465) %
Amphetamines	67.0	76.1
Amyl nitrite	58.9	63.9
Cannabis	83.9	89.0
Cocaine powder	23.7	46.5
Crack cocaine	5.7	11.6
Ecstasy	62.3	62.1
Heroin	5.4	8.9
LSD	65.6	56.3
Magic mushrooms	26.2	32.4
Solvents	27.3	21.8
Tranquillisers	14.4	15.2
At least one	91.1	93.1

time for a few members of the cohort during adulthood. There was a small increase in drug offers and availability from the age of 18 to 22 with over nine in ten having been in situations where drugs were available to them for free or to purchase at the age of 22 (93.1 per cent, up slightly from age 18). Patterns of drug offers have remained broadly consistent since the age of 18 with cannabis being the drug respondents were most likely to have been 'offered' and the remaining top five drugs consisting of amphetamines, amyl nitrite, ecstasy and LSD. In respect of easily accessible drugs, respondents identified cannabis, solvents, amphetamines, ecstasy and amyl nitrite.

The percentage of respondents having been in offer situations increased by a small amount between the ages of 18 and 22 for most drugs. The most notable exception to this occurred for cocaine, for which offers rose substantially from 23.7 per cent to 46.5 per cent by the age of 22. When our cohort was 18 years old, we noted that cocaine was not as accessible to this cohort as some other drugs and predicted that this may not remain the case for their younger peers, reaching adulthood in a climate of increased availability of cocaine in the late 1990s. This rise in offers for cocaine is consistent with our prediction. The reduction in the reporting of having been in drug-offer situations for LSD and solvents may be a product of sample attrition and anomalous reporting, but may also mirror the changes in pre- and post-millenium substance availability and popularity. LSD is no longer widely available whereas cocaine availability became far more widespread in the late 1990s and early 2000s and the increased prevalence in this cohort mirrors national trends (Aust *et al.*, 2002; Condon and Smith, 2003; Ramsey *et al.*, 2001).

Ever tried a drug

Lifetime prevalence of drug use increased throughout the study. By the age of 18 almost two-thirds had tried a drug at least once. As we noted earlier, the increase in incidence of drug trying during late adolescence at the transition to adulthood contradicts conventional views of drug use as 'adolescent rebellion' and invites alternative explanations. By the age of 22 (see Table 4.9), the proportion of respondents who had ever tried a drug increased to around three-quarters from about two-thirds four years earlier. Lifetime prevalence is broadly similar at the age of 27 with a small reduction in reports of having ever tried a drug. It is likely that biographical reconstruction or forgetting may in part explain this reduction in prevalence, since the more substantial drops in reports of drug trying tend to be amongst those drugs associated with use in early adolescence (amphetamines, amyl nitrite, LSD and solvents). It is important that we do not over-emphasise lifetime prevalence rates; by this stage in the lives of the cohort, a substantial proportion of respondents included in this statistic will be one-off triers or ex-triers. Indeed, as we discuss in more detail later, we found a reduction in the frequency of recent or regular drug use during adulthood.

Table 4.9 Comparison of lifetime illicit drug taking (age 18, 22 and 27) by individual drug

	Year 5 (n = 529) %	Year 9 (n = 465) %	Year 14 (n = 217) %
Amphetamines	32.9	41.8	36.6
Amyl nitrite	35.3	45.2	38.2
Cannabis	59.0	69.9	68.2
Cocaine powder	5.7	24.6	29.1
Crack cocaine	0.8	2.4	2.4
Ecstasy	19.8	28.5	27.2
Heroin	0.6	0.9	0.5
LSD	28.0	28.8	22.2
Magic mushrooms	8.5	12.6	11.3
Solvents	9.5	10.3	3.8
Tranquillisers	4.5	5.8	3.8
At least one	63.1	75.8	72.0

The trying of specific drugs

The lifetime prevalence rate for cannabis increased by just over 10 per cent from the age of 18 to 22 and remained broadly similar from the age of 22 to 27 (see Table 4.9). From the age of 18 to the age of 22, drug-trying rates increased for all drugs. For some of the stimulant based 'dance drugs' (amphetamines, amyl nitrite, and ecstasy), this increase was substantial. For cocaine, the increase was approximately five-fold (from 5.7 per cent to 24.6 per cent). The only drug for which there was an increase in lifetime prevalence from age 22 to 27 was cocaine (up by 4.5 per cent). This indicates some of our samples were willing to try cocaine for the first time in their mid twenties. During young adult-hood, lifetime prevalence for most drugs dropped slightly, and in some cases substantially by the age of 27 compared to age 22. Previously, we noted that lifetime prevalence of magic mushrooms declined from the age of 15 onwards; however, it increased back to similar levels by the age of 22, reflecting national trends with increased availability and use of magic mushrooms linked to the growing use of vacuum pack technology which facilitated the sale of fresh (and therefore legal) mushrooms (Measham, 2004a) before this legal loophole was closed and psilocin became a Class A controlled drug in all its forms in the Drugs Act 2005. Lifetime prevalence rates for ecstasy, cannabis, magic mushrooms and crack cocaine remain broadly similar throughout the twenties. The data collected from the sample in young adulthood highlights the willingness of some to try stimulant drugs and cannabis for the first time during this stage of the life course.

More recent drug trying and drug use

Potentially regular drug use during adulthood, in the form of past year and month prevalence, are presented in Table 4.10. Prevalence of recent or regular drug use for at least one drug declines from the early to the late twenties, suggesting a gradual decline in frequency of drug use in adulthood. Although past year drug use remained consistent from the age of 18 to 22, it substantially decreased from over half to just over a third by the age of 27. At the age of 22, we asked survey respondents to indicate whether they had taken each individual drug in the three years that intervened between our survey at the age of 18 and our next survey at the age of 22. This 'retrospective recall' method for assessing drug use in the intervening years is not as accurate as having conducted surveys during those years, but does allow us to attempt to reconstruct changes in drug use between surveys. The prevalence of past year use of at least one drug steadily increased until the age of 20 when 58.2 per cent report having taken a drug in that year. This is followed by a steady reduction in past year drug taking from the age of 20 to 22 which mirrors the increase from 18 to 20 years (see Table 4.11). For our cohort, then, the age of 20 may represent an important transition year, whereby drug taking begins to decline. However, the decline after the age of 20 (mirroring the increase prior to that age) is gradual, and we still find that just over half of the sample engaged in at least some drug use during each of those years. Although we do not have retrospective recall data for the intervening years between the ages of 22 and 27, we can see that over this period, past year prevalence rates decline by an average of about 3.5 percentage points per year.

We do not know the precise point during which drug use begins to decline more sharply, but it is clear that as our cohort go through their twenties, drug use becomes less likely for them. However, it is important to note that even by the age of 27, a substantial proportion of them (about one third) were past year drug users, putting their use at a roughly similar overall level to what we found for the cohort around the age of 14–15.

In respect of individual drugs and past year use, cannabis was most popular followed by LSD, amyl nitrite, amphetamines and magic mushrooms during early adolescence. Prevalence of past year cannabis use increased dramatically from the age of 16 (11.3 per cent) to 17 (44.0 per cent) and has remained consistently much higher than for all other drugs. From 18 onwards, the sample's past year drug use began to change as they reached adulthood in the late 1990s (see Table 4.11). Whilst cannabis remains the drug reportedly used by the most respondents in the past year, amphetamine is the second most popular drug until at 22 (in 1999) when it is replaced by cocaine. Past year prevalence for cocaine quadruples from the age of 18 to 22, from 1995 to 1999; mirroring national trends in increased cocaine use at that time (Ramsay *et al.*, 2001). Whilst ecstasy was popular as a past year drug at 18, we

Table 4.10 Prevalence of lifetime and more recent illicit drug taking (age 18, 22 and 27)

	Year 5 (n = 529) %	Year 9 (n = 465) %	Year 14 (n = 217) %
Lifetime	64.3	75.8	72.0
Past year	52.9	52.1	34.1
Past month	35.2	31.2	19.5

witness a gradual decline in its use from 18 to 22. By age 22 it is the third most popular drug to have been taken in the past year, again reflecting national trends in the late 1990s. There have also been substantial reductions in the reported use of amyl nitrite and LSD from the age of 18. The key drugs for past year use in hierarchical order by the age of 22 are: cannabis, cocaine, ecstasy, amphetamines and amyl nitrite.

Indeed, for many of the drug users by their twenties, cannabis is the only drug they report using in the past year (although of the 81 cannabis-only past year drug users, all but one of them had previously tried other illicit drugs – for more detailed discussion, see Parker *et al.*, 2002). In early adulthood these data show there are both changing patterns of drug use and emerging signs of moderation in frequency of drug use which continue into the late twenties. By the age of 27, the key past year drugs in hierarchical order are: cannabis, cocaine, ecstasy, amyl nitrite and amphetamines, all at much lower prevalence than previous years with the exception of cocaine and ecstasy.

Past month use is often used by researchers as a proxy for regular use. As we have argued elsewhere (see Aldridge *et al.*, 1999), the use of this statistic as a proxy for more regular use is likely to be less problematic amongst our cohort members as adults than when they are adolescents. A similar pattern to past year prevalence occurs with past month drug use (see Table 4.10). Past month use of any drug remains fairly stable

Table 4.11 Past year prevalence of illicit drug taking (age 18–27) by individual drug

	Year 5 (n = 529) %	Year 6 (n = 465) %	Year 7 (n = 465) %	Year 8 (n = 465) %	Year 9 (n = 465) %	Year 14* (n = 217) %
Amphetamines	24.0	25.6	20.9	17.1	11.0	2.8
Amyl nitrite	20.4	23.1	17.2	13.9	10.3	4.2
Cannabis	47.8	45.7	47.3	46.9	46.8	28.0
Cocaine powder	4.0	5.2	8.2	14.2	16.2	15.5
Crack cocaine	0.4	0.2	0.6	0.6	0.9	0.9
Ecstasy	17.4	14.0	15.1	14.9	14.5	9.4
Heroin	0.2	0.0	0.2	0.0	0.2	0.0
LSD	15.2	15.1	10.3	4.3	2.8	0.5
Magic mushrooms	4.2	4.9	4.2	1.1	1.7	0.9
Solvents	1.1	3.9	0.5	0.0	0.0	0.0
Tranquillisers	1.5	2.2	1.9	1.1	1.1	0.5
At least one	52.9	56.3	58.2	56.8	52.1	34.1

* Intervening year data was not collected at Year 14 as the recall period was too long

from the age of 18 to 22 at around a third of respondents, and then declines to just under a fifth by the age of 27.

We also collected data on frequency of past month drug use. At the age of 22, almost a third (29.3 per cent) of drug users report taking drugs monthly, of which a fifth (20.1 per cent) are weekly drug takers with a small minority (4.9 per cent) of these using drugs daily. The mean rate for monthly use is three episodes. Just under a quarter of respondents (23.5 per cent) reported taking drugs less than once a month but several times per year. The patterns of use for individual drugs are broadly similar to past year drugs.

By age 22 past month use of individual drugs in hierarchical order are: cannabis (25.8 per cent), ecstasy (8.3 per cent), cocaine (7.0 per cent), amyl nitrite (4.1 per cent) and amphetamines (3.7 per cent). By age 27 the number of key past month drugs is reduced. In hierarchical order they are: cannabis (13.6 per cent), cocaine (7.5 per cent) and ecstasy (5.2 per cent). The prevalence rates for amphetamines and amyl nitrite are below 1 per cent. In respect of frequency for individual drugs at age 22, cannabis was used once a week or more by 14.4 per cent, of which 5.0 per cent are daily users. The mean rate of use is three episodes. The frequency of cannabis use reduces by age 28: 8.8 per cent use it once a week or more but the proportion of daily users remains fairly consistent at 4.6 per cent. The frequency of use for cocaine and ecstasy is much lower than cannabis with few using these drugs on a weekly basis in young adulthood. As we have suggested elsewhere (Measham *et al.*, 2001; Parker *et al.*, 2002) this indicates that stimulant drugs are reserved for more occasional use, with consumption often associated with weekend visits to bars or clubs.

It is clear, then, that by adulthood, drug users not only had chosen drugs which they regularly used but they also began to moderate their use of them. Whilst cannabis, cocaine and ecstasy remain the most popular three drugs for recent or regular use, their frequency of use declines during young adulthood. This decrease in recent and regular drug use has been observed as an epidemiological feature for several decades. It is to be expected as young people progress through the life course and negotiate transitions to adulthood, identified in other studies of youth and young adult drug use (e.g. Shiner, 2009). Reasons for moderating or desisting from drug use will be discussed in Chapter 6.

Impact of gender, social class and ethnicity

We noted earlier in this chapter that one of the striking features of drug use by the respondents in their teens was the lack of any major or statistically significant gender differences in drug trying, leading us to suggest that gender was no longer the straightforward predictor of or protector from drug use that traditionally it was seen to be. There were some minor gender differences in terms of drug offers and drug trying, however. Slightly more females were in drug offer or trying situations than males in the early teens. This pattern was reversed from the age of 15 onwards, with more males reporting having been offered drugs and trying them and with a growing gender gap throughout the late teens regarding recent and regular drug use. This pattern remains the same at the age of 22 (see Table 4.12) with a quarter more males taking drugs in the past year than females and substantially more reporting past month use than females. Although by the age of 27 there is symmetry in drug use statistics by gender, this is most likely a product of attrition of male drug users in the sample.

Throughout the study, we have found some minor differences in respect of social class (defined by school catchment area) in terms of drug offers and drug trying rates, although again not statistically significant. Early in adolescence, respondents from schools with predominantly working-class catchment areas were more likely to be offered drugs and to try them. However, by the age of 17 respondents from schools with predominantly middle-class catchment areas were more likely to be offered drugs and to have taken them recently. This pattern continued into adulthood, although the differences became smaller. From the age of 22 onwards, we witness a reversal of this pattern: respondents from schools with working-class catchment areas are more likely to take drugs although the differences are relatively small.

We previously noted that because of sample attrition we cannot make any robust analysis of drug offers and use by ethnicity. Attrition has continued to impact disproportionately upon the ethnic composition of the sample such that it is predominantly white. We provide new prevalence data in respect of ethnicity, drug offers and use but merely do so for information and consistency and make no attempt to draw conclusions from it.

In later years of the study, we redesigned our surveys and reduced the number of questions measuring experiences associated with specific drugs. We continued to assess how the sample felt about the last time they took drugs and all times that they had used them (see Table 4.13). On the whole, respondents held positive attitudes about the last time they took drugs. Over two-thirds at the age of 22 described their last drug-taking experience as 'very good' or 'good' as did over half of respondents at the age of 27. The proportion of respondents who describe their last drug taking experience as negative is relatively small

Table 4.12 Gender, class and race by offer and use statistics (age 22 and 27) for at least one drug

| | Total % | Gender | | Class | | Race | | | |
		Female %	Male %	Middle %	Working %	Black %	Asian %	White %	Other %
Year 9	(n = 465)	(n = 197)	(n = 266)	(n = 318)	(n = 145)	(n = 6)	(n = 17)	(n = 434)	(n = 6)
Offer	93.1	92.5	93.9	94.0	91.0	100.0	70.6	93.8	100.0
Lifetime	75.8	73.2	79.2	74.8	77.9	100.0	47.1	76.7	66.7
Past year	52.1	45.0	61.7	50.0	56.7	66.7	23.5	53.1	50.0
Past month	31.2	25.2	39.1	28.9	36.2	66.7	6.3	31.8	16.7
Year 14*	(n = 217)	(n = 125)	(n = 85)	(n = 151)	(n = 59)	(n = 4)	(n = 5)	(n = 200)	(n = 1)
Lifetime	72.0	72.4	71.3	71.2	73.8	75.0	20.0	73.0	100.0
Past year	34.1	34.1	34.1	32.5	38.3	25.0	0.0	35.3	0.0
Past month	19.5	19.2	20.0	17.9	23.7	25.0	0.0	20.0	0.0

* Data on drug offers was not collected at Year 14

Table 4.13 Respondents' perceptions of drug experiences (age 22 and 27)

	Year 9 (n = 319) %	Year 14 (n = 149) %
The last time I had drugs was . . .		
Very good	15.4	8.7
Good	54.5	45.6
Equally good and bad	22.9	32.9
Bad	4.7	9.4
Very bad	2.5	3.4
All the times I've had drugs were . . .		
Very good	14.5	10.8
Good	53.5	43.9
Equally good and bad	26.1	35.1
Bad	4.1	6.8
Very bad	1.9	3.4

although there was an increase in reporting of negative experiences from the age of 22 to 27. It may be that younger drug users are less willing than older users to admit to less-than-ideal drug experiences; equally, adult drug users with more experience in drug taking may have fewer of the memorable and highly positive experiences associated with early use. Perceptions of last drug-taking experiences are mirrored in attitudes to all drug experiences for the sample. A further assessment of the sample's experiences with drugs can be gleaned from their reasons for drug use selected from a list of 20 options when they were age 22. Here and elsewhere (Measham *et al.*, 2001; Williams and Parker, 2001) we have noted that drug users weigh up the costs and benefits of their drug use, with the primary reasons for taking drugs being hedonistic, sociability and the desire to create 'time out' in a work–play balance based on learnt decision making as to when and where to use alcohol, cannabis, ecstasy and cocaine in particular.

Summary

During the first five years of the study, we concluded that the cohort experienced unprecedented rates of drug offers, experimentation and regular drug use, predominantly for cannabis but accompanied by LSD, amyl nitrites, amphetamines and, in late adolescence, ecstasy. We found that a minority – between one in four and one in five – were regular users.

Moving into adulthood, despite biographical reconstruction and sample attrition, the findings for this sample are fairly predictable. The drug patterns we have discovered should be considered in tandem with the results for alcohol discussed in Chapter 3. Lifetime drug offers have remained high at around nine in ten with a considerable increase in the availability of cocaine and a decrease in the availability of LSD mirroring the national picture at that time. By young adulthood, around three-quarters of the cohort have tried a drug. Cannabis dominates the picture yet cocaine prevalence increased substantially in the late teens, in the late 1990s, and by the age of 27 was the second most frequently taken drug. Turning to regular use, in line with pre- and post-millennium and adult trends, the sample have begun to moderate the frequency of their drug use in young adulthood. We observed a decline in past year and month prevalence from the age of 22 onwards. By the age of 27, self-reported past year drug use has fallen to a third of the sample and past month drug use has fallen to around a fifth. During this period of the life course, patterns of drug use also changed: some became cannabis-only users, whilst others continued to use cocaine and ecstasy and rejected LSD and amphetamines. Stimulant drugs are still reserved for occasional weekends compared to cannabis which is used more often. The gender gap in respect of drug-use statistics continued to grow in young adulthood but has levelled out by the age of 27. Class catchment area differences remain relatively small throughout the teens and twenties and do not predict involvement with drugs. In terms of drug-trying experiences, on the whole, the sample continues to rate these positively in adulthood.

5 Pathways

Drug abstainers, former triers,
current users and those in
transition

Overview

This chapter begins with a reproduction of the 'pathways' chapter from
the first edition of *Illegal Leisure*. We follow this with an update entitled
'Pathways: Update from 18 to 27 years' that documents the changes in
the drug pathways that occurred for our cohort in adulthood.

The pathways analysis

Initial developments

In this chapter we break with the conventional approach to measuring
and presenting the prevalence of illicit drug use. We move beyond the
analysis presented in the last chapter of seeing prevalence as a dependent variable by simply comparing those who have tried a drug with
those who haven't and attempt to provide a more multi-dimensional
analysis. What have our samples, and core cohort in particular, been
thinking and concluding about the use of drugs and how does this
relate to their behaviour – if they *use* drugs, which drugs, how many
drugs and how often? Basically, we attempt to identify and distinguish
those engaging in current, regular and sustained drug use from those
who are not but might in the future and those who are not and have no
intentions of ever trying illicit drugs. We call this a drugs pathways
analysis. It provides a far more sophisticated understanding of young
people's drug use than that described in Chapter 4.

As we built up a developmental picture of the samples' alcohol,
tobacco and drug use and looked for characteristics or factors which
correlated with and might explain particular profiles we began,
implicitly at first but then explicitly, undertaking this drugs pathways
analysis. Thus, in Year 4 we began to test out our hunches that the

sample were clustering around typical behavioural repertoires and decision-making processes in respect of alcohol, tobacco and illicit drugs. We used three separate questions to compute these pathway categories: the past-drug-use/recency question for the 13 'listed' drugs; future intentions for drug use for the listed drugs; and a self-nominated four-option 'statement' question in which the respondents indicated that which best described their view of themselves, young people and drug use:

1   I take drugs myself. I think taking drugs is OK if you're careful and you know what you're doing.
2   I do not use drugs myself at the moment, but it is possible that I might in the future. I have no problem with other young people using drugs.
3   I do not use drugs myself and don't expect to. I have no problem with other young people using drugs.
4   I don't use drugs and I don't expect to. I don't think people should take drugs.

We then set about looking at whether the data supported our second outline hypothesis that there were two clearly distinctive pathways: *abstainers* and *current* (probably regular) *drug users* and another group in between. This third group in fact split empirically into *former triers* (or ex-users) and those *in transition*. The initial analysis which includes very detailed description of the reliability and validity issues was, as noted above, undertaken when our respondents were 17 (see Aldridge *et al.*, 1996). In this chapter, by also using Year 5 data, when respondents were 18 years old, we further develop the analysis. In particular, we look at the core cohort (n = 223 including interviews with 86) who were with the study for the full five years and for whom we have complete data to build up the pathways retrospectively. Thus, we also look back from Year 5 to Year 1 attempting to identify key factors which have tended to affect or predict particular pathway journeys.

The construction of the drug status variables at 18

Abstainers were all those respondents who indicated never having tried any of the drugs in the list and who also indicated that they never *intended* to try any of the drugs. Abstainers nominated themselves into either the third or fourth of the four statement categories regarding themselves, young people and drug use.

The group of *former triers* comprised respondents who indicated having taken, often experimentally, at least one of the drugs in the list, but who simultaneously indicated that they intended never to take drugs again. Former triers or ex-users, nominated themselves into either the third or fourth statement categories regarding young people and drug use.

The group of *current drug users* comprised all those respondents who reported having had at least one drug, indicated that they might or would try again at least one drug in the list, and nominated themselves into the first of the four statement categories regarding themselves, young people and drug use ('I take drugs myself'). Finally, those *in transition* were respondents who indicated that they either would or might try drugs at some point in the future, either for the individual 13 listed drugs or by nominating themselves into the second of the statement categories regarding young people and drug use, 'I don't take drugs myself at the moment, but it is possible that I might in the future.' The respondents in this group may or may not have already tried or used drugs as indicated in the past-drug-use/recency question. The rounded frequency distribution for this drug status pathway variable at Year 5 is shown in Figure 5.1.

The criteria for differentiating between abstainers and former triers

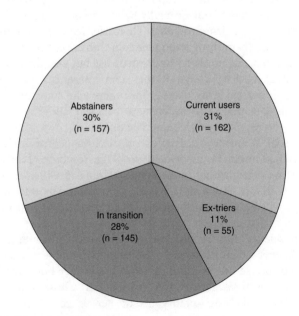

Figure 5.1 Drug status at age 18

from others in the sample are straightforward and the justification and face validity of the categories is transparent. The other drug-status categories, current user, and those in transition, however, require some investigation into the content and internal validity in terms of both the *prima facie* meaning and usefulness of these categories and the extent to which the respondents classified into these categories behave in ways we would consider predictable and definitive.

Validation of drug-user categories

Of the various surveys of young people's drug use in Britain, none, so far as we are aware, has attempted to estimate prevalence rates of current drug users. Most have instead focused upon the estimation of drug-use prevalence rates based on *recency of use* measures (that is, how long ago the last occasion of usage occurred: within the past month, past year, or prior to the past year), similar to the one we have employed in each administration of the survey. Therefore, there is no available standard against which we can compare our estimate of prevalence rates of current drug users as a validation technique. Internal validity, however, can be addressed by exploring the responses to other questions answered by respondents in the current-drug-user pathway.

Current users are all those respondents who had ever tried a drug, intended to do so again and, crucially here, who nominated themselves as drug users ('I take drugs myself'). This latter feature is key therefore in differentiating them from respondents in transition who had already tried a drug (who also intended future drug use but who did not nominate themselves as drug users). If this nomination is a valid way of differentiating current drug users from others who have tried a drug, then we should find key differences between these two groups, particularly on recency and frequency of drug use.

What 'usual' frequency of drug use most closely corresponds to the frequency that might be associated with the response 'I take drugs myself'? How often would someone use drugs in order to indicate agreement with this statement? Obviously, the criteria used to make this assessment will be different for each young person and will vary also considerably by drug taken, drug availability and could, perhaps, for some respondents, even be unrelated to frequency of use at all. None the less, there is a common-sense validity in assigning a particular frequency to drug use that we should want to consider both regular and sustained, as well as current. A respondent whose usage is too infrequent is unlikely to qualify his or her usage as 'current'. We anticipated that 'less than once a month' would probably most likely correspond to occasional, non-regular, and possibly even non-current usage.

Respondents were asked to indicate the frequency of their past month usage for each of the drugs they had taken. For respondents in the current user group, the average past-month-use frequency for all drugs combined was 15.06, a figure substantially higher than that found among respondents in the transition pathway who had ever had a drug, who on average had done so less than once in the month prior to the survey (mean of .83). Clearly, then, the feature that distinguishes these two groups in terms of their construction (self-nominated drug user, 'I take drugs myself') also distinguishes between them in terms of their frequency of drug use: respondents who agreed with the statement 'I take drugs myself' on average had past-month-usage frequency that was more than 18 times that of the respondents in the transition pathway who had ever already taken a drug but had not agreed with the statement. Agreement with the statement thus has strong behavioural connections of the kind we would expect.

How accurate is our estimate that the current regular drug user is one who uses drugs at least, but probably more than, once a month? If our estimate of current regular use at a frequency of more than once a month is correct, then we should find that the majority of our current users had had a drug within the past month. In fact, we find that for 148 (91.4 per cent) current users the most recent use of at least one drug occurred within the past month, compared to only 18 (25 per cent) respondents in transition who had ever had a drug. Furthermore, among current users, 51 (32 per cent) had had a drug within the past week and 64 (40 per cent) either on the day they filled in the question-naire, or the day before. Again, these comparisons show reassuringly marked differences in drug-use behaviour when self-nominated drug status is taken into consideration.

Validation of the 'in-transition' category

The group we have identified as in transition (145, 28 per cent) is, unsurprisingly, much more diverse than the others in terms of respond-ents' drug-taking histories. Thirty-two (22 per cent) of respondents in this group have never had an illicit drug, though all of them either intended to do so, or thought that they might in the future. At the other end of the drug-use continuum, 28 respondents in transition (about one in five of the group) had consumed a drug within the past month, but for the majority (19, i.e. 68 per cent) this occurred on only one or two occasions. The remaining 26 of the respondents who indicated more frequent usage had consumption levels ranging from three to 20 occasions within the past month. Does this suggest that this sub-group of frequent users in transition are respondents that we should consider current users, even if they themselves did not? If, in fact, they are similar to our group of self-identified current users in all but the self-identification, we may wish to place less confidence in using self-identification as a tool for classification.

In fact, however, if we compare the cluster who had used a 'listed' drug more than once in the past month to the current users, we find they were much less likely than the current-drug-user group to have had a drug as recently as the past week and significantly less likely to have ever had amphetamines, amyl nitrite, cocaine and ecstasy. These frequent in-transition users also had tried significantly fewer drugs in their lifetimes (mean of 2.7 compared to 4.4 for current users), as well as in the past year (1.8 compared to 3.2), past month (1.2 compared to 1.7), and past week (.25 compared to .98).

Similarly, the in-transition group who had never tried a drug also differed significantly from the group to which they might reasonably be compared, the abstainers. For 'drug offers' the non-users in transition were significantly more likely to have been offered a drug than abstainers (94 per cent compared to 71 per cent of abstainers); and for specific drugs this difference in offer rates held true for amphetamines (59 per cent of non-users in transition compared to 35 per cent of abstainers); amyl nitrite (50 per cent compared to 25 per cent); cannabis (88 per cent compared to 54 per cent); cocaine (19 per cent compared to 4 per cent); ecstasy (56 per cent compared to 37 per cent); anabolic steroids (13 per cent compared to 3 per cent); and tranquillisers (9 per cent compared to 3 per cent). Table 5.1 provides an overview of this analysis based on 521 respondents.

The drugs attitudes scale (DAS)

A further device was used both to validate the drug-status pathways analysis and extend its analytic power. As well as comparing the drug-use patterns for each pathway group, we also created a drugs-attitude measurement scale. Did each of our four pathways groups hold different attitudes about drug use and were these consistent with their self-reported behaviour?

Thirteen statements were devised in order to assess attitudes toward drugs and drug use:

1   Taking drugs is OK if it makes you feel good.

2 Taking drugs always leads to addiction.
3 I have a negative attitude towards drugs.
4 Taking drugs is always dangerous.
5 Most of my close friends take drugs.

Table 5.1 Drug-taking attitudes, behaviours and intentions for the Year 5 sample and by drug status

Drug status	Sample (n = 521) %	Current users (n = 164) %	Former triers/users (n = 55) %	In transition (n = 145) %	Abstainers (n = 157) %
Drug-taking behaviour					
Recency					
Never	36.3	0.0	0.0	22.1	100.0
Prior to past year	11.1	0.0	67.3	14.5	0.0
Within past year	17.5	8.5	23.6	44.1	0.0
Within past month	11.7	20.7	9.1	15.2	0.0
Within past week	23.4	70.7	0.0	4.1	0.0
Number of listed drugs taken					
(drug triers only)	(n = 332)				
Mean no. taken in lifetime	3.3	4.4	1.7	2.3	–
Mean no. taken in past year	2.1	3.2	0.4	1.3	–
Mean no. taken in past month	1.0	1.7	0.1	0.3	–
Mean no. taken in past week	0.5	1.0	0.0	0.1	–
Future drug-use intentions					
(excluding abstainers and former triers)	(n = 309)				
Expecting to re/try at least one drug (excluding cannabis)	71.5	90.2	–	50.3	–
(excluding abstainers and former triers)	(n = 309)				
Mean no. drugs expected to re/try	3.6	4.6	–	2.5	–
Attitudes	(n = 474)				
Mean 'DAS' scores	37	47	35	37	29

6   People who take drugs live life to its fullest.
7   I could no longer respect someone who I found out took drugs.
8   Taking drugs is morally wrong.
9   Older people worry too much about the dangers of drugs.
10 People who take drugs have mostly good experiences with drugs.
11 Cannabis should be made legal.
12 Taking drugs is just a bit of fun.
13 Most people who take drugs will eventually have problems.

For each of the statements, respondents were asked to indicate their level of agreement on a Likert-type scale that ranged from (1) 'agree strongly' to (5) 'disagree strongly'. Possible scores on the scale could therefore range from 13 to 65, with higher scores representing more 'pro-drug' attitudes. Actual scores ranged from 13 to 62, with a mean for the cohort of 37.26 (SD = 9.31).

A principal-components factor analysis of the items in the scale confirmed evidence for the reliability and internal validity of the DAS as a uni-dimensional scale. One factor accounted for 43.7 per cent of the variance among items, and factor loadings for each item ranged from .51 to .79. A two-factor solution was neither empirically justified nor theoretically interpretable. The Cronbach's alpha coefficient was .89, indicating that the reliability for the scale was high.

Mean scores on the DAS between pathways were all in the expected direction. Thus, the current users had by far the highest pro-drug attitudes scores (mean 46.5) followed by respondents in transition (36.8), former triers (34.5) and abstainers (28.9). A one-way analysis of variance showed that differences in drug-attitudes scores between groups were statistically significant, and post-hoc comparisons (Scheffe) showed that each group differed significantly from the others except the small difference between former triers/users (34.5) and respondents in transition (36.8). And, providing further confirmation for the validity of the in-transition group, we found that even the frequent drug users in transition (identified above) had significantly less pro-drug attitudes (39.4) than the current user group (46.5). Similarly those in the in-transition group who had never tried a drug had significantly more pro-drug attitudes (37.6) than abstainers (28.9).

In conclusion, the drugs pathways analysis seems robust. Each pathway is measurably distinctive by attitude to illicit drugs, self-definition of drugs status and drug-taking behaviour (frequency, recency and number of drugs consumed). 'Future intentions', as we shall see when we compare pathways at Year 4 with Year 5, is a more complicated and necessarily elastic measure.

Drugs status groups

Abstainers

In the next chapter we look at the cost-benefit analysis which most drug users apply to assess whether they should take a particular drug. However, abstainers have also had to become drugwise during the 1990s and their critique of recreational drug use has its own sophistication and evolution. We did find a few 'classic' abstainers in our study who simply held the line:

> I've had it drummed into me even since I was little how bad it is and what it does to people [Who by?] My mum and dad. Watch documentaries on it. I've seen how it's affected friends. I've seen people get into debt. I think if you're the kind of person that can enjoy yourself you don't need it. I don't think anyone needs it. And, just the fact I'd be too scared . . . . I feel very strongly . . . I've never been tempted and I don't think I ever will be, or I know I never will be. [How do you feel about other people doing drugs?] It's upsetting that healthy people need to take things to give them a bit of a lift because it's the effects afterwards. [Different views about different drugs?] I don't really know a lot about drugs. I know the different names but I don't actually know what each one does. But I know a drug's a drug and they're all bad.
>
> (Ellen)

However, such watertight perspectives, particularly from someone who pubbed and clubbed, were rare and whilst it is obviously possible to find an interview setting with mid adolescents undergoing anti-drugs education whereby their views of those who take illegal drugs are wholly negative (Shiner and Newburn, 1996), such responses were atypical of this study. Why abstainers have had to become drugwise and how they are adapting to drug offers and drug use around them is an important plank in the normalisation thesis (Perri, 6 *et al.*, 1997; Wibberley, 1997).

Abstainers are not usually risk takers and they readily admit that the thought of taking drugs scares them.

> [Why don't you take drugs?] They're expensive, I don't like injections. I don't like smoke as well. I don't like inhaling things . . . . I don't want to damage my lungs, some people have reactions don't they just try it once and bang . . . . I'm scared about that as

well. I wouldn't want to put myself in any situations. . . . I couldn't handle it.

(Samantha)

Because I'm scared really what they're going to do to me. I'm scared of not being in control and losing my mind and not knowing what I'm doing. It's just really my own personal choice – morals I suppose. [Health?] Not really . . . I suppose it can kill you in the long run. I just don't think you need drugs to have a good time. I know people who can't go out without having Es.

(Josephine)

Yet both these outgoing and sociable abstainers did not regard their attitudes and moral perspectives as applicable to others. They felt each young person had to make up their own minds.

I feel quite strongly personally . . . but people should each make their own decisions especially where drugs are concerned. [Different views on different drugs?] I think if you try pot I think that's OK but once you get into that circle that you've got contacts, the druggies, they think they can try other drugs, they start to experiment more and I think that's how it progresses.

(Josephine)

I used to think they were really stupid but now I think well if you want to do it, do it but don't encourage me to. The people that I hang around with *know* not to put them under my nose . . . . I hate seeing people off their faces . . . I feel really responsible if I'm with them. [Different views about different drugs?] I think I'm calmer about Es and whizz and stuff like cannabis . . . rather than someone who's taking heroin or cocaine.

(Josephine)

These complex and coherent perspectives about the risks and dangers of taking illicit drugs were routinely found in the interviews with abstainers. They were clear about their self-prohibition but also acknowledged the 'right', however foolish, of their peers to take drugs. They judged drug users on the basis of how responsible their use of drugs was and which drugs they took. In short, they distinguished between responsible recreational drug use and a hard drug career: 'Everyone's got their own opinion. If they do take drugs then they're a bit daft but it doesn't bother me, like my cousin takes them (cannabis and amphetamines) and he's alright' (Tim). 'In a lot of ways I feel sorry for them. They've made a choice, it's their problem. I just let them get on with it' (Paul).

One of the changes brought about by the widespread and early avail-ability of illicit drugs in the 1990s is that abstainers cannot easily avoid social relationships with drug users. It is getting harder to change friends and peer groups and be insulated by like-minded peers and, thus far, more realistic to be upfront and accommodate difference.

> Only from a personal point of view I'd never do them, but as far as anyone else is concerned it doesn't bother me. Provided I don't get any pressure, it doesn't bother me.
> [And do you?] No not from the friends I've got. [Do they do drugs when you're out with them?] Yes.
>
> (Tony)

Such a strategy is not without its difficulties:

> [Have you ever felt awkward, upset about this?] I feel awkward sometimes when we're in a group and they say 'oh I'm going to get some drugs does anybody want some', I maybe feel isolated, not that I'd ever try, but I feel as if I'm not part of that group anymore, they then are in their own little group taking them as it were. [Do you feel pressured at all by that?] No, they may offer me, but they never pressure me. They say fine if you don't want any, fine.

However, there is a bottom line.

> It was a couple of years ago now really, one of my closest friends started taking drugs on a regular basis and I had to cancel a holiday with her and the friendship just split up really, I don't see her any more. [When you say you cancelled the holiday . . . was it because you just weren't to go with her because of it?] Not only that, but we were going with parents as well and they found out and they weren't very happy about it. [Do you know what she was using?] She was taking speed, and I think she was taking ecstasy, but I can't be sure on that. She was smoking cannabis as well. [Did you just gradually move away from her, or did you have a big bust up?] It happened gradually at first, at first I wasn't really bothered about it but her personality changed, she just changed completely into a different person, I just couldn't handle the change in her behaviour.
>
> (Linda)

Overall abstainers having grown up with drugs, and having had to reject and negotiate so often around drug offers and drug-taking situations, have themselves become drugwise. They feel that, by and large, and certainly by late adolescence, their abstention is respected by triers and users and they in return come to accommodate soft-drug recreational users not least because they might be a romantic partner, brother, sister or friend. This is, many of them feel, a sad and unfortunate state of affairs but it is a social reality with which they feel they must come to terms. Basically if you are outgoing and sociable and feel you have the right to enjoy yourself and party, pub, holiday in the sun or club without drugs then you must accept that others will behave differently. As one abstainer put it:

> Drugs are always going to be there, no matter what you do about it, they'll always be there. Kids will always want to try them, and if they get away with it they'll try it again. If they've got the money they'll have it. And, to be honest there's nothing you can do about it. All you can do is to tell them how bad it is for them, and that's about it.
>
> (Ben)

Former triers

The least crowded pathway is for former triers or ex-users. Whilst some have extensive drugs careers which they have now left behind, most of this cluster have been experimenters or users only briefly. In some ways, for instance attitudinally, former triers are closer to abstainers. Similarly, by declaring that they do not intend to try drugs again, these former drug takers share an abstentionist perspective. However, behaviourally this pathway group have actually tried or indeed used illicit drugs and it is this experience which also brings them closer to drug users and those in transition who have also experimented.

One young man, a trainee accountant, who began using cannabis at 16 and then started using amphetamines alongside alcohol changed pathways at 17. He continued to socialise in the same drug-using group but had not taken an illicit drug for six months when interviewed.

> Basically it's (cannabis use) been part of our social life to have it every now and again. It mellows us out and puts us in good moods, that sort of thing. But it's not important to me at all and I can live without it. Like I say I haven't touched it for six months I

suppose I've tried it all now. I know what it's like, rather than have the temptation being there for years and years.

(Tom)

'Growing out of' adolescent drug use was seen by several interviewees as underpinning their giving up. One young woman continued to keep in the same peer network but stopped taking drugs (cannabis and amphetamines) several months before the interview. She put her decision to quit down to several factors: her mum finding out, feeling ill on several occasions, but most of all realising that she preferred drinking and clubbing. Looking back, her brief career was about:

Just having a good time, everyone's doing it, so everyone's the same and there was nothing else to do when I did it with them and I was 14 to 16. There was nothing else to do . . . now because I'm older and can go to clubs and that.

(Anne)

Several respondents in this pathway group only ever tried one drug on one occasion: 'It was weed. I had just a puff of one. That's all I had, I didn't have the whole thing, just a puff. I was with friends and they were saying "go on just try it, try it" . . . I really hated it, I never touched it again' (Alice).

A final key definer for ex-users and triers was that many gave up because of a bad or very bad drug experience, often with LSD or, in the case of our most salutary account, 'tablets' purporting to be MDMA. When he was 16 one of our now ex-user interviewees went clubbing with his girlfriend. They bought tablets in the club. He took one and his girlfriend took two: 'My girlfriend, she just dehydrated, just collapsed. She was drinking beer, and you know beer, it doesn't actually quench your thirst does it? She just collapsed' (Daniel).

This young woman died several days later and our interviewee has not taken an illicit drug since, although he now drinks heavily.

In transition

Conceptually, this pathway is the most difficult to define. Because this cluster are reviewing and revising their drugs status, there is a sense in which they are on a roundabout rather than taking a clearly signed route. At Year 4, three-quarters of the in-transition group had tried a drug and felt they might do so again in the future. The other quarter had no direct personal drugs experience but felt they might want to try a drug in the future. As we shall see, over half of this group actually change status and move down another pathway during Year 5 thereby giving further justification for this conceptualisation. We should also remember that this cluster, although clear they were drug *users*, had fairly pro-drug attitudes and this in particular distinguished them from the abstainers. Thus, one young man in transition, a keen sportsman, committed to a healthy lifestyle, was happy to have a friendship network of drug users despite the fact he'd never tried an illicit drug himself. Asked if he had any strong feelings about drug use, he replied: 'No, not bothered at all. I've no thoughts about it whatsoever, no feelings.'

This interviewee made a clear distinction between 'soft' drugs and hard drug use. He had no truck for junkies but felt cannabis was benign. Asked about his future intentions: 'Maybe . . . depends what mood I'm in. Depends how much I'd had to drink. [Situation?] Who I'm with I suppose. [Which drugs?] Cannabis only' (Craig).

An 18-year-old female, keen on sport, who had tried cannabis, LSD and magic mushrooms did not regard herself as a drug *user* because she settled for occasional binges of combination drug use involving alcohol, cigarettes and cannabis. She again felt comfortable with this status within her peer network. Typically of those in transition who used drugs, she did so less often than current users: 'Usually do it when it's available, they're there, and they just say "do you want to try it" or "do you want to today?" and I just say yes or no' (Sophie).

Another non-trier who'd used the cost-benefit assessment and decided against drug trying felt she was becoming increasingly agnostic through time.

> I don't really feel strongly about it, it's just up to now I've chosen not to. Like I said before, each to their own, it doesn't really bother me. . . . I feel more strongly towards say ecstasy or cocaine or heroin. I'm more against them. [In the future?] Yes I could do. [Situation?] Either with family or friends. [What might influence your decision?] Just the consequences really. [Which drugs?] Cannabis . . . I'm a bit indecisive about these hallucinogenic drugs cos I think they're a bit too dangerous for my own liking.
>
> (Alison)

A 'big drinking' male interviewee felt similarly:

> When I was younger it was very important, because it was sort of like being clean if you know what I mean. You haven't had nothing so you're clean. Getting older, it's not as important now, as I said

... I'm tending to go that way a bit now as if I want to try something, but I haven't decided yet.

(Ben)

Moving into adulthood and going to university or having access to the nightclub scene was identified by several in-transition interviewees as being a likely change in set and setting which might well stimulate their drugs initiation or diversification into dance drugs. One young man who was beginning to experiment with amphetamines could see his first E around the corner.

> Just to experiment really. That's it. Just to experiment, just to try them. I suppose the atmosphere of clubs makes me want to try them . . . not really because my friends are doing it, it's because I want to experiment myself. I mean, my friends never ever pressure me at all, no peer group pressure at all, its basically my choice.
>
> (Lee)

Current drug users

The next chapter is dedicated to describing journeys through adolescence which result in young people becoming drug users and here we shall only briefly outline this pathway status group. We have shown that current users hold the strongest pro-drug attitudes and many speak with some disdain at the hypocrisy of alcohol- and tobacco-loving adults *vis-à-vis* cannabis and the way anti-drugs campaigns include cannabis as a 'drug of death'.

> I think it's sad really that people are so concerned about pot, a harmless drug. I say harmless, I'll take it for granted that its harmless for the moment because as far as everybody knows it is, apart from the tobacco in it. When there are so many things that people should do something about . . . all the funds that go into . . . can you imagine all these thousands of people working making leaflets against cannabis, how sad is that.
>
> (Ricky)

Drug users take far more drugs more often than those in transition and demonstrate they have learnt to distinguish between drugs and their effects.

> Favourite combination, yes, speed, cannabis and alcohol. It's all

three in all kinds of situations. [Order?] Probably have a drink first and then it'll be the speed and then a lot later on we'll probably have the cannabis.

(Vicky)

And they enjoy their drug use and as we shall see have far more good times than bad.

You're in a really good mood, it's more inside, nobody can annoy you no matter how gorgeous or how skinny the girl that stands next to you, it just doesn't really bother you, you feel like you're the nicest person in there. It gives you confidence.

(Diane)

[Where do you usually take drugs if you do?] Mainly in a nightclub. Or, there was a phase we went through . . . there's like a brook near a waterfall, and a waterfall sounds dead peaceful at night time, and there's this big concrete slab, and about eight, nine of us used to go up there and we used to sit and have a spliff, and it used to be dead relaxing. A friend of mine got a jungle tape and it was really relaxed and there was like soul breaks in it, and we put that on these speakers you get with a Walkman, and sat there looking at the waterfall mist and looking at the stars, and everyone's just like falling asleep. It's wicked. Just lay there. Such a warm night, we just sat there smoking, just really chilled out, relaxed.

(Gary)

Those taking the drug-using pathway expect to continue to take or try drugs in the future but also to modify or restrain their behaviour.

[You haven't used LSD for a couple of years now . . .?] Yes, I think I've matured with drug use. At first I was into trying anything, now I know what I like, what I don't like. I don't particularly like taking amphetamine, the after effects, but when you're on it it's alright. I probably will give that up, and probably, I've not taken LSD for a long time, but if I do take it again I'll probably just take one tab just for old time's sake. But with weed I wouldn't mind carrying that on. I don't know if I definitely will or not, but I'd like to.

(Adam)

This early risk taker who left school at 16 in the midst of a heavy polydrug period also reminds us that his peers are joining the current-users pathways just as he is restraining his use.

I would say a lot more (of them) are into it now. When I started I was young, it seemed mad to others of my age but once we left school they were also using drugs whereas they had criticised me in the past. Seems they have now caught up.

(Scott)

Others leaving sixth form and setting off for college, expecting new adventures, thereby remind us that here is another dynamic, undulating drugs pathway:

I think it'll all change when I go to Uni. I'll go to a lot more clubs hopefully. [Which drugs do you plan to use in the future?] Whizz, more whizz. Probably weed will stay the same. [Anything else?] No that's about it. [More or less often?] More often. [Amounts?] Probably increase but I won't try anything new now, I'll stick to what I know.

(Kate)

The making of drug pathways

In this section we take the drugs status of our core cohort at Year 5, as they enter young adulthood, and look back down the pathways from which they've come from when they were 13 and 14 years old. In short, we analyse what factors, decisions and behaviours in early and mid adolescence correlate and predict drugs status at Year 5.

First drug offers and first drug trying

It is quite clear from Tables 5.2 and 5.3 that there were situations, actions and decisions back in early and mid adolescence which helped shape the particular pathway journeys taken. We can see that abstainers were least likely to be in drug-offer situations in early and mid adolescence although as time went on they, too, nearly all encountered such situations. However, even at 13–14 years of age nearly three-quarters of current users had already been in such situations. Former triers and ex-users, as we can see, are a small but more complex cluster. Some were in fact early risk takers who were both in offer situations at 14 and had also, by then, tried their first drug (34.8 per cent). We also find that at around 18 years of age (Year 5) another significant minority became abstinent and declared themselves as ex-users and former experimenters. The in-transition cluster consistently take the middle course and were more likely to be in offer situations than abstainers and obviously by definition more likely to have tried a drug. There is an incremental

Table 5.2 Year in which respondents first reported being in a drug-offer situation for any drug for the cohort and by drug status at Year 5

	Cohort (n = 223) n	%	Drug status category			
			Current users (n = 64) %	Former triers (n = 23) %	In transition (n = 64) %	Abstainers (n = 72) %
Offer situation never reported	10	0.0	0.0	0.0	0.0	0.0
Offer situation of any drug first reported						
Year 1	121	54.3	73.4	65.2	53.1	34.7
Year 2	38	17.0	12.5	8.7	29.7	12.5
Year 3	21	9.4	12.5	8.7	4.7	11.1
Year 4	23	10.3	1.6	8.7	7.8	20.8
Year 5	10	4.5	0.0	8.7	4.7	6.9

Table 5.3 Year in which drug use first reported for the cohort and by drug status

	Cohort (n = 139)* n	%	Drug status category		
			Current users (n = 64) %	Former triers (n = 23) %	In transition (n = 52) %
Use first reported					
Year 1	55	39.6	46.9	34.8	32.7
Year 2	23	16.5	18.8	17.4	16.5
Year 3	17	12.2	17.2	8.7	12.2
Year 4	26	18.7	15.6	8.7	18.7
Year 5	18	12.9	1.6	30.4	12.9

Note: * only respondents in the cohort who have never had a drug included. Never reported n = 84

steadiness about their initiation over the five years. Current users, however, clearly have the longest drugs careers, nearly half having already tried a drug at 14 and nearly all the remainder initiating by 17.

Smoking and drinking by pathway status

The discovery that current users, at 18–19 years of age, had been far more likely to have begun smoking tobacco in early adolescence and to have sustained and indeed increased this consumption pattern through into young adulthood is highly significant both statistically (see Tables 5.4 and 5.5) and epidemiologically. Abstainers, by contrast, demonstrate that not smoking is another important related decision they make. Over two-thirds of abstainers have never smoked and only a tiny minority have ever been regular smokers (see Table 5.4). Once again, the in-transition group sit very close to the mean taking the middle ground, being more likely to smoke than abstainers and former triers but far less likely than current drug users.

Drinking is far more normative than smoking in the UK and the majority of all young adult Britons drink every week. We must thus expect most abstainers in any representative sample to indulge in

Table 5.4 Smoking status for the cohort at each year and by drug status

	Cohort (n = 223) %		Current users (n = 64) %	Former triers (n = 23) %	In transition (n = 64) %	Abstainers (n = 72) %
Year 1 (n = 214)						
Ever smoked	71	33.2	57.4	26.1	34.4	13.0***
Current smoker	41	19.2	37.7	8.7	16.4	8.7***
Year 2						
Ever smoked	116	52.3	77.8	52.2	57.8	25.0***
Current smoker	55	24.8	50.8	21.7	20.3	6.9***
Year 3						
Ever smoked	129	58.1	85.9	56.5	65.1	27.8***
Current smoker	64	288	59.4	26.1	23.8	6.9***
Year 4						
Ever smoked	142	63.7	92.2	69.6	73.4	27.8***
Current smoker	61	27.4	62.5	30.4	18.8	2.8***
Mean no. smoked yesterday	53	8	9	9	8	5 n.s.
Year 5						
Ever smoked	150	67.3	93.8	73.9	78.1	31.9***
Current smoker	85	38.1	81.3	43.5	32.8	2.8***
Mean no. smoked yesterday	66	11	11	8	12	0 n.s.

Note: *** p ≤ .001

drinking. This is the case with over two-thirds beginning drinking around 14 and only 22 per cent never engaging in weekly drinking (see Table 5.5). This said, abstainers reach their weekly drinking far later than all the other pathway groups. Again, the former-triers group appears to contain some early risk takers, a third (34.8 per cent) who begin weekly drinking in early adolescence, and another cluster who begin regular drinking at around 17 when access to pubs and age presentation at off licences make social drinking accessible. Current users, with the exception of a couple of respondents who don't like or drink alcohol, were already drinkers by 14–15 years of age and three-quarters were weekly drinkers by 16.

Risk-taking indicators

This same patterning by pathway group holds for all the other 'deviance' or risk-taking indicators utilised in the study. For early sexual experiences (more than a kiss!) under the age of 16, abstainers were far less likely than current users to have had a sexual experience

Table 5.5 Drinking status for the cohort at each year and by drug status

	Cohort (n = 223) %		Drug status category			
			Current users (n = 64) %	Former triers (n = 23) %	In transition (n = 64) %	Abstainers (n = 72) %
Current drinking never reported						
	7	3.1	1.6	0.0	0.0	8.3*
Current drinking first reported						
Year 1	187	83.9	95.3	87.0	89.1	68.1
Year 2	17	7.6	3.1	8.7	7.8	11.1
Year 3	9	4.0	0.0	4.3	1.6	9.7
Year 4	1	0.4	0.0	0.0	0.0	1.4
Year 5	2	0.9	0.0	0.0	1.6	1.4
Weekly drinking never reported						
	21	9.4	1.6	4.3	4.7	22.2***
Weekly drinking first reported						
Year 1	49	22.0	26.6	34.8	25.0	11.1
Year 2	49	22.0	32.8	8.7	25.0	13.9
Year 3	40	17.9	15.6	13.0	20.3	19.4
Year 4	42	18.8	18.8	34.8	12.5	19.4
Year 5	22	9.9	4.7	4.3	12.5	13.9

Note: * = p ≤ .05; *** = p ≤ .001

(p<.001). At 16, 76 per cent of abstainers reported not having had sex but only 41 per cent of current users did so (p< .01). Former triers (61 per cent) and those in transition (53 per cent) were also less likely to have had under-age sex than current users (see Newcombe *et al.*, 1994).

Exactly the same patterning occurs when we look at our cohort's involvement with the police and criminal justice system. At Year 5, just over half (54 per cent) of the cohort had been stopped by the police including 28 per cent of current users. However, 81 per cent of abstainers had still never been stopped by the police (p<.001). Statistical significance remains between these two contrasting pathways for being arrested (p<.01) and being cautioned or convicted (p<.01).

However, whilst all this shows defining differences between users and abstainers, it should not detract from the other vitally important conclusion – that despite the war-on-drugs rhetoric about the link between drug use and crime, hardly any of the cohort are seriously delinquent and over two-thirds (67 per cent) of current users have no cautions or convictions either. Moreover, just being out and about increases one's risk of being stopped and arrested.

Drugs pathways into young adulthood

In this section we identify and discuss the continuity and change in the cohort's drugs status between Years 4 and 5. The period coincided with the cohort having an 18th birthday and obtaining many of the official trappings of adulthood. For many it was a time for leaving home and going to college or university, for others jobs and wages kicked in.

Abstainers

Figure 5.2 illustrates the longitudinal changes in the abstainer cluster. One abstainer became a current user whilst a handful became former triers by briefly experimenting with drugs during Year 5. Two of the 14 in this category tried only one drug before quickly returning to abstention as former triers. In Year 5, 16 per cent moved into transition; half of whom only made an attitudinal change by declaring that it was now a possibility they would take a drug in the future. The remainder actually tried one, usually two, drugs during Year 5 and acknowledged they would probably do so again, thereby further confirming their shift out of abstention.

All this said, 75 per cent of this pathway group who had never taken a drug during their whole adolescence maintained this position on into young adulthood. Whilst there are clearly grounds for believing the

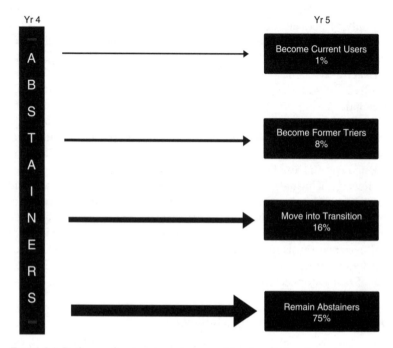

Figure 5.2 Pathways for abstainers between Year 4 and Year 5

abstainer group will further diminish in size, it is also very likely that the majority of these abstainers will sustain their status.

Former triers

Former triers and ex-users are a small proportion of the cohort but as we can see from Figure 5.3 they continue to review and redefine their status. During Year 5, 43 per cent continue as former triers and if we include the four respondents who were anomalous reporters by 'forgetting' at Year 5 if they had once tried a drug (as discussed in Chapter 2) then over half have remained on the same pathway.

This said, the remainder have moved back towards drugs with 11 per cent becoming current users and no less than 38 per cent moving into transition. Of the 18 in this latter pathway half had used a drug, primarily cannabis, very recently. The remainder had only made the intellectual or attitudinal shift by declaring that they might take another drug in the future. Overall, in terms of actually imbibing a drug during Year 5 only 13 of these 47 former triers actually indulged.

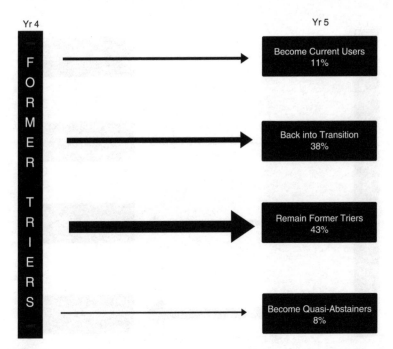

Figure 5.3 Pathways for former triers between Year 4 and Year 5

In transition

By definition we should expect considerable movement in the in-transition cluster. Figure 5.4 confirms this. No less than 50 (37 per cent) of the cluster became current users. This is a substantive shift because it involves a major behavioural change. Most of these new current users (44, 88 per cent) had already tried a drug. Primarily what we have measured is the operationalising of their intentions several months before. Having taken one or more drugs in the past and expecting to do so in the future, this group then quickly moved into a level of drug use which defined them as current users. Nine respondents became former triers and nine became abstainers during Year 5, sharing a shift away from drugs. For the half (49 per cent) that remained in transition, two-thirds (45) had already had a drug. Overall, therefore, we must accept that the majority of those who take the in-transition pathway are more likely to move towards rather than away from regular drug use.

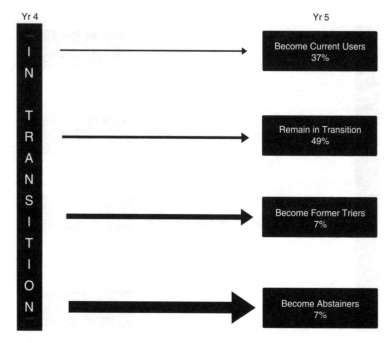

Figure 5.4 Pathways for those in transition between Year 4 and Year 5

Current users

This pathway group (n = 164) have undertaken the least personal change *vis-à-vis* drugs (see Figure 5.5). No less than 80 per cent remain current users by attitude, future expectations and drug-taking behaviour during Year 5. With only two respondents giving up drug use to become former users, the only other shift was for the 16 per cent who moved 'back' into transition by no longer agreeing with the statement 'I take drugs myself.' This does not mean they no longer ever take drugs. In fact, half were past-month users of cannabis. We are here probably measuring a reduction in frequency and range of drugs used as well as temporary abstention.

Summary

We have shown how the four discrete drugs pathways our samples have taken during their adolescence are conceptually robust. The abstainer, former-trier, in-transition and current-drug-user pathways

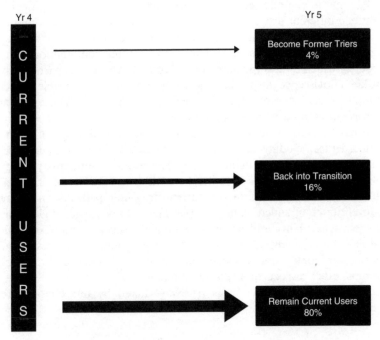

Figure 5.5 Pathways for current users between Year 4 and Year 5

are identifiable by attitude, future expectations about drug use and actual drug-trying and drug-taking behaviour. Abstainers hold anti-drugs attitudes, have never taken a drug and never intend to. Former triers and ex-users hold fairly negative attitudes to drug use and whilst they have tried or used illicit drugs during their adolescence they have no intention of doing so again. Those in transition hold fairly positive drugs attitudes, most have tried drugs but, importantly, all feel they might use drugs in the future. Current users hold pro-drug attitudes, they use one or more drugs regularly and expect their drugs careers to continue into the future.

Whilst each of these pathways are 'static', young people by reflecting on and reviewing their attitude to and use of drugs can switch pathways. We have shown by plotting young people's decision-making journeys that as our samples move into adulthood there is a continuing increase in the proportion who are becoming current users and a reduction in the number of abstainers. Most young people who become drug users move gradually into regular drug use and so spend periods in transition.

All this is complicated by the fact that today's youth distinguish between different drugs in a fairly sophisticated way whereby those in transition for instance are more likely to use the 'softer' drugs such as cannabis whereas current users have a larger, often combination, drug repertoire including amphetamines and ecstasy. Abstainers, particularly in late adolescence, also accommodate those who are 'sensible' recreational users of soft drugs thereby also showing drug wisdom consistent with the normalisation thesis.

Finally, whilst current drug users have the most florid, risk-taking antecedents, including early smoking, drinking and sexual experiences, they do not have strong delinquent tendencies nor fit into any typology of abnormal development. Whilst there will be a minority of drinking, drug-taking delinquents in the current-drug-user pathway, most are conventional 'bounded' young people. This is to be expected given the greater accessibility and accommodation of drug use amongst 1990s adolescents whereby, as we have seen, today's young drug users are of both sexes, come from all social and educational backgrounds and are in most other respects quite conventional.

We turn now to the drugs pathways taken by our cohort into adulthood.

Pathways: an update from 18 to 27 years

Earlier we described how we developed and identified specific drugs pathways – typical routes through which adolescents navigated their way through drug decisions from the age of 14 to 18. We found that at any one survey year, respondents in our cohort had a drug use status that fitted into one of four discrete categories describing their drug journeys up to that point in their lives: *abstainer, former trier, in-transition* and *current user*. A drug status at any one point in time, however, was always subject to future change, and mapping these changes is what we called the drugs pathways analysis. The advantage of this drug pathways approach has been to move beyond the crude prevalence statistics (lifetime, past year, and past month use) that continue to dominate quantitative approaches to understanding youthful drug use, in spite of our earlier demonstrations that past month and past year use represent poor proxies for regular drug use amongst adolescents (see also Aldridge *et al.*, 1999).

Since members of our cohort have become adults, we have observed a reduction in abstainers and an increase in current drug users. In this chapter update we revisit this 'pathways' analysis, focusing on data collected when respondents were predominantly age 22 in 1999.

The pathways analysis

The construction of the drug status variables at age 22

As in previous data collection sweeps, we assessed drug pathways using past drug use/recency data for 13 individual drugs; future use intentions for these drugs and the self-nominated option statement question. From the age of 22, we constructed drug status categories that were modified slightly from those used originally, namely *abstainer, current user, ex-user* (previously referred to as 'former triers') and the new category, *opportunistic user*. The definition for abstainers, current users and ex-users remains the same from that employed when the sample was 18. These three categories remain empirically robust. However, the 'in-transition' grouping was no longer appropriate because we only had two sample members who fitted the criterion: who were not drug experienced but thought they might take drugs in the future. These two respondents were instead classified as abstainers. This loss of the in-transition category reflects the fact that as the adolescents in our sample moved into adulthood, their drug-taking decisions were less transient and fluid. Instead of in-transition users, we found we had a group of respondents who could more appropriately be termed *opportunistic users*. All of these respondents had some drug experience but, at the time of the survey, did not consider themselves to be current drug users, but nevertheless thought they might take drugs again in the future. We will discuss in more detail later in this update section the distinction between these opportunistic users and current or ex-users. The distribution for the drugs pathways variable at the age of 22 is presented in Figure 5.6.

As would be expected, there have been some changes in drug status for the cohort from the age of 18 to 22. The abstainer group has reduced again, this time by 5 per cent. There has also been a reduction in the number of current drug users from 31 per cent to 28 per cent in this four-year period, whilst the ex-user and opportunistic user groups have grown by 5 per cent and 4 per cent respectively.

The construction of the drug status variables at age 27

The survey carried out when members of the cohort were 27 employed a questionnaire that was substantially shorter than previous versions. One question that had been key in defining drugs status in earlier survey administrations was the 'self-nominated' drug status question. The final survey administration only collected recency data for 11 drugs to create

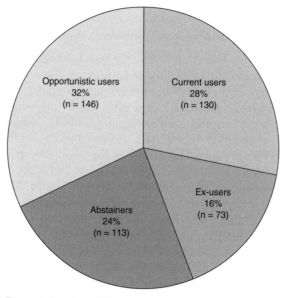

Figure 5.6 Drug status at age 22

Note: Three respondents are not classifiable in terms of drug status

the following drug status categories: *drug abstainer* (respondents who had never tried a drug in their lifetime); *drug desister* (respondents who had not had a drug in the past year); and *current drug taker* (respondents who had taken a drug in the past year) (see Williams, 2007). These categories have been applied to the data collected at age 18 and 22 to illustrate change (see Table 5.6).

As we have already noted above, the drug abstainer group decreases over time: from age 18 to 22 it reduces by a third. By the age of 27, less than a fifth of the sample report never having used a drug. This is an important finding, because it demonstrates that initiation into drug

Table 5.6 Comparison of drug status at age 18, 22 and 27

Drug status	Age 18 (n = 529) %	Age 22* (n = 465) %	Age 27* (n = 217) %
Drug abstainers	29.9	24.5	18.6
Drug desisters	39.3	47.4	47.9
Current drug takers	30.8	28.1	33.5

* Two respondents were unclassifiable in terms of drug status at both age 22 and 27

taking continues past adolescence and into adulthood, even though the proportion of drug desisters also increases over the period (from 39 per cent to 47 per cent). Thus, these overall decreases in use hide a proportion of the sample who initiate for the first time. This suggests a remarkable willingness to experiment amongst those who were adolescents of the 1990s – even if for the first time in their mid-twenties. Interestingly, despite these fluctuations from decreasing numbers of abstainers to increasing numbers of desisters, the core group of current drug users has remained fairly stable in number (although different in composition) with around a third of the sample reporting current use.

Validation of current user and opportunistic user categories

Previously in this chapter, we discussed how the categories of current user and in-transition were distinct from each other in terms of frequency and recency of use in expected ways. Similarly, we find an expected distinction between the current user and opportunistic user groups at the age of 22. Current users were far more likely to have taken at least one drug in the past month (84.4 per cent) compared to opportunistic users (21.7 per cent). Moreover, current users were more likely to have used drugs in the past week (55.0 per cent) compared to opportunistic users (7.2 per cent). None of the opportunistic users had taken a drug on the day they completed the questionnaire whereas 16 (12.4 per cent) current users reported doing so. Substantially more current users (49.2 per cent) also reported that they usually take drugs once a week or more compared to opportunistic users (1.4 per cent). Current users also have a greater mean rate of monthly drug use. They reported using drugs on average 15 times per month compared to three times per month for opportunistic users. These drug status categories are therefore clearly distinct from each other in respect of frequency and recency of use. Opportunistic users are also different to ex-users because of their future drug use intentions. All indicated they would take at least one drug again in the future.

Drug status groups

In this section we describe three of the drug status categories using the data collected from interviewees during Year 9 of the study, when the cohort was 22 years old. The qualitative data collected from current drug users is discussed in the following chapter and therefore not discussed here.

Table 5.7 Mean score on the drug attitudes scale (DAS) at age 17, 18 and 22

Drug status	Age 17 (n = 536) mean score	Age 18 (n = 529) mean score	Age 22 (n = 465) mean score
Current user	43.99	43.39	43.03
Ex-user	31.39	31.94	27.33
Opportunisitc user	36.00	34.14	34.54
Abstainer	27.00	26.76	25.40
All	34.34	34.56	33.73

Note: High scores on the DAS equate to more pro-drug attitudes and lower scores to less pro-drug attitudes

Abstainers

The abstainer category consists of a quarter of the sample at the age of 22 and reduces to just under a fifth by the age of 27. The drugs attitude scale analysis (see Table 5.7) demonstrated abstainers held the most anti-drug attitudes with their attitudes becoming increasingly more steadfast over time. Interestingly, the quantitative data collected at the age of 22 indicated that almost three-quarters (72.9 per cent) had at least one close friend who had tried drugs, suggesting that most associate with drug users (see Parker *et al.*, 2002). Their interview data revealed almost two-thirds (61.5 per cent) of abstainers held tolerant attitudes towards drug users. They were willing to accommodate 'sensible' recreational drug use, usually involving the consumption of cannabis:

> . . . if they're just sort of smoking cannabis I don't have any problems, I don't have any problems with somebody doing that. I've been in, sort of a room and people have been, and that doesn't bother me as long as it's not, as I say, right in my face. I mean any harder drugs I do object and I would leave the company.
>
> (33661, female abstainer, age 22)

Few abstainers viewed all drugs as bad. Repeatedly, many commented 'it's up to them' and discussed drug use as an individual choice: '. . . at the end of the day it should be just like down to the individual and if they want to let them' (63554, male abstainer, age 22).

Many drug abstainers had never had the desire or curiosity to try drugs. As Williams (2007) notes in her analysis of the qualitative data collected from the sample at age 28, abstainers perceived serious risks associated with drug use and their family members or partners also held anti-drugs attitudes.

Despite a level of tolerance of 'sensible' recreational drug use, a few did recall occasionally feeling upset if drugs such as cannabis were used in their presence:

> [Since you were eighteen, have you ever been in a situation where you felt awkward when people were smoking cannabis around you or taking other drugs around you?] Only once or twice at university when we lived in halls of residence and it was just like strictly banned and people would be taking it, but that was about it. [Cos you thought you might get in trouble?] Yeah, cos it was like in, sort of, as far as they [university staff] were concerned it was an illegal offence. You'd be thrown out of university if you were around it.
>
> (43332, female abstainer, age 22)

Some also recalled occasions where they felt pressured to take drugs by friends, which made them more steadfast in their anti-drug attitudes. In these instances, they maintained their drug-free status by no longer associating with friends who took drugs. In spite of some fairly intransigent positions amongst some of the abstainers at the age of 18, it is interesting to find that some nevertheless became drug users in adulthood.

Ex-drug users

The ex-user group remains the smallest category at the age of 22. Drug desisters, however, comprise almost half of the sample at 22 and 27. In the next chapter update we will discuss in detail what has led these respondents on the path to desistance, focusing particularly on their social relationships and transitions to adulthood.

Ex-users had a variety of drug experiences. Some had taken a range of drugs regularly in the past, others occasionally and others were one-off triers. The following interviewee, who was a drug abstainer until she was 19, describes her brief experience of illegal drugs:

> . . . it was at my boyfriend's house and his Mum and Dad were away and his brother-in-law had managed to get hold of some [cannabis] cos he smoked it quite a lot. And we just sat there and got absolutely wasted. It was great actually, it was a really good

night but I've just never gone near it since. I've just, it doesn't really appeal to me any more.

(83F03, female ex-user, age 22)

This interviewee recalled smoking cannabis as a pleasurable experience yet it is not something she wanted to repeat. Others recounted bad experiences with drugs, particularly LSD or ecstasy, which curtailed their drug-trying journeys.

Although many ex-users declared in their survey at age 22 they would never take drugs again in the future, when they were asked to describe their drug-using behaviour and future intentions during their interviews, some were less inclined to be so adamant about future abstinence. The following interviewee had taken amphetamines, cocaine and cannabis in the past:

I mean cannabis, I would, cos I don't think that's as bad as a lot of drugs; alcohol's probably a lot worse in some senses. So, yeah, cannabis but not, I don't think I'd be interested, well I know I wouldn't be interested in trying any other drugs. I mean I tried the ones I wanted to when I was younger, that's it now, I've done that.

(33678, male ex-user, age 22)

Some were willing to consider taking drugs again in the future, especially cannabis. The data collected at the age of 27 revealed that individual respondents' earlier predictions of their future drug journeys were fairly accurate. Although some of the most adamant ex-users returned to drug taking again, those who thought they might take drugs again were generally proved to be correct in their prediction. Some returned to previous levels of regular drug use, others 'dabbled' again for a short time. Some took a variety of drugs whilst others limited their use to cannabis. One of the strengths of a longitudinal study such as this, in following respondents through their twenties, is its ability to identify how drug status can over time be fluid, flexible and subject to change, not just in adolescence, but well in to adulthood (Parker *et al.*, 1998a; Williams, 2007).

Despite movement from ex-user to current user status, there are still some steadfast ex-users who achieve a sense of pride in choosing not to take drugs:

[And how important would you say not taking drugs is to you?] It is quite important, I must say, it's quite a, quite proud of myself for not doing it actually cos in today's society there's so much about.

(43×28, female ex-user, age 22)

However, maintaining a drug-free status could at times be challenging, especially when interviewees continue to associate with friends who take drugs. The following ex-stimulant user explains how she declines ecstasy when her friends offer it to her:

> Just said 'No, thanks'. They said 'Come on' and I just said 'No'. They said 'Oh go on it'll be good' and I just said 'No'. That was 'Right, fine'.
>
> (73A02, female ex-user, age 22)

Throughout the study, after abstainers, ex-users have been the group most likely to express anti-drug attitudes. Some ex-users are not as committed to abstinence as they initially contend, however, when the subject is explored further in interviews.

Opportunistic drug users

When the sample was age 22, we identified a new drug status category – opportunistic users – which comprised almost a third of the sample. This group expressed the second most pro-drug attitudes of the sample after current users. As with other drug status groups, they became less pro-drug with age. Similar to the ex-user group, these respondents had a range of drug experiences. Some had always been opportunistic users whilst others became so by this stage. The following interviewee, a cannabis-only user, recalled occasions when she had smoked it more frequently in the past:

> [Can you describe to me your drug taking since you were 18, has it been regular, occasional or no consistent pattern?] It increased for about nine months when I went to university in [the North East], but since then it has been very occasional, you know, sometimes just non-existent and you know I don't even think about it. [Yeah and how long a period would that be non-existent?] About a year, because when I was in my third year I didn't have any for about a year and then again until just recently for about a year.
>
> (43343, female opportunistic user, age 22)

Others also described the frequency of their drug use as intermittent, as another cannabis-only user explains:

> . . . it's fits and starts really, some, maybe if we're looking at it real-istically, some months I could have more than others. I mean,

there's some months that I don't have any at all, so I mean, it's not really a drug that's a part of my life in any respect really. I mean it's, it is when I'm, when I'm out and with people that are doing it but as far as myself going out to buy it for my own use and to actually do it myself and purchase it for me own use then no, I don't, I don't do that. I'm more a, I suppose a blagger, take it off other people (laughter).

(13095, male opportunistic user, age 22)

The opportunism present in this interviewee's account is typical of this drug pathway. There is a 'take it or leave it' attitude amongst this group. Many will not buy drugs themselves but if they are offered they may decide to take them. Others had not taken drugs for a few years but are reluctant to categorise themselves as ex-users as they believed they may take them again in the future: 'I can't say I will not again cos I know I'll smoke marijuana and stuff like that again but as for anything else, no.' (23174, female opportunistic user, age 22).

We can observe how some of these drug users are refining their drug choices and limiting themselves to only considering cannabis in the future. However, similar to the ex-user group, some did start to take a range of drugs more frequently.

The making of drug pathways

We established from the quantitative data collected during the first five years of the study that abstainers were less likely to be in offer situations than other drug status groups, and current users have the longest drug careers. We also discussed how current users were more likely to have started smoking tobacco in adolescence and to be current smokers compared to other drug status groups. In terms of alcohol, current users were also more likely to have started their drinking careers earlier than other drug status categories. The majority were weekly drinkers by the age of 16. In this section we continue this analysis, focusing on smoking and drinking behaviour at the age of 22 and 27 before moving on to consider other risk indicators.

Smoking and drinking by pathways status

As we previously found, current drug users are significantly more likely to have smoked tobacco compared to all other drug status groups (see Table 5.8). When smokers were asked if they describe themselves as regular smokers, the differences between drug status groups are small.

Table 5.8 Smoking and drinking status at age 22 by drug status

	Drugs status at age 22				
	Current drug user %	Opportunistic drug user %	Ex-drug user %	Abstainer %	Total %
(n size)	(n = 129)	(n = 144)	(n = 73)	(n = 113)	(n = 459)
Ever smoked	65.1	34.0	31.5	5.3	35.3
(n size)	(n = 83)	(n = 53)	(n = 24)	(n = 6)	(n = 166)
Regular smoker	77.1	71.7	66.7	66.7	73.5
Mean no. smoked in past week	63.0	53.8	60.0	62.3	59.7
(n size)	(n = 65)	(n = 38)	(n = 17)	(n = 4)	(n = 124)
Mean no. years a regular smoker	6.9	5.6	6.2	5.0	6.4
(n size)	(n = 130)	(n = 146)	(n = 73)	(n = 113)	(n = 462)
Ever drank alcohol	100.0	100.0	98.6	92.9	98.1
(n size)	(n = 129)	(n = 142)	(n = 72)	(n = 111)	(n = 454)
Drink alcohol weekly	91.5	88.0	79.2	67.6	82.6

Current users, abstainers and ex-users smoked a greater mean number of cigarettes in the past week than opportunistic users. Turning to the mean number of years respondents reported smoking regularly, all who are drug experienced have smoked for a longer period of time than abstainers. The differences in lifetime alcohol consumption are relatively small, yet it is noticeable that *all* current and opportunistic drug users have tried alcohol and current users are also significantly more likely to drink alcohol on a weekly basis compared to other drug status groups, particularly abstainers.

There are some interesting changes in the drug status of current smokers by the age of 27. Although the differences were not statistically significant, it is perhaps surprising to note that abstainers (40.0 per cent) were more likely to be current smokers than current drug takers (33.0 per cent) or drug desisters (25.8 per cent). Turning to alcohol, the patterns of lifetime consumption remain the same. All current drug users have drunk alcohol compared to 96.8 per cent of drug desisters and 93.3 per cent of abstainers. There is a statistically significant relationship between drug status and weekly alcohol consumption. Current drug users (79.3 per cent) are more likely to be weekly drinkers compared to drug desisters (75.8 per cent) and abstainers (56.7 per cent).

We have found on the whole that current users are more likely to be smokers and drinkers. It is not surprising then that they rate their general health less positively than other drug status groups. Overall, almost eight out of ten (79.5 per cent) of the sample felt their general health was good or better. When we examine this by drug status, current users are significantly more likely to rate their health less positively than those from other groups. Just over two-thirds (68.5 per cent) of current users assessed their general health as excellent or good compared to 85.8 per cent of abstainers, 82.7 per cent of opportunistic users and 82.2 per cent of ex-users.

Risk-taking indicators

We found during adolescence that current users were more likely to report involvement in 'deviant' behaviour, such as sex before the age of 16 and involvement with the police and criminal justice system. At both the age of 22 and 27, we again find similar patterns of involvement with the criminal justice system. Less than a tenth (7.4 per cent) of the sample had been cautioned or convicted for a criminal offence by the age of 22. Current users, however, (16.4 per cent, n = 20) were significantly more likely to have been cautioned or convicted compared to other drug status groups. The key offences relate to their lifestyles and include: drugs possession, being drunk and disorderly, assault or wounding, drink driving and drugs supply/intent to supply. In contrast, only one abstainer reported being cautioned, for being drunk and disorderly. Data collected at the age of 27 indicates that current users are more likely to have been cautioned (15.6 per cent) for a criminal offence compared to abstainers (0.0 per cent) and drug desisters (3.4 per cent). However, drug desisters (5.0 per cent) are more likely to have been convicted of a criminal offence compared to abstainers (0.0 per cent) and current users (3.8 per cent). Similar offences were reported in the late twenties.

Drugs pathways into young adulthood

In the first edition of *Illegal Leisure* we identified the longitudinal changes and continuity in drug status up to the age of 18. Using an even longer exposure we can now observe changes in drug status from the age of 17 to the age of 22 (see Table 5.9).

As we noted previously, this time period encompasses some key transitions to adulthood when many of the sample left home to go into

Table 5.9 Drugs status at age 17 and 22

		Drugs status at age 17				
		Current drug user	*In-transition*	*Ex-drug user*	*Abstainer*	*Total*
Drugs status at age 22	*n size*	*87*	*107*	*38*	*139*	*371*
		%	*%*	*%*	*%*	*%*
Current drug user	102	65.5	29.0	21.1	4.3	27.5
Opportunistic drug user	117	11.5	46.7	47.4	20.9	14.3
Ex-drug user	53	23.0	15.9	21.1	12.9	31.5
Abstainer	99	–	8.4	10.5*	61.9	26.7

* Three respondents who disclosed trying a drug at age 17 indicated they had never tried a drug at age 22

higher education (and some returned to the parental home again), as well as for most starting full-time employment. Between the ages of 17 and 22 there has been considerable movement between drug status categories. We might expect the 'in-transition' group to be subject to change; however, there has been a surprising amount of movement from the abstainer category to other drug statuses during this time. We can also observe some continuity, for some at a slower pace, in terms of drug use for current and opportunistic users. Around eight out of ten of the current drug users at the age of 17 are still drug involved at the age of 22 (65.5 per cent current, 11.5 per cent opportunistic). Three-quarters of those previously 'in-transition' are also currently drug involved. This suggests we have a group of long-term recreational drug users, around three in ten of the cohort by the age of 22.

Examining the drug status groups, for all drug status groups there is some continuity in drug status between the ages of 18 and 22 (see Figures 5.7 to 5.10). Two-thirds of abstainers and current users retain this status four years later, as do two-fifths of ex-users and half of opportunistic users. These findings again point to the existence of some long-term recreational drug users. There have, however, been changes in drug status amongst the cohort during those four years. Almost a third of abstainers at the age of 18 have at least some drug experience by the age of 22, although few are current users. Amongst ex-users at 18, two-fifths remain ex-users at 22, whilst a further two-fifths have reported some drug taking at 22. One fifth of opportunistic users at 18 become current users, whilst 16 per cent no longer intend to take drugs at the age of 22. Finally, a quarter of the current users became opportunistic users, and a small proportion became ex-users.

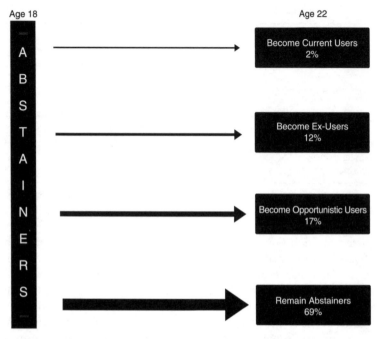

Figure 5.7 Pathways for abstainers between the ages of 18 and 22

This longitudinal analysis also allows us to examine anomalous reporters, or 'recanters' – those who report drug use at one point in time that they do not disclose in subsequent survey administrations. We find evidence of recanting of past drug use amongst the ex-user group at 18, almost one fifth (17 per cent) of whom declare at 22 they have never taken drugs. Similarly, we have some recanting of past drug use within the opportunistic user group, with almost one in ten (9 per cent) reporting they have never taken drugs. As we suggest in Chapter 2, there may be a number of reasons for recanting, including inadvertent errors made when filling in the questionnaire, and the kind of biographical reconstruction of past experiences that we found accounted for much adolescent recanting. However, we think it likely that at least some level of intentional non-disclosure may also play a role amongst these adult recanters. As we noted in Chapter 2, the groups with the highest levels of recanting (ex-users and opportunistic users) were constructed in such a way that *not* identifying as a drug user was a defining criterion. Both groups therefore include those engaging in at least some drug use at 18, but unwilling to self-designate as drug *users*. We find virtually no recanting amongst the current users who do self-identify as drug users.

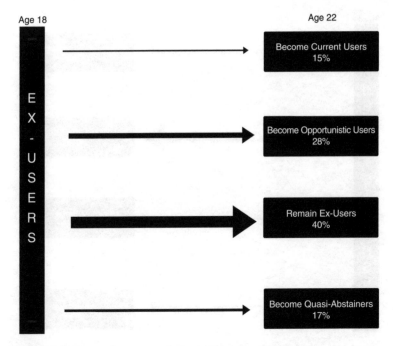

Figure 5.8 Pathways for ex-users between the ages of 18 and 22

It is amongst individuals who may be less comfortable – more ambiva-lent – about their drug taking, perhaps because their social worlds involve conflicting expectations, that recanting occurs amongst more than a few respondents.

Summary

During the first five years of the study we identified four robust drug pathways and noted how the sample switched between them as they progressed through their adolescence. The proportion of abstainers reduced over time whilst the number of current drug users grew. We also found current drug users were more likely to be risk takers (Plant and Plant, 1992) in terms of smoking tobacco, drinking alcohol, early sexual encounters and involvement with the criminal justice system compared to other drug status groups.

Our analysis of the data collected since the age of 18 has revealed a considerable amount of movement in drug use status from adolescence to adulthood, and throughout early adulthood. This finding in itself

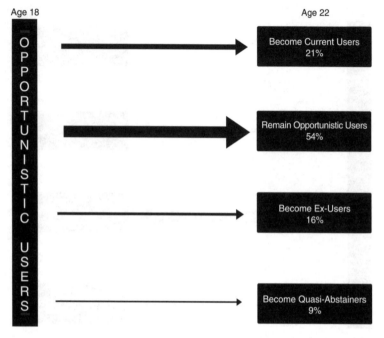

Figure 5.9 Pathways for opportunistic users between the ages of 18 and 22

demonstrates the complexity of drug use careers for this generation. As would be expected, we now have fewer abstainers. By the age of 27 only a fifth of the cohort are abstainers: those who have never tried any illegal drugs and plan never to use drugs. The current user pathway has remained relatively stable in adulthood and at just under three in ten at ages 18 and 22, and about a third at age 27. There has also been an increase in the proportion of ex-users (or drug desisters) and opportunistic users. This is consistent with the signs of moderation in adulthood that we identified and discussed in Chapter Four. However, as we have noted, some of the cohort who were categorised as ex-users or opportunistic users at the age of 22 went on to become regular drug users in their later twenties. This suggests there is still the potential for movement between drug status groups in the future.

Regardless of fluidity between drug pathways, there is persistence within the current user group, some of whom have long-term recreational drugs careers by their late twenties. Almost eight out of ten of the current users at the age of 17 were still drug involved at the age of 22 as were three-quarters of those from the in-transition group. As we have

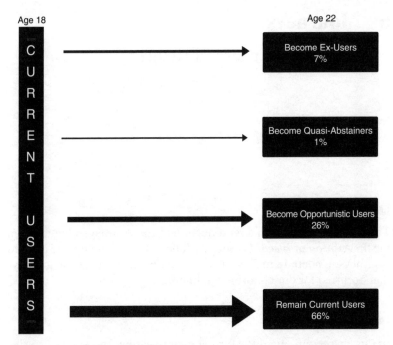

Figure 5.10 Pathways for current users between the ages of 18 and 22

shown, current users are generally risk takers who are more likely to smoke tobacco, drink alcohol regularly and to be involved in criminal activity. Furthermore, they also rate their health less positively than other drug status groups. These respondents continue to take cannabis, cocaine and ecstasy (identified in Williams and Parker, 2001) into their twenties, mirroring national trends in legal and illegal drug use in the late 1990s and early 2000s (Condon and Smith, 2003; Measham, 2004a), selecting and combining these drugs for specific reasons.

Overall, the sample has become more anti-drug in attitude perhaps in line with their shift from specific drug pathways and the increased advantages to them of developing more conventional adult identities. Despite these attitudes, abstainers who are the least pro-drug are still generally willing to accommodate 'sensible' recreational drug use and particularly the consumption of cannabis.

6 Journeys
Becoming users of drugs

Overview

This chapter begins with a reproduction of the 'Journeys' chapter from the first edition of *Illegal Leisure*. We follow this with an update entitled 'Journeys: Update 18 to 27 years old' that documents the drug journeys that occurred for our cohort in adulthood.

Introduction

In this chapter we offer little further quantification. Instead we describe and illustrate the 'journeys' which young people make as they try certain drugs and weigh up whether a particular drug can or will, on balance, be used more regularly. In making these experimental, sometimes existential, journeys drug triers and users become far more *drugwise* as they make and remake what are clearly identifiable *cost-benefit assessments* about regular drug use.

We have already seen that committed abstainers hold distinctive attitudes and expectations about illicit drug use which 'protect' them from this journey although they are often interested and concerned onlookers. Here we focus on those who have tried or use drugs. We rely heavily on their oral histories given at around 17 and 18 years of age. Their drugs journeys are of course tied up in the general pace and drama of adolescence as they face up to educational challenges, career decisions, mutating friendships, sex, romance and a changing relationship with parents. Being *drugwise* is one of the extra responsibilities which 1990s' adolescents face because they must grow up in a world in which drugs are an everyday reality.

We listen to young voices actually describing how they get their drugs, what actually happened the first time and how they assess risk before trying again. As we have already seen in respect of alcohol, risk assessment is part of the cost-benefit calculation and it involves weighing up for each drug the likelihood of bad or frightening experiences, the health risks, the impact of 'getting caught' by teachers, parents, employers or the police. These are weighed against the pleasure and enjoyment of particular drugs and their ability either to blank out stress and distress or, most often, help deliver cost-effective, deserved 'time out' through relaxation and enjoyment from the grind of ordinary, everyday life.

This drugs wisdom, the knowledge basis, is of course far from complete and rarely wholly accurate. Indeed, as we shall see, there are many versions of 'the truth' as each young person attempts to compute their own position from the plethora of often contradictory information they receive from friends, schools, parents and the media. One significant process in all this is the role of drugs stories – community 'folk tales' about what has happened to drug-trying young people locally. These tales are microcosms of the 'global' stories presented by the media. They are told and retold to support the views and perspectives of the raconteur. Thus stories about people being excluded from school, 'tripping' on the college bus or being hospitalised after an excessive night of clubbing on drink and drugs all become important contemporary folk tales.

Getting drugs

Drugs availability

In early adolescence those young people we have called 'risk takers' are far more likely to have been in situations where drugs were available. Thus we find our early drug takers have many more stories about being in these situations, even at school: 'There used to be open dealing in the corridors. You could shout out and ask if anyone had any trips and several people would say "yeah I've got some".' (Year 5, joint interview, two female polydrug users).

Quite often availability and initiation were combined, as in this situation when one interviewee looked back on being 14 and being given her first drug (LSD):

Acid, strawberry. [Who were you with?] At a school concert, I was with my mates about twenty of them . . . one of my mates in school he had to ask his cousin.

[What did you think?] It took about two hours before I noticed anything then I was dead aware of everything.

(Claire)

However by mid adolescence, around 15 and 16, these situations were encountered by the majority of our respondents rather than just early drugwise experimenters and users: 'We used to go to a Teens Scene, and at the end of GCSEs we all went down to the beach and there was plenty of them around there' (Sandra, polydrug user).

By late adolescence most respondents and interviewees had been in a whole range of situations where drugs were available and talked about:

> They were always available with the people I knew from school. And some bloke on the train offered me some for free. [What did you say?] I told him I didn't really want any. [Anywhere else?] Parties I suppose . . . just being passed around . . . pot, acid, really anything.
>
> (Martin, cannabis-only trier)

> Yes . . . in any number of places – pub, the park, at school, just generally around, street corners. They don't have to be friends, they're not really dealers either, they're sort of friends of a friend of a dealer and it all gets passed down, I don't really think there's any proper dealers (around here).
>
> (John, cannabis user).

> Pubs, clubs, on the street, parties. That's about it really. [Friends?] Friends, well not close friends but people you know through people you know. [What drugs?] Es, LSD, speed, cannabis.
>
> (Ian, non-user)

> Pubs, friends' houses. [Dealer friends?] Well yes for free and then dealers. If you see people you know and you say 'alright' they just say 'Oh I've got this, you can have some.' [Who's offering the drugs generally?] Mainly friends, but a few people I know they deal and that, so they've offered. [For money?] Sometimes, if it's a dealer it's for money but if it's a friend they'll say, just have a bit . . . just weed. I can have weed on tick. Whizz, and I've been offered trips and things like that for free, but nothing like that interests me.
>
> (Karen, cannabis user)

> Yes loads of times *The Scream* and one time we were in *Trios* in town, we got offered tablets twice, by the same fella, you know asking again . . . Oh and at *Pandora's* one time. That was speed.
>
> (Amy, trier, non-user)

Friends as dealers

In these everyday worlds we are penetrating, a far more blurred line between user and 'dealer' emerges than the 'war on drugs' discourse discussed in Chapter 1 could contemplate. Whilst our interviewees (n = 82) had been offered drugs by dealers and strangers, the majority of their experiences of being in drug-offer situations were related to friends, acquaintances and friends of friends.

> I've got two sets of friends and I take them (cannabis) with both. With this (town) having a beach it's either down the beach or in this friend's house that I was telling you about before. [Where do you get your stuff?] I know some guy at school who can get it, although he's not a dealer he knows someone who's not a dealer who can get it. [Reliable quality?] The quality's not bad but getting it's a pain in the arse quite frankly . . . I never think I'll be able to get it in time and if I do I think it'll be rubbish stuff, until I'm stoned, then I realise that it's not actually that bad. [How far in advance do you get it?] Usually it's oh I'll get draw for next week, ask around and people say oh I can get it you by Friday.
>
> (John)

> My friend's house, her boyfriend sells pot but if he's got any spare he'll pass it round, don't have to pay, or sometimes we'll pay for it.
>
> (Lisa, polydrug user)

Most drug users were as likely to have drugs 'for free' as purchased, thus again blurring the dealer–user line whereby some drugs have become seen, like cigarettes, as symbolic signs of friendship to be given freely. For his 18th birthday one male, regular user, who usually paid for his drugs was asked by one of his friends: 'it's your birthday, if you want we'll club together and get some drugs for you?' (Martin).

One interviewee, a cannabis user at 17, noted how younger children saw her, because she was a drug user, as a potential source of drugs.

> I've had little kids ask me. A few lads about twelve, asked me to go and get them something (cannabis) and I just said no. Because I think its wrong at that age.
>
> [Would other people get stuff for them?] A few of my mates drugs yes, and, ale as well. I know people who go and get them ale.
>
> (Karen)

Whilst refusing to get drugs 'for children' is one thing, a significant minority of drug users in our samples had obtained drugs for other friends, usually 'for free', sometimes with 'clubbed together' resources and sometimes to cover the costs of their own drugs bill. One experienced polydrug user, whose parents accepted her lifestyle, ran a fairly extensive supply system for friends and particularly 'friends of friends'. Whilst this began as:

> I'm normally the stupid one who sorts everything out for everyone. It soon became a well-organised process. [How often do you sort people?] Weekly. Depends what's going on, if there's any special occasions . . . for other people I've got whizz, Es, trips.

This young woman also worked out that having cannabis around, to sell, carried other risks: 'I used to do quite a bit of dealing, but it just meant that I'd smoke more, I used to smoke it (supplies) before I'd sell it, so it wasn't a good system' (Louise).

We did interview one young man whose dealing moved beyond the home and acquaintances into a local nightclub. His situation reminds us how, for a minority, drugs careers and delinquent careers can intertwine. He and a friend working as bar staff came to an arrangement with door staff whereby they sold amphetamines, LSD and ecstasy: 'some nights we were walking out with about £600 in our pockets. It wasn't bad but things started getting heavy when CID came in'.

It was not just police interest that dissuaded this young man. He quickly realised that just above the informal, usually hassle-free drug-getting arrangements of 'friends of friends' of a dealer there was a commercial business at work which used fairly aggressive market-protection strategies.

> We were cutting out Towling's main dealer, we were cutting out . . . Eastmoor's main dealers and they weren't very happy, and they started coming down quite heavy . . . I think the worst was . . . I was at college and all these guys surrounded the car I was in and said 'get out the car otherwise we're going to shoot you through the window'. The police turned up . . . everything got sorted.
>
> (Gary, polydrug user)

Similarly, two female friends from the sample found themselves followed by the police to a drug dealer's house and arrested, charged and cautioned.

> Once on the train two CID told me to get off the train. We recognised them. They'd followed me from Beachtown. We'd been

walking round town all day smoking, right off it. They took all my details and gave me a caution. I only had £10 or an eighth's worth of weed on me but I must have led CID right to the weed hut (the dealers). I haven't been back since. I don't think I'd be too welcome.

(Year 5, critical incident interview)

This same pair had become nightclubbers and ravers and had many tales to tell about door staff and dealers in clubs. Stories about trouble, 'taxing' and the more serious and dangerous end of drug dealing helped draw the line about where relative safety ended and potential trouble began. Thus whilst simply buying drugs from dealers in nightclubs was risky in terms of quality, it was relatively safe in terms of not meeting any heavy-duty people but things change radically if you get involved with door staff, club 'territory' or selling for profit. Similarly, getting your drugs via the friend of a friend of a dealer was relatively safe in terms of both quality and avoiding police surveillance. However, start to move up the chains and networks either to get better value supplies or to make money for yourself and the drugs–crime connection is made and you become of interest both to the Drugs Squad and more organised criminal dealers.

Finally, a tragic 'dealing' case needs reporting. One of our respondents and her friend were caught trafficking in cocaine and they are both serving lengthy sentences in a South American jail. Whilst we only have information supplied by letters and an interview with one mother, it appears that the two girls became 'mules' for a Nigerian man who persuaded them to smuggle cocaine. This was one case where a local story became a global story – where a community tale and a media sensation merged.

In summary, the steep climb in availability and offer rates described in Chapter 4, whilst they help us measure the significant penetration of illicit drugs into the social space of adolescence, failed to capture the routinisation of all this, the frequency of repeated availability and offer situations. Moreover, drugs are not 'pushed' at young people as the war-on-drugs discourse would have it. Most obtain their drugs from friends of friends and have genuine difficulty in perceiving these acquaintances as dealers committing a potentially serious criminal act. Whilst a handful of our cohort became more instrumental dealers and moved into making a financial profit, most low-level 'dealers' in our cohort at most covered the cost of their own drug use. This accommodation, some might say colonisation of drugs 'supplying' within youth culture, is an important feature of the normalisation debate to which we will return.

Trying drugs

Initiation

We have already noted that initiation, measured as 'incidence', but which drove up our prevalence of trying rates, takes place throughout adolescence. Cannabis dominates as the first drug ever tried throughout.

> That was pot . . . I think I was about 13 . . . with my sister and my mates. These lads who had it, we got in with them, they'd been smoking it for a while; but it was our first time. [How did you know what to do?] I didn't, they did it for us, it looked dead complicated to me. [Had you smoked cigarettes before?] Yes I've been smoking since I was about eleven. [Was the spliff easy to inhale?] No, it choked me at first. [Get any effect?] Oh, very easy. I'd only had a couple of pulls and I was sitting there giggling my head off. It was brilliant. Because like when you're at school, and all of your homework and all the teachers moaning and you, you know . . . so the first time, I can remember that night, I felt brilliant. [Anything bad about it?] No. Only when I came in and my mum and dad looking at my eyes. I was terrified . . . but they didn't know.
>
> (Lisa, drug user)

These early experiences are often reviewed and perhaps redefined with time, as in this next case by a young women who became a serious drug user by 17.

> Yes I was drunk at the time and I was in a nightclub. I was only 14. I used to have a Saturday job and we all went out. It was only pot but at the time I thought it was brilliant. And I was drunk and I most probably didn't understand and probably not even smoking it properly. That was the first time, that was pot that was it . . . it was different, it was just a bit more relaxed. I just personally think there's nothing wrong with it. OK, 14 is a bit young, but it's not really a hard drug or anything.
> [Did you know what to do?] No. Not really at the time, we were just looking at everybody else . . . because you don't know you just pick up what other people do.
>
> (Zoe)

We noted in Chapter 4 that in mid adolescence amphetamines and LSD were also common initiation drugs.

Speed, sixteen with five friends. [Where did you get it from?] My friend's boyfriend's mate. I just dabbed it they snorted it. [How did you know what to do?] Well basically they'd done it before and just said do you want to snort it and I said no, so they said well put it in a cigarette paper and I said oh no and then they said well just dab it then and take it that way. So they gave me the options . . . it tasted completely horrible. [Did you think it was worth it?] After the very first time no. [Anything positive?] When it started to come up on me then I felt it was easier for me to talk to people and to go along with people and I felt more relaxed and open. [Anything negative?] At the end I didn't feel very well. I wasn't hungry, I felt a bit depressed as well even though I'd only taken it the once. [Any other drugs at the same time?] Just alcohol. [And the feeling?] Not very easy at first, my mates were actually speeding when I was still bobbing along . . . they said 'oh it'll work, you'll find out when it works'. I think it was an hour and a half before I'd actually . . . for it to come up on me. [How long were you up for?] All night, all morning, it was well into the next day before we actually got any sleep. [How much had you had?] We bought it in fivers and we split it into £2.50s worth each. Maybe that was it, I'd never had it before, so maybe I'd taken too much for the first time.

(Vicky, regular drug user)

LSD in particular sometimes proved an unpleasant first-time experience. An experienced regular polydrug user at 18, one young woman recalls her initiation:

The first drug I took was LSD. It was horrible . . . once I came up – all the lads had taken them before – none of the girls had because we all took them together this night – they said you'll go home and you won't want to go in, you'll be that frightened, that paranoid, you won't want to go in. I thought 'Yeah yeah' but then I got outside and I was standing outside my house for two hours, I didn't want to go in. I was supposed to be in at 10 o'clock and I got in at midnight. So I got battered for coming in late. It was horrible. I came in and put on some videos and some music and then it was alright.

(Kate)

Yet although LSD warning stories were common they tended to become more instrumental in later adolescence given that, despite its unpredictability, most users had early positive experiences of trying it.

Me and my friend took LSD when we went to a travelling fair. There was me and my friend and three others, and I think the other people got a bit fed up of us, because we just spent the whole time laughing and messing around, which was a good experience when I was on LSD. Then we went back to the fair the following year, we didn't find it funny at all because we weren't on drugs. That kind of situation, if I was to go back there again I might take LSD again. [It made it better?] It made it better, yes. And, we went to Stratford with school, to see a play, and we were on LSD and we were just laughing all the way through that. That was weird . . . Shakespeare . . . we found Shakespeare extremely funny.

(Elaine)

In later adolescence first-time use may well involve ecstasy as the initiation drug. This, as we have already discussed, is related to new ventures and values linked to obtaining adult status. One young woman holidaying with her parents reported her first experience on ecstasy as follows:

I met them in a bar. Three lads from Stockport and some girls. And we were just drinking like you do and went into a club and they were all taking it. They offered me some and I said no at first and then I was a bit curious so I said yes. And actually I was amazed at the amount of energy I had . . . it was so different to how I imagined and a lot better than I thought it would be . . . you just felt really good about yourself, and confident.

(Joanne)

Asked if her parents guessed she'd been on ecstasy, she replied: 'no, no they think I'm far too sensible!'

Those who initiated on ecstasy tended to be over 16 and many accepted that their interest in dance music and the excitement of the dance club scene led to contemplation which, once in the setting, produced the trigger: 'I suppose the atmosphere of clubs makes me want to try . . . it's not really because my friends are doing it, it's because I want to experiment myself' (Lee, occasional drug user).

Reasons for trying drugs

It is very difficult to write authoritatively about why anyone first tries an illicit drug. A myriad of factors may be at work. Clearly age, gender, race, the setting, the actual type of drug and probably the people one is with, will interact in a complex way with the disposition of the person, both generally and at the particular time for any individual decision. In the last chapter we showed how abstainers hold particular attitudes and beliefs and possibly are distinctive personality types. They will respond quite differently to the same setting compared with a more adventurous 'curious' person. To further complicate matters, reasons for trying or experimenting with a drug are likely to be different from those motivating repeated use. We analysed the motivational accounts given by our interviewees as to why they had or hadn't ever tried a drug given almost all had had such 'trying' opportunities or knew how to create them. *Availability, curiosity* and the presence of *peers* and *friendship networks* who could provide the encouragement, reassurance and know-how were seen as most important. These factors were then mediated by each interviewee's view of themselves and their own *moral* perspective and views of *risk* for health, fitness or vocation, and in early to mid adolescence in particular, the views or potential responses of their *parents*.

The impact of all these factors will be different for each person and indeed as we saw in the Pathways analysis the weight given to each factor by a young person may well change through time.

Drug-trying interviewees nominated curiosity and friendship patterns and influences as the most important factors involved in initial experimentation and the trying of a range of drugs. These factors usually combine, as explained by a cannabis user who has also tried LSD and amphetamines but was, at 18, becoming more cautious:

> Mainly curiosity. Me and my close friend . . . you hear that people have good times on drugs, so you feel like doing it yourselves. [Any other things?] Not really, just the fact that they were around. If there'd been other drugs around at the time (when 15 years) say maybe ecstasy, then I might have done but it wasn't really in our age groups.
>
> (Elaine)

> I suppose that all my friends were. Just wanted to try it. It's all very well saying how bad things are, but until you've tried it you don't really know these things do you.
>
> (Sandra, polydrug user)

The dominant view of why young people take drugs, portrayed in the media and encapsulated in government policy, relegates curiosity and choice in favour of peer pressure. Yet it is extremely difficult to measure peer pressure. Even if one observed a drug initiation in a peer-group setting, it would be problematic, merely using personal accounts, to make a safe assessment. Furthermore young people are encouraged in their wider education to be self-assertive and not be unduly influenced by others and many young people would not wish to be perceived or perceive themselves as being a 'victim' of such pressure. Moreover, the rejection of peer pressure as a significant factor was almost unanimous amongst our interviewees (only five of the 63 interviewees who were asked or answered the specific question about peer pressure felt they had been affected by it).

For the majority, certainly at 18 and looking back, the statements below were typical:

> I've not really been pressured into taking them or anything. I'd say that every time that I've done something it's been my own decision.
>
> (Martin, polydrug user).

> What level of mood I'm in . . . the place I'm in, the environment and the people I'm with. [What about when you first started taking drugs?] I think the first reason I started was because everybody else was and I thought well I'll just try it. [Any peer pressure?] No, nobody would pressure me to do it, I just saw everybody else having a good time and good laugh.
>
> (Vicky, polydrug user)

Interestingly, however, when we undertook a content analysis of the interviews, we found that several more interviewees described events and recounted episodes where at least one interpretation could be that they had been strongly influenced by their peers.

> When we got into the gang, everyone was doing it in the club, and I was going to say no because of my brother (serious drug problems) but my mate said 'come on we're having them, you have to have them too because you might feel like the odd one out, like the weirdo if you're not doing it'. I'd say one of the reasons why was because everyone else was doing it.
>
> (Helen)

This young woman did appear to come from a fairly dysfunctional family and was receiving counselling. The interviewer suggested she was fairly vulnerable in a number of ways. Another young woman felt that she had been under pressure at 14.

> When I was in school, I had my first trip, it was with my best friend and her sisters, and I didn't really want to and they were

saying 'go on, go on', so I had half . . . and I've never touched trips since.

However, at 16 she began a drug-using career which has continued into dance-club-related ecstasy use.

> Curiosity, friends I suppose and I was 16 when I was going out with my boyfriend and he used to always go to the Big Bar and I never used to drink and they always seemed to be on a different planet, and I always used to wonder, and I used to feel left out I suppose and I wanted to know what kind of wavelength they were on.
>
> [So drugs?] Just to say I'd tried them once really, And just to know for myself if I liked them or I didn't want them.
>
> (Diane)

Questionnaire surveys of young people's drug use appear to be able to quantify their decision-making processes. Indeed it is not difficult to set a closed question asking a sample 'do you think young people try drugs because their friends encourage them?' and conclude that peer pressure is significant. Ask a sample of 18-year-olds who've made up their minds about drugs whether they feel they've been pushed or pressured into their conclusions and they will no doubt deny this, thereby apparently rejecting peer pressure. This gets us nowhere. We have a set of phrases in official drugs discourse – peer pressure, peer preference, peer influence – to which we might add peer example and peer support. In the end, adolescence is a life phase where peers are central to most decisions and activities and we can have the same unhelpful debate about whether school performance, participation in sport, joining community groups or whatever is related to peer behaviour. And even if we could isolate and quantify the effects of peers, we can do little about this. The dominant way of caring for and controlling children and teenagers is to herd them together in schools for most of their waking hours for most weeks of each year and for at least 11 years. Moreover, the key thing young people want to do in their free time is to be with their friends.

A myriad of variables can be identified in drug-initiation and drug-trying events. We have shown that availability of drugs, disposable income, curiosity, friends who do drugs, friends who don't do drugs, drugwiser acquaintances who can guide and support novices, being drunk, have a certain outlook on risk taking and rule breaking, parental influences, religious and moral frameworks, the impact of 'drugs stories' may all be found to impact on decisions. However, beyond identifying the complexity and multifaceted nature of drug-trying events, it is probably impossible to weight different factors in any generalisable way. It is most certainly unsafe to collapse this complexity into monocausal 'soundbites' such as peer pressure.

The cost-benefit assessment

Each drug is different

Before describing the cost-benefit assessment which broadly guides each young person's journey into becoming a user of one or more 'recreational' drugs, we need to recall the general consensus which emerged from the surveys about the positive and negative effects of each of the main recreational drugs. In this section we concentrate on cannabis, amphetamines, LSD and ecstasy, these being the most widely used drugs (solvents and magic mushrooms as 'trying only' drugs are not discussed here and poppers are only referred to in the context of dance drug use).

Heroin and crack cocaine are important to our analysis only because of their symbolic value. Despite their apparent sophistication about their own drugs of choice, 1990s' adolescents maintain a fairly stereo-typical imaging of hard drug users as dangerous, diseased, dishevelled injecting 'junkies' and 'saddos' who commit vast amounts of crime to fund their habit. For most of this age cohort the idea of taking hard drugs and actually injecting a drug is anathema: a rubicon they will not cross. If heroin and crack are at one end of the spectrum, cannabis is at the other. Cannabis is regarded, even by many abstainers, as a relatively safe drug and certainly no more dangerous than alcohol and tobacco. Its predictability, steady quality and price and 'sociability' are cele-brated along with its ability to induce relaxation, reduce stress and mediate sleep patterns.

The 'middle three' have a more ambivalent status. Few who are drugwise doubt the potential positive enjoyment of LSD, amphet-amines and ecstasy but there are risks with each and the unpredict-ability of any particular dose causes many potential triers or users to reflect carefully as they make their cost-benefit assessment.

The key point is that those moving into regular drug use judge each drug or combination on its merits. They begin with the premise that each drug is different. They see themselves as far more sophisticated about this than their elders, be they parents or politicians, who, they conclude, tend to see drugs as generically bad and dangerous.

The assessment formula

As we have shown in Chapter 5, trying drugs, usually for free via a friend, is not the same as using drugs regularly. Regular use is an act of consumption which involves, directly or indirectly, the *purchase* of the chosen drugs, which in turn involves a decision about expending limited disposable income. The fact that these transactions are *illegal* and that there is a risk attached to being caught with drugs at school, college, work or through routine policing is also relevant. Each drug also carries a potential health risk. The exact nature of this risk is diffuse and hard to quantify but divides into several components. There is an *immediate* risk of a bad experience, incident or accident. The longer-term *health impact* of a particular drug or combination may be relevant but again hard to quantify. Possible *dependency* and addiction is another potential concern. Then there are the side or *after effects* of drug-using episodes. For some, these unwanted effects are significant 'risks' but for many experienced users they are seen as part and parcel of knowing and understanding a drug. So what would be regarded as a dreadful risk for an abstainer would be seen as the accepted consequences of 'getting out of it' by an amphetamine user.

Finally, we need to place *leisure and pleasure* in the formula. Drugs are used because they give enjoyment. Young drug users who spend their disposable income on alcohol, cannabis or ecstasy etc. are, in their own minds, making rational decisions about hedonistic consumption. Essentially, they are using a *cost-benefit equation*. Whilst it would be unwise to suggest that every young drug user in the study utilised this formula comprehensively and explicitly, almost all our interviewees alluded to most components of the formula in giving their motivational accounts and describing their decision-making journeys into recreational drug use.

Before illustrating each component of the cost-benefit equation, we should remember to place all this in context since, by definition, we are only capturing a brief period, mainly around 16–18, in this 'journeys' analysis. Given that we know that the 'onset' of drug use spans adolescence and continues into young adulthood then the nature and sophistication of decision making will be mediated by age, intellect and maturity whereby the quality of decisions at 14 is likely to be very different from those taken at 19. Undertaking high-risk behaviour with little insight into the possible consequences is sometimes referred to as adolescent's perceiving themselves as *invulnerable* (Plant and Plant, 1992). One young woman although quite unaware of the terminology had no doubt about its impact.

You kind of go through a phase when you're 14–15 when you do a lot of things like that (take trips at school) and then when you get older you realise that, when you're at that age you think that nothing can happen to you, whereas when you get older you realise that it is actually dangerous. I don't think pot is dangerous I'll do that again.

(Elaine)

Other interviewees recognised they had failed to understand the significance of early drug trying but put a quite different spin on their conclusions.

The money. Your sleeping patterns. You get in with some bad people. [Money?] I used to go out four nights a week, and I had a part-time job and all my wages and more, I ended up owing nearly £400. [Did you pay it off?] Yes. I stayed in for four months. [And sleeping patterns?] I used to have speed all the time, so I never used to sleep and when I started getting to sleep it was 6 o'clock in the morning . . . and I was getting up for school. [Bad people?] One of my mates is only 17 and he's been involved in an armed robbery . . . but I've never been in trouble with the police. [Do you see your drug use as normal, OK or unusual, a problem?] It was a problem I suppose . . . I've decided not to make it a problem now. I used to sit there and think . . . I wished I wasn't curious. If I hadn't had the first one . . . or if I hadn't done them till I was 18 it would have been different . . . like I used to do a lot of sport at school, now I don't do anything . . . I passed everything then I failed my medical to get into the army because I'd been doing the stuff I was doing at school.

(Claire)

For this respondent the costs to her finances, her health, her energy and her career prospects had all proved far greater than she, as a 14-year-old, had been able to calculate. With these provisos we can now describe the various facets of the cost-benefit assessment.

Relaxation, enjoyment and a 'buzz'

In Chapter 4 we summarised the positive and negative effects our survey respondents attached to each widely used drug. We noted that those who had used a particular drug listed far more positives than negatives. Cannabis users and polydrug users who include cannabis in their repertoire speak confidently about its enjoyment value: 'I just like the effect, it relaxes me. And you can buzz off it sometimes if you're stoned, just buzz off the littlest things' (Lucy, cannabis user).

> It's sort of, when you go out and try and enjoy yourself and it's a sort of way of bringing on the enjoyment I suppose. It helps you relax. It's just something to do. It's sort of basically getting a bit of a buzz really.
>
> (Neil, cannabis user)

> [Cannabis?] It just relaxes me. I'm able to get into things a bit better . . . It gets a lot of pressures out of you, cannabis just makes me feel a bit easier.
>
> (Jason, polydrug user)

Poly drug users note the distinctive role of cannabis in their chosen drugs repertoire. One young female, single parent, noted:

> When it's pot, it's just to unwind, when I'm with the baby all day and night in the week, if you ever get a free night it's to unwind really, relax, have a change. [What about speed?] That's whenever I go out, you know with the baby I'm tired all the time. When I start getting ready to go out of a Saturday night, so it makes us a bit energetic.
>
> (Lisa, polydrug user)

Another polydrug user compared ecstasy with her more regular diet of alcohol and cannabis:

> Favourite . . . E, even though I don't take it anymore. [Why E?] Because you just feel so different, it's just, I can't explain, it's just such a wonderful feeling. You see everything in a different light, everyone seems so nice, and everyone's dead friendly. When everybody else is having it as well, you can do what you want and no-one thinks you're a dick. [What effects do you particularly like about it?] The good feeling. The feeling that you can go on all night. [Where do you prefer to have it?] At a club, an all-night club.

Having realised that ecstasy brought on her asthma attacks, this young woman had reluctantly removed it from her repertoire. Asked about her favourite combinations she noted:

Usually just have alcohol and weed and cigs as well. If I'm on a whizz as well I smoke weed but not usually if I'm on E. [Your favourite combination?] Yes, alcohol and weed. [Order?] Usually have weed first then go out for a drink. [The aims?] To try and get happy and relaxed. [Anything else?] No that's about it.

(Kate, polydrug user)

Risks and dangers

Family responses

Parental condemnation of their children's drug use appeared to be total at the beginning of the 1990s. Indeed the development of widespread recreational drug use in adolescence for the first time produced genuine concern amongst most adults. In early adolescence our samples were almost unanimously of the view that if their parents found out they were taking drugs then 'mega' trouble would follow. This situation still held for the majority of interviewees even at 18. 'I know my dad would go absolutely mental cos he works with loads of people that have gone over the boundary and took too many drugs. He works as a counsellor. My mum would go mad as well' (Sandra, drug user).

[Do your parents know you take drugs?] No, oh God no. Terrible. They'd go absolutely mad, they really would. I don't think they'd throw me out or anything, but I think it would put something between us.

(Suzanne)

However, near the end of the study there were signs that this clash of minds was not inevitable. A third of drug-taking interviewees confirmed that one or both parents knew something about their drug use. Cannabis is perceived by both parties as 'the least worst' drug both for parents to hear about and children to admit to: 'Problems? No not really, my mum asked me not so long ago if I had ever taken cannabis, I said yes, that was really hard on her but I told her I don't take it regularly' (Neil, drug trier, cannabis user).

One interviewee arrested via a routine police stop was charged with possession of cannabis for which, after admitting the offence, he was given a police caution. His parents, although very shocked, 'were sound about it. It's just that if I get caught again the last one will be brought up. It worries me a bit but not to a great extent . . . They don't know about anything else' (Martin).

What this young man's parents didn't know is that their son's favourite drugs combination, of ecstasy and amphetamine, makes up a regular weekly clubbing diet. Polydrug users were typically economical with the truth, feeling the cannabis card was the only one to play at home.

> I'd be a dead man . . . my mum would kill me and my dad, because he's taken it he'd chat with me and talk about it. He's already said he wouldn't mind me smoking gange. He said 'if you're going to do it, just tell me. I'll probably join you on a session', but he said 'if you ever got into any heavy stuff, I'd kill you'.
>
> (Gary, polydrug user)

Few respondents felt their parents could cope with any more than cannabis admissions.

> Yes mum knows about cannabis. [Was she shocked about it?] She was when she found out but I gave her a leaflet . . . I don't think they'd appreciate me doing ecstasy but with cannabis they accept it as a social thing.
>
> (Andy, polydrug user)

Parental 'ignorance' is seen as the main reason for potential disagreement and trouble. So even upon entering young adulthood, when the authority element in the parent–child relationship declines, interviewees felt it was not usually worth standing their grown-up ground and pointing out that their drug use is recreational and nothing to worry about. Parents simply think the worst.

> . . . my dad. He's just completely against it. [Because its illegal?] Yes. Well and because he doesn't like drugs. [Are the arguments about drugs regular?] Yes. But I just say it's my life. He knows I smoke the weed, I've told him so there's nothing he can do about it . . . [Can he differentiate between different types of drugs?] No. He puts them all together. He thinks, like, when I said I smoke the weed dad would say I was a druggie. He thinks you have to inject it into your arm or something, he doesn't know the facts . . . you can't get through to him.
>
> (Lucy, cannabis user)

Concern for parental feelings via 'white lies' was not unusual but we should remember the mum whose daughter is in a South American prison and the parents of those teenagers whose delinquent and drug careers overlap and bring chaos to family life. Adolescent behaviour can also be beyond the pale and thus extremely painful and difficult for parents:

> At first they didn't have a clue. They knew I smoked weed and tolerated it, as long as it was in my bedroom. They would just leave me be. They couldn't stop me. Then I came back one New Year's Eve and they clicked. My parents do my head in now because one, they blame everything on drugs if we argue about anything, and two, they know I don't do weed but they don't believe I've stopped taking other stuff. I used to rob lots of money, £200 or more. That's why there's locks on all the upstairs doors. If you went upstairs you'd see all the locks. I argued with them, broke windows, got chucked out. I left school, blew a thousand pounds in three weeks, lived with my mate. In the end they just tolerated it, in the end. They had no choice. I smoked spliffs all day. I got kicked out, left school. I had a thousand pounds in a bank savings account and I blew it. I moved in with my mate 'cos her parents went away. Dad phoned me every day to ask me to come home. I came home when her parents came back.
>
> (joint interview Year 5, female polydrugs users)

Friends and partners

The risk of causing trouble and upset in the family home extends, naturally, to equally significant others, namely friends and partners. Traditionally, self-selecting friends with similar outlooks, interests and attitudes has mediated tensions caused by difference which becomes dissonance. Outgoing, smoking, drinking socialisers befriend fellow-revellers and eschew abstainers. Equally, such risk takers would not be chosen companions for more cautious, rule-keeping adolescents. Whilst this self-selection continues to operate, it is clearly no longer able to prevent disagreements surfacing. We saw how the impact of differential attitudes to drug use distinguished abstainers from drug users and those in transition in the pathways analysis. Yet once we explore relationships within drug user networks we find similar discord. This is because through the cost-benefit assessment distinctive personal limits are defined. One young woman who had a frightening experience with ecstasy has 'never touched it since' yet her friends continue to use dance drugs.

> My friend said 'you should have half and go to the cinema' ('to get

back your confidence with ecstasy') but I just don't want to get . . . but everybody . . . I'm abnormal to my friends, they used to have them in school . . . to them, I'm abnormal for not ever wanting to do it again.

(Diane)

Similarly, an amphetamine-using respondent felt caught up in club-drug culture expectations.

I was in the toilet with my best friend and she took drugs and she was a lot older headed than me and she brought another girl and there were four of us all together and she said her friend had bought two Es . . . a half each. 'No I don't take them' I said and Tara started going off her head . . . 'what do you think you're doing, she just bought you one, you should take it', so I said 'well I don't want to take it' so we ended up having a fight about it, a proper fight, and ended up getting thrown out of the club because I wouldn't take it. And I said never, not one would ever touch my lips. I'd take a whizz but not an E because I've heard all the . . . you have your first one and you're dead.

(Suzanne)

Such experiences can lead to reassessment about friendship patterns and support the importance of peer preferences.

I was involved as well, we took an E, or I think it was and they didn't know what it was or anything, it was awful, they were just off their heads . . . it really scares me. Yes and then they took another one and mixed two types. They didn't know if it was off or any-thing, they were really stupid, they were drunk as well at the time, so that made it worse and it was just really scary. I hadn't seen them like that before . . . I think I've grown away from them since that, after that incident. Me and my other friend have just stayed away.

(Natalie, reducing drug user)

As with drinking together so taking drugs together can set friends against each other.

I've had arguments with my friends occasionally. [What are the arguments about?] It's me as well as my friends, but I've got a friend in particular who tends to get quite aggressive sometimes when she's taking drugs and she'll tend to snarl and snap at you a lot, so it tends to cause arguments between us. And myself, I tend to be more aggressive with her back, so it does cause problems that way.

(Sandra, drug user)

Romantic relationships were regularly discussed in the context of drug use. Most often it would be along traditional gender lines whereby there were far more boyfriends under scrutiny for excessive drug use and a lecture the day after.

He didn't actually tell me he took cocaine, I heard it from his brother and the first time he had it he got it free and then the second time he got it free as well because it was a close friend of his who had it. I just thought if he was going to get it free all the time he'd keep taking it. To me cocaine is like a very very hard drug, whereas LSD doesn't seem that bad.

(Elaine, drug user)

My boyfriend, when he was smoking skunk, he gets extremely paranoid off it – I haven't had any of that particular type and he thought I was carrying on with one of his friends, so it got out of hand and there was a fight, and it was all totally innocent. It was just his imagination running away with him.

(Karen, polydrug user)

Occasionally all roles are reversed as the female user is required to save the male abstainer from hedonism:

My boyfriend was on about taking a trip. He's a bit snobby, so it was dead upsetting. He's always been dead law abiding and strict, and someone who keeps me on the straight and narrow. And he was on about taking them as well so it was a bit worrying.

(Sandra, polydrug user)

In summary, because drugs are illegal and because they produce 'attitude' from almost everybody, the potential drug user has to consider the import of their usage on significant others. Whilst parental wrath and indeed upset and pain is usually a major consideration during adolescence, this mutates with the move into young adulthood so that protecting parents from unnecessary worry apparently justifies either continued denial or being very economical with the truth. Friendships can also be disturbed or even fractured because disagreements emerge about the acceptability of both drugs taken and styles of use. Romantic relationships in particular seemed to produce disagreements and the need for compromise or change in respect of drugs. All this said, the fact that there is so much debate amongst young people about each other's drugs views is also indicative of the significance of penetration of 'recreational' drug use into mainstream youth culture.

Health risks and bad experiences

Weighing up the chances of frightening experiences and/or damaging one's physical or psychological health is the central plank, the spinal column, of the cost-benefit assessment. Whether one is an abstainer, trier or regular user, reaching conclusions about this aspect of risk, certainly by late adolescence, appears to be universal. However, longer-term health risks are rarely mentioned spontaneously although when prompted some regular drug users will acknowledge that they have a general worry about the longer-term effects of their habits.

> I do worry about it in the future I think, it's not a worry so's I wouldn't do it, I just worry about, like if I was pregnant or something and I didn't know, and I'd taken something, that kind of thing. My friend, she's a year older than me, and she drank and she had a trip, and she didn't know (that she was pregnant), but I always wonder how John is going to . . . because he's fine now, but maybe when he goes to school . . . because they don't really know do they.
>
> (Diane, polydrug user)

The absence of spontaneous mention of distant 'morbidity' in normally flowing accounts is compatible with the notion of adolescent invulnerability. Yet we must juxtapose this with the acceptance of vulnerability in spontaneous, animated discussion about bad experiences and *immediate* health risks which, usually in the form of 'drugs stories', dominate the cost-benefit discourse of our young subjects.

This said, we also need to distinguish between bad experiences and effects on health, which for abstainers and cautious triers would be defined as negative outcomes and real risk, but which for regular users with particular levels of risk tolerance are basically to be endured as part and parcel of using a particular drug. Regular poly users often accepted the occasional 'whitey' from too much cannabis, the possibility of flashbacks after LSD or insomnia after amphetamines.

Because when you take speed, if you take too much, you can't go to sleep, and when you've had pot, I take it to sit down and relax and I know I'm going to have a good night's sleep, but with speed I'm tossing and turning all night and getting up and going to the toilet and coming down stairs. I can't get settled when I've had speed, even though you've been dancing all night.

(Lisa)

Ecstasy and polydrug users in dance clubs had their own package of after effects which many perceived as an acceptable, expected price.

Pains in the legs the next morning from dancing. [Anything else?] From smoking weed I get really bad munchies and I feel really guilty for eating all this chocolate. [Any other disadvantages?] No. I've got a sore jaw the next morning, and I've got ulcers off where I've been chewing gum. [Does your drug use effect any other part of your life?] The next day I can't really seem to concentrate or anything, I can't do anything too demanding, I'm just tired. It's the same as if you've got a hangover though. It's not like – I've got a friend, she used to take quite a lot – I go out every one or two months, have half or three-quarters, and she used to give it a week to recover and then she used to really look a mess and her skin went horrible.

(Diane)

[Does it affect any other aspects of your life?] Yes. [In what way?] Smoking it at college I don't want to do any work, so college work goes down. If I'm taking whizz or something at a weekend it takes me a week to come down properly, so I can't be arsed to do anything during the week.

(Kate)

Sometimes diagnosing the cause of minor ailments is difficult in that drug use may or may not be relevant.

I suffered from a lot of headaches at one time. I went to see a doctor about my headaches, but I told my mum I was suffering from headaches, and she said 'well you need to go to the doctors, I'll take you', and I said 'no, I'll go on my own'. [Did you tell him/her about drug use?] Yes. I told her I'd occasionally taken speed. [What did she say?] Well she obviously told me it was bad for me and should try and knock it in the head. She said it could be (to do with speed), she couldn't exactly be sure of it, but she asked me how often I'd taken it, and I told her it was about once a week, but she didn't actually think it was enough to actually cause headaches unless I was taking it in huge amounts. [How was she with you?] She was really just down to earth, she wasn't at all funny with me or anything. [Did you actually believe it might be related to speed?] Yes, I did actually. [Did you do anything about it, or carry on taking it?] I personally thought it was because of the speed I was suffering the headaches, so I told my doctor and I told my boy-friend about it, so he went berserk, and he told me he wasn't going to let me take it anymore, and I should calm myself down. But I still suffer from them anyway. I went for an eye test and all that kind of thing to see if it was that, but it wasn't and then I just gradually started taking it again.

(Louise)

Other illnesses were clearly drug related:

We went to the doctors because I got complications, I went for a scan, I had kidney problems, and he just said 'have you been on drugs' I said 'no'. He goes 'I know you're lying to me', I said 'how do you know, you're not me'. He goes 'well I'm your doctor, I've known you since you were a baby', so I go 'well OK then, if you think I've been taking drugs, what do you think I'm on?'. He goes 'the symptoms you've got and your health problems', he said 'there's loads of drugs inside you . . . anyone could tell that you've been taking drugs, you want to lay off it, or your kidneys . . . going to be . . . damaged'. I said 'so?', I said 'it's my life I'll do what I want'. He goes 'fine, Helen, I'm your doctor, I'm here to advise you on things' but I wasn't interested, and then he just come to ours one night . . . and my dad goes 'we know about the problem'. He just left a few leaflets and that and said 'if you want to do what you want to do in the future you've got to stop it now', I just told him to mind his own business, 'you're not my father are you, you're just a doctor, nothing to do with me'. So he just walked away, but now I get on fine, and keep going to him and getting tablets.
[Have you told him now?] Yes, he knows, he's one of the people who helped me through the drug things as well, he helped me through, he just said 'I'm glad you got your head together'.

(Helen)

This young woman would perhaps be described on her family doctor's records as anxious, depressed and perhaps volatile by way of a warning to colleagues who might have to treat her. This reminds us that young people take drugs for different reasons and that vulnerable and damaged adolescents are probably even more likely to seek solace in drugs but, in turn, be more susceptible to 'misusing' them. Another respondent looking back on a very troubled adolescence was beginning to realise her own low self-esteem could not be permanently overcome chemically.

> Because . . . it's weird when I take drugs I don't stop eating, and I can go to sleep straight away. Everyone else I know they won't eat for another two days, and they won't go to sleep. I go straight to sleep and I'll have pudding, chips and gravy on the way home. I don't know what's wrong with me. So I thought what's the point, I'm just going to get even fatter. I think the only reason why I took a bit of whizz was because I was putting on weight, and I thought 'I'll take some of this, and I'll lose some weight'. But I didn't get nowhere . . . I have put on a lot of weight since last year.
>
> [Is that since you stopped the whizz?] No, it's more boredom really. I just can't remember what I used to do. I used to go to the army cadets on a Thursday and a Tuesday, and then I stopped all that.
>
> (Suzanne, polydrug user)

One of the key reasons for defining and assessing risks associated with drug use is to avoid bad experiences, sudden illness or loss of control as a direct consequence of drug use. Drug stories are thus important to cautious users and abstainers because they can be used to affirm or reaffirm their declaration not to take any or particular drugs.

> LSD? I told you about my friend (bad trip). I'm scared to take it. I've always been scared to take it but that backed up my idea about being scared because my friend kept getting flashbacks and had to go for drugs counselling.
>
> (John, cannabis user)

> My mate's boyfriend, he got a tablet when he went out to a club, but it was a dodgy one. One of his mates when they were coming home, they were driving, they had to keep stopping the car, he was throwing up everywhere. His other mate couldn't hear nothing, and he just felt like shit all night, he hadn't slept all night, and in the morning he went to the doctors and he was dehydrated and

everything. And he said 'if you'd left it another day and not really drank enough', he said 'you would have been dead'. So that was a scare, and he hasn't been out for a few weeks. [Has he had another tablet?] No, that was the last time. He has trips now.

(Lisa)

I know someone who was at a club with all his friends and he took drugs, and he was dancing, and he didn't have anything, no water or anything to drink, and he had a bit of fit on the floor and his mates started to panic, and just one of his mates sorted him out, rang the ambulance, and he was taken off and sorted out. [Did you know that you're recommended to drink water?] Well I knew that it's not a good idea just to dance all night and dehydrate, he should have drank water.

(Ian, drug user)

Having experimented with cannabis, LSD and amphetamines a male, who now uses only cannabis, discussed how he felt about being part of a group of friends with a more extensive drugs repertoire. Quite incidentally, he showed how he'd reached his own limits through recognising the health risks attached to two of these drugs.

I'm not really bothered I suppose, as long as the only drugs they have is cannabis, but LSD and speed, I wouldn't want them to have that all the time, because with speed, as you know, you can lose a lot of weight with it, and it can do your bones in as well, and with LSD it just sends you off to another planet if you keep on having that every day. [If they used LSD and speed regularly, what would you do?] I'd try and stop them, because it's not good for you at all. If you have them about once every fortnight it's not so bad. [How often do they use speed and cannabis?] About once a fortnight at most.

(Jason)

For some users the bad experience involves abandoning a particular drug either permanently or at least for a while. One dance drug nightclubber modified her views on drinking and taking ecstasy 'tablets' after one serious incident.

I felt really bad, I stopped dancing, actually sat down and just took myself home. I was sweating cobs as well, I was really, really sweating. I think I did the sensible thing by just calming myself down, sitting down and going home. Because if I would have stayed there . . . well . . . God knows. [Not what you wanted?] . . . was expecting, just to be a little bit more lively, just to have a bit of a dance and that, because when you've had a few drinks you get tired don't you, when you're really drunk. [How much did you spend?] £25 on alcohol. The tablets were £10 each. We actually got them cheap as well, they were saying 'because there's a group of you we'll give you these for so much . . . I felt embarrassed afterwards, I didn't feel as safe as normal, like I thought I was going to faint . . . I was sick the next day . . . the day after I just didn't feel like nothing to eat at all.

(Natalie, polydrug user)

Another polydrug user related her own scary moment merely as a cautionary tale, just one of those things that happen occasionally. She continued to use amphetamines but took greater care with combination use.

It was while I was actually taking the drug, I'd taken speed, I'd taken a bit too much for my body to cope with I suppose, and I felt sick and I started actually being sick and shivering and cold, and then I blacked out. [How much had you had?] Quite a lot, and I'd been drinking as well, so I think it was a combination of the two.

(Vicky, drug user)

Through observing these sorts of drink–drug mishaps, other dance drug users regard them as serious enough to repackage a weekend repertoire. One respondent who had used all the main recreational drugs avoided getting drunk at nightclubs. She'd start her Saturday night with a spliff of cannabis before moving on to her preferred clubbing combinations.

Ecstasy and Rush – just for that moment, I wouldn't want it all night. Not all the time, maybe every twenty minutes. [What order?] Before, usually in the car, because I have to take it (ecstasy) dead early for me to come up because it takes ages. If I take it when I get in there I come up when everyone's going home. Take Rush in there and maybe one half of lager. I've never been drunk on a tablet, I've seen what other people are like, I like to know what I'm doing. [Anything else? Cannabis at all?] Yes about four o'clock in the morning.

(Diane)

In summary it is the immediate health risks and the chance of having bad experiences particularly with amphetamines, LSD and ecstasy, perhaps combined with alcohol, which dominate the risk concerns of young drug triers and users. Yet the consensus we find at the two ends of the spectrum about cannabis on the one hand and heroin and cocaine on the other is harder to identify with these middle-range drugs. What is an acceptable bad experience for one is a bridge too far for another and the cost-benefit equation cannot fully explain these subjective understandings and thresholds. Significantly, whilst pharmacologists and addiction experts (Saunders, 1997) are debating the long-term effects of regular use of drugs like ecstasy, our respondents rarely made spontaneous reference to them.

Conclusion

In attempting to describe and analyse drug decision-making journeys we have identified a set of repeated elements which are found in the motivational accounts of our interviewees and respondents. In this chapter we have tried to illustrate how clusters of young people journey down particular drugs pathways as they gain experience, take on new information, learn more about themselves and the personal effects of particular drugs. We are also illustrating why so many drug-taking opportunities are rejected, why cannabis-only users won't even try another drug, why for some LSD is a taboo drug whilst ecstasy is acceptable and so on.

The cost-benefit equation is a conceptual tool, a dynamic framework to help us understand these journeys. It should not become a mechanical explanation nor should it be used to filter out contradictions. Our young subjects are not immune from exaggerations or distortion nor can they always even adequately define their own relationship with drugs. We have identified some quite damaged and vulnerable young subjects, others with delinquent tendencies and others again who have, by normal standards, excessive appetites for psychoactive highs.

The cost-benefit equation, for instance, *cannot* fully explain whether or not this latter group will continue to journey down polydrugs careers which could end up in dependency and disorder. It does not pretend to include theories of addiction in that growing dependency is often invisible to the user. Whilst the interviewer may have identified signs of psychological dependency this young woman made no such connection.

> Every time I go out and I don't have it, I think 'oh I'm dying for one . . .' but I can go out and not have anything, but I would prefer to.

[What are you getting out of it?] A good night. I just feel like having that feeling. That's it really. [Do you crave it?] When I go out, in Beachtown not so much, but if we went to town and I was seeing everybody else. I wouldn't sit here (now) and go 'oh my God I need a tablet', but if you hear the music or something that reminds me of it, I think 'ooh I just fancy one of them'.

(Diane)

In this chapter we have built on the pathways analysis by offering an appreciative perspective of the actual experiential journeys our drug triers and users took during their adolescence, based on the in-depth interviews conducted when the samples were becoming 18. We have hopefully brought to life the issues of drugs availability and the key role friendship and acquaintance networks play in obtaining drugs. The vast majority of our drug users get their drugs via 'friends of friends' or 'friends of dealers'. Aside from the nightclubbers in the sample, direct contact with professional drug dealers is a rare event and sometimes an unhappy one. The dealer–user distinction is both extremely hard to make within this world of recreational drug use yet suddenly abundantly clear when 'real' dealers appear.

In offering oral histories of their drugs initiation and early trying experiences, interviewees emphasised personal curiosity and the support, sometimes encouragement, occasionally 'pressure', of friendship networks. Most first-time experiments were with cannabis and were benign. LSD and amphetamines and, in late adolescence, ecstasy, were occasionally more problematic and often became significant events captured in a 'drugs story'. Becoming a drug user involves a greater commitment and a more complicated self-assessment. The elements of this assessment were so often repeated in each interviewee's accounts that they can be brought together within the cost-benefit equation. This equation assumes that most young people are *drugwise* and that they differentiate between the range of drugs readily available on the youth market in terms of their effects, both positive and negative.

Our young drug triers in the early 1990s nearly all rejected heroin, cocaine powder and crack cocaine out of hand as drugs with dreadful reputations because of their addictive potential and the dangers lurking in the subterranean worlds in which they are dealt and used. Hard drugs currently have no place in the normalisation thesis we have been assessing. Cannabis on the other hand is perceived as a fairly safe drug. The middle three – amphetamines, LSD and ecstasy – are more equivocally defined and when we explore attitudes to and the acceptability of these drugs we find the cost-benefit equation in full flow.

The regular consumption of one or more of the available drugs usually involves a purchasing decision. However, for the 'supplier' this transaction is illegal, as is possessing each drug. This risk has to be assessed in terms of stigma and censure by parents, partners, friends, teachers and the criminal justice system. Personal relationships and career opportunities might be damaged. The immediate health risks, including scary moments and bad experiences, must also be gauged for each drug or combination. Longer-term health risks are rarely assessed, probably because of the lack of available information and lack of agreement amongst the 'experts'.

All these risks and possible costs are compared with the enjoyment that can be obtained from using a particular drug. Here drugs 'culture' offers added value in that being with friends and partners whilst using drugs is usually an important, enjoyable social event. It is part of 'time out' from the grind of most days. But the drug users segment because they reach different cost-benefit conclusions. For many, primarily cannabis users, the 'brilliant' weekends described by the nightclub poldrug users are obtained at far too high a risk.

The cost-benefit assessment is a useful conceptual tool in helping to understand the key elements in each young person's decision-making journey but, unlike the pathways analysis, it cannot explain or predict outcomes. It is not a theory nor should be seen as an always explicit, fully utilised equation to be reduced to a drug user's handbook of rational consumption, for whilst rational decision making usually guides, it may not dominate. Thus, we have identified how a minority of quite damaged and vulnerable young subjects have 'misused' drugs to their cost and how others with delinquent tendencies have got involved in situations which can hardly be described as 'recreational'. This journeys analysis cannot predict how individuals will turn out since it makes no attempt to assess individual propensity to physical or psychological dependency on drugs. Furthermore, numerous other factors would be needed for theory development. On the other hand, the articulate and animated debates we have captured demonstrate how deeply entrenched recreational drug use has become in contemporary British youth culture and how to journey through adolescence in 'modern' times makes almost all young people drugwise.

We turn now to an updated discussion of findings from our cohort in relation to their drug journeys into adulthood.

Journeys: update 18 to 27 years of age

Introduction

This chapter has described the cohort's drug journeys by analysing the in-depth interview data collected at the age of 17 and the critical incident interviews at 18. These journeys involved a complex interaction between individual and structural factors (such as gender, age, ethnicity, personality, employment), access to and availability of different drugs, the setting in which they were to be taken and with whom, the weighing up of the costs and benefits associated with different drugs, curiosity and moral perspectives. We found that the key turning points in the cohort's drug journeys were linked to education, career decisions and social relationships such as family and friendship networks. These factors are still important for the continuity or (re)commencement of drug use in adulthood.

In this update we develop the analyses by drawing on the experiences of drug-using interviewees further to understand continuity, change and desistance in drug use journeys as the cohort has reached their late twenties. As detailed in Chapter 2, these analyses take advantage of our methodological shift over the course of the research to relying more on in-depth qualitative data to answer our research questions about drugs journeys into adulthood. Drawing on the data collected at the age of 22, Williams and Parker (2001) predicted that transitions to adulthood would be a key determinant for moderating drug use in adulthood. As in their teens, protracted transitions and delayed adult life stage markers such as leaving the parental home, buying or renting a home, marriage and parenthood – in sociological terms 'extended adolescence' – had led to the continuation of drug use further into young adulthood for this cohort. Although many respondents began to negotiate their key transitions in their early twenties, it was too soon at this point to conclude how these would ultimately influence their drug journeys. As described in Chapter 2, the interviews on which this chapter update is largely based were conducted when the cohort were 28, and the analyses of these, alongside comparisons with earlier interviews, was the work of Lisa Williams for her doctoral research (see Williams, 2007[1]). There are key analytic insights gained through this PhD research which are

---

1   The full PhD thesis can be viewed as a pdf document (www.law.manchester.ac.uk/ staff/lisa_williams). A monograph detailing many of the findings from the thesis is under contract with Willan/Routledge, entitled 'Bridling the Horse: Drug Journeys from Adolescence to Young Adulthood'.

outlined in this chapter and will be described in more detail in future publications. Williams examined different risk perceptions amongst interviewees and concluded they can change during the life course to justify current behaviour. Further, she found changing social relationships, the drug status and attitudes towards drugs of those in such relationships were important when making decisions whether or not to take drugs. Finally, in exploring the significance of transitions to adulthood, she concluded it is not the transition *per se* which impacts upon drug journeys but the nature of transitions. In addition to this work, we also present some analyses here for the first time.

We revisit the cost-benefit approach to understanding drug use; a perspective and approach employed by interviewees discussed earlier. We now focus on what interviewees at the ages of 22 and 28 disclose as priorities – such as friendships, intimate relationships and transitional biographies – which impact on the drug use decision making process. We begin however by exploring some of the pleasures, functions and associated health risks they consider when making a cost-benefit assessment.

The cost-benefit assessment

Assessing the pleasures, functions and health risks

A growing number of researchers are critical of the over-focus upon risks associated with drug use at the expense of describing pleasures and functions (Aldridge *et al.*, 1999; Duff, 2008; Ettorre, 1992; Measham, 2002; O'Malley and Valverde, 2004; Williams, 2007). As we found in adolescence, drugs continue to be used in a leisure context from late teens and into adulthood, with a specific range of pleasures and functions perceived in relation to different drugs. For example, cocaine is described functionally by the young adults who spoke to us as a drug that provides a short burst of energy, lowers inhibitions and increases confidence. Drug users also reported taking it concurrently with alcohol as they perceived it made them feel less drunk and in turn facilitated further alcohol consumption:

> . . . the only reason when I'd ever do it [take cocaine] is to give me some energy and not to feel sick when I'm drinking. [Yeah.] That is it. And not to get drunk, cos you don't get drunk on it.
>
> (53404, female current drug user, age 28)

When making drug use decisions, interviewees also consider the risks they perceive to their health, safety and general well-being (Aldridge, 2008; Aldridge *et al.*, 1999; Williams, 2007). In adolescence, they tended to identify the immediate negative effects of drug use such as 'whiteys' (nearly passing out) from cannabis and scary hallucinogenic trips from LSD. These costs were still discussed across the transitional years and the immediate after effects of drugs, in the form of the 'come down', were a key concern. Although many drug users complained about the come down, few had desisted from taking stimulant drugs as a result. In adulthood, however, some had moderated the frequency and quantities of their stimulant drug use, as described in Chapter 4, and were beginning to ask themselves whether the 'come down' was a price worth paying. In particular, as time becomes more limited in adulthood, the whole 'package' of drug use – including the come down – becomes a temporal indulgence in a time-limited world:

> It takes me about three or four days to recover from it as well. (laughs) You just get . . . I just get absolutely knackered by it now. So I think I get to the point now where I think, 'Well is it really worth it for one day of running around like a dickhead? Is it worth it being shattered for like the next week?' So I'd rather now have a few glasses of wine and get a bit tipsy, you know, do that rather than be worn out.
>
> (23a04, female current drug user, age 28)

As this interviewee illustrates, some were beginning to consider alternative ways of spending their leisure time, including by trying alternative, legal drugs, to achieve a desirable state of intoxication. Later we discuss how risks and negative effects are assessed in conjunction with their life course position, for instance, current employment status.

We noted earlier in the chapter how the cost-benefit assessment was in full operation in late adolescence when amphetamines, LSD and ecstasy were considered. Cocaine and heroin were often dismissed as far too risky for this cohort in the mid 1990s, whilst cannabis was perceived as relatively benign. The vast majority had drawn the line at heroin and cocaine, which they perceived to be 'hard' drugs. However, as we have noted, there has been a substantial increase in the prevalence of cocaine use for this cohort beginning in their late teens, during the late 1990s. With increasing availability and use across the UK during this period, the cohort reported they had friends who could inform them about the effects of cocaine, and some therefore decided to try it. Consequently, through time and via indirect and direct experience, cocaine came to be seen as no longer too risky. Indeed, compared to other stimulant drugs such as amphetamines, some reported their preference for cocaine and the less harsh or less lengthy 'come down' in the days after taking it.

Throughout adolescence there was a notable absence of debate amongst our interviewees about the long-term health risks associated with drugs, consistent with typical adolescent attitudes to risk and their sense of invulnerability. What starts to become apparent is the greater salience of health risks with age. *Ex-users* in particular now tend to prioritise long-term health concerns in their decision making. Some are concerned about the effect past drug use may have upon their current and future physical and psychological well-being. These concerns were even disclosed as a reason for desistance. Drawing on Reith (2004), we can see that drug risk perceptions can be understood as justifying current behaviour (Williams, 2007). Thus, abstainers perceive serious risks, for instance addiction or death, which justify their choice not to take drugs; drug users generally perceive short-term and manageable risks which justify their decision to continue to take drugs; and ex-users perceive long-term risks which justify their decision to no longer take drugs.

Interestingly, drug users also attribute more serious risks in respect of specific illegal drugs that they do not take. In support of this attribution we found that risk perceptions changed during the course of the study (Williams, 2007). For example, many in adolescence perceived there to be a not insignificant risk of death associated with ecstasy use and presented this as a reason for not trying it. The possible dangers of ecstasy were particularly salient for this cohort, reaching their mid teens in the mid 1990s. Very close in age to Leah Betts when she died, our cohort was exposed to the full weight of the anti-ecstasy post-Leah Betts media coverage and public health campaigns which suggested that 'one pill can kill' (see also Critcher, 2000; Forsyth, 2001; Henderson, 1997; Measham *et al.*, 1998; Murji, 1998). However, when those who had previously rejected ecstasy became late adolescent or early adult users of the drug, they no longer attributed the risks of danger and neurotoxicity to the drug and instead their concerns about ecstasy focused more on the short-term negative effects of the 'come down'.

Even though drug users as a rule tended to perceive manageable and acceptable effects, at times, a few did recall experiencing more serious harms or risks that they attributed to their drug use; for example, dependency or damage to physical health. Even in these cases, this did not lead to complete desistance. Instead, these interviewees recommenced their drug journeys at a later stage of their lives but at a slower more conservative pace.

During late adolescence, the cohort had revealed learnt drug wisdom as they became increasingly 'drug wise'. As they progressed through early adulthood, they continued to modify this drug wisdom and increasingly refine their risk management strategies to maximise the pleasures and minimise the problems associated with their drug use (see also Moore and Measham, 2006). To manage the effects of the ecstasy and cocaine 'come down', many smoke cannabis and a few take valium to aid sleep. In addition, many combine drugs for a specific function or pleasure:

> . . . if you do a little bit [of ketamine] all the time then it can really enhance your pill, it really, really does. [. . .] when I go out I like to do [ecstasy] pills and I think coke brings you down off your pills. [Do you think it sort of straightens you out?] It does, whereas whizz [amphetamines] because it's a constant it goes on for hours, it's like prolonged and you're there for a long time instead of going up and down with coke. And when you're having your pills you can still feel your pills because it's just, it's like you're in a higher state, but you've plateaued with your whizz so when you take your pill you're actually going higher.
>
> (83820, current drug user, age 28)

This dynamic accumulated drug wisdom continues to inform the cohort's cost-benefit assessment. They also use this approach to assess when, where and which drugs to use. For some, perceived and actual risks to their health or well-being are beginning to outweigh the perceived functions or pleasures, and subsequently lead them to moderate their consumption or even desist from drug use (see also Aldridge 2008; Aldridge *et al.*, 1999; Williams, 2007). For others, such risks are still perceived as acceptable and/or manageable and they continue to take drugs in adulthood.

The importance of social networks

Previously we noted how social relationships played an important role in drug journeys. Friends, and occasionally girlfriends or boyfriends, provided access to drugs in a variety of settings. In adolescence, admission or discovery of drug use risked causing problems with parents. In making the transition to adulthood, however, relationships are prioritised differently. Friends are still important but many are now in settled intimate partner relationships. The survey data revealed that by the age of 27, almost two-thirds (64.9 per cent) are married or cohabiting with a partner. The majority have left the family home and thus any concerns about parents discovering their drug use have diminished. Here, we explore the impact that social relationships continue to have upon drug journeys in respect of providing access to drugs and social accommodation of drug use.

Many interviewees, at the age of 22 in 2000, noted that they had even greater access to drugs than in the preceding decade, illustrating how fluctuations in access and availability in recent years have impacted upon the cohort: '. . . it's [drugs] everywhere now. [. . .] I've got the same friends it's just that everyone seems to have drugs on them now' (63485, male current drug user, age 22).

Whilst friends continue to be a key source for illegal drugs, so too are intimate partners, particularly for the young women in this study (see also Measham *et al.*, 1998; Williams, 2007). With easy access to drugs resulting from these key life relationships, some made the decision to take them. Friendship and intimate partner relationships, as we found in adolescence, are often mutual. Friends and partners may 'sort' each other for drugs via their social networks with the purchase of drugs from known sources considered to be a risk reduction strategy. Many discussed how they trusted their friends, partners and also dealers they regarded as 'friends' to provide them with access to reliable drugs and, as we found previously, they rarely bought drugs from unknown sources (see also Measham *et al.*, 2001; Williams, 2007). Thus, social relationships and sources of drug supply continue to be a key element of the cost-benefit assessment in adulthood.

Despite greater access to drugs during their late teens and early twenties, some interviewees reported availability diminished by their late twenties. Over time, friendship patterns or intimate relationships changed or ended, and thus often so did access to different drugs. The following case study illustrates how changing friendships impact upon drug journeys. A female interviewee, who was an ex-user by the age of 28, first tried ecstasy when she was at secondary school with access through friends. A new set of friends at university provided her with access to ecstasy, cannabis and amphetamines, and she incorporated her use of these drugs into going clubbing. During vacations, however, she no longer had easy access to these drugs and stopped taking them until she went back to university. After graduating, when she returned home to live with her parents, she re-contacted some old school friends and started to take cocaine for the first time:

[So when did you first try coke?] Yeah, that wasn't until I was about 22 because when I was at Uni and in school it kind of wasn't really, it wasn't that, it was known, but it wasn't half as readily available as it is now. [Yeah.] And I was living in [the North West] and it was me friend's, we started hanging around with me friend's brother who was older than us and we kind of started trying it that way really.

(63534, female ex-user, age 28)

With easy access to cocaine, in line with the national pre and post millennium picture of increased availability, this interviewee and her friends took it regularly for approximately a year. Such accounts highlight how changing friendships impact upon drug use decisions. Likewise, changing intimate relationships also influence drug journeys. For example, another female ex-user began smoking cannabis regularly at university with her boyfriend. When the relationship ended her cannabis consumption reduced dramatically: '... once I had split up from that relationship, that was it really. And it's just been like on and off really since then, you know, I've smoked occasionally with friends' (43331, female ex-user, age 28).

What is crucial for the continuity of drug use in the context of social relationships is the drug-using status of those involved which in turn affects access to drugs and levels of social accommodation of drug use (Williams, 2007). It is evident that drug use is socially accommodated within specific social relationships (Pennay and Moore, 2010). A female ex-user explains her decision to take cocaine with her friend:

... this girl who I was friends with, like her boyfriend started dealing it, I don't think he still deals it now, but at one point he started dealing it so like he just had it, so we just had it.

(13079, female ex-user, age 22)

There is an inevitability in this interviewee's account of her decision to try cocaine: it was available within her social network, acceptable to her friends and therefore she decided to try it. Others also disclosed how drug use was socially accommodated within their intimate relationships, influencing their decision to take drugs. When a female current drug user was 17, she tried amphetamines for the first time and began taking them regularly with her partner. She acknowledges the influence he had upon her decision: '... he sort of introduced me to that whole drugs scene really. I kinda worshipped the ground that he walked on ...' (83890, female current drug user, age 28).

As social relationships changed, either because friends or partners began to reduce their own drug consumption, completely stopped or because these relationships ended, drug use might no longer be socially accommodated. An ex-amphetamine user describes the dilemma she faced in deciding whether to take drugs, depending upon who amongst her friendship group she went out with on a particular night:

> ... I'd consider having it [amphetamines] if I went to the club but, I suppose with the different people I go to clubs with I find it awkward bringing, you know, well, just talking about it with them. Cos some of them don't agree with taking drugs anyway. [Yeah.] And some of them do. But it's, I don't know I, I'd quite happily do it myself but I don't want to, you know, impose it on other people.
>
> (83x43, female ex-user, age 22)

We sometimes identified discord in intimate relationships during adolescence: male drug users in particular might be subject to scrutiny by their female partners. Thus, drug use by one partner was not always mimicked or accommodated by the other. Many in this situation therefore decided to reduce the frequency of their drug use, to stop taking specific drugs or to curtail their drug journeys, although this sometimes only occurred for the duration of that relationship. A male current drug user recalled why he reduced the frequency of his stimulant drug use in his twenties:

> She [his partner] didn't take any drugs, she didn't agree with it either. [Yeah.] She wasn't bothered about me smoking pot, but anything else [sharp intake of breath], that'd've been a killer.
>
> (23144, male current drug user, age 28)

Evidently, stimulant drug use is not socially accommodated within this interviewee's relationship, an illustration of what Pennay and Moore (2010) refer to as micro-normalisation. When this relationship ended and he began to spend more time with friends, he started taking cocaine regularly again.

Social relationships are therefore a further factor considered in the cost-benefit assessment, with some relationships providing opportunities to start or extend drug use, and others restricting drug use. Whilst relationships may therefore have a causal effect on drug taking, the reverse could also occur, with a particular drug-taking stance (either pro or con) affecting the likelihood of a relationship's success. A male ex-user illustrates:

> I think the people she [his partner] was with and the culture that was associated to her, they weren't my type of people. And I think because of that I think may be, you know, if she was doing drugs or whatever she was doing, because of what it was associated to, I

didn't quite enjoy it. I didn't really want to go to the places she was going. And turning up at a house at three o'clock in the morning seeing everyone monged off their heads on a Saturday night and I was like, 'I'm not really up for this to be honest' and she was like, 'It's great, we're having a laugh'. These different people monged off their heads, 'It's hilarious!'

(73739, male ex-user, age 28)

Because of his partner's leisure and friendship choices, he ended both this relationship and his stimulant drug journey. Others reported that drug use fulfilled a specific function or provided pleasure in the context of social relationships. For example, interviewees described how stimulant drugs could increase confidence and reduce inhibitions, which in turn provided opportunities for bonding or 'having a laugh' with drug-using friends or partners. Thus, for some, these functions or pleasures outweighed the possible resultant negative effects and perceived risks associated with illegal drug use.

We previously discussed the significance of peer pressure, peer influence and peer preference upon drug journeys and noted how it is difficult to measure. In adolescence, the sample recounted drug decisions which *could* be interpreted as responses to peer pressure. Pilkington (2007) argues that our understanding of drug use decisions should move beyond the notion of peer pressure. She asserts such decisions are a combination of youth cultural practices as responses and resistance to structural determinants. Here we have shown that youth cultural practices embodied in peer relationships with friends or partners provide access to drugs and therefore may facilitate drug use, rather than pressuring the unwilling into use. These peers may influence drug-taking repertoires, as well as the frequency and quantity of drug use. Measham *et al.* (1998) and Williams (2007) found both similarity and difference in respect of frequency, quantity and types of drugs used within social relationships. Some females in this cohort, for example, recalled that they took drugs more frequently during the course of an intimate relationship with a drug user than they had done before. A female current drug user accounts for her frequent use of heroin and amphetamines in her late teens and early twenties as influenced by her intimate partners:

... I've only really taken it to heavy extents when I've had people around me, you know, like strong figures around me have done it and that's where I've sort of joined in. So sort of knowingly, but not, because you don't, you just sort of do it.

(23a04, female current drug user, age 28)

Thus, when drug use is socially accommodated in an intimate relationship, some women may find it difficult to refuse to take drugs. In their twenties respondents rejected the notion that they were pressured to take drugs by a partner, just as in adolescence they had refuted the idea of being pressured by their friends. Instead they describe their partners as providing reassurance about drug use. However, to refuse to take drugs may have been perceived as a risk to the relationship in the cost-benefit assessment. Nevertheless, we also found clear evidence of differences in drug repertoires between friends or partners. For instance, a female current drug user at age 28 reported her friends take ecstasy and ketamine but she refuses to even try them. We have shown here how the social relationships the cohort established over time have influenced their decisions whether or not to take drugs. We now turn to explore structural factors which are also significant when making decisions about drug use.

Transitions to adulthood

In contemporary times, sociologists have noted how young people's transition to adulthood is protracted (Coles, 1995; Furlong and Cartmel, 1997; Roberts, 1995). As we noted earlier, the extension of adolescence for young people has had an impact upon the drug use decisions of this cohort. Youth transitions research traditionally explores three key transitions to adulthood: from education to work; leaving the parental home; and marriage and parenthood. Life course criminology also identifies similar milestones on the road to desistance from crime (see Catalano and Hawkins, 1996; Laub and Sampson, 2003; LeBlanc, 1997; Sampson and Laub, 1993; Thornberry, 1987). Research with drug users has found that as young people adopt adult roles which demand their attention, drug use declines (Bachman *et al.*, 1997; Kandel, 1980; Vervaeke and Korf, 2006). As we alluded to earlier, it is not the transition *per se* which impacts upon drug journeys; it is the nature and quality of the transition which is significant. For example, type of employment gained may lead some to moderate their drug taking. MacDonald and Marsh (2002) assert that transitions are interdependent and in addition to the traditional three, they explore transitions in drug careers (from recreational to dependent use), criminal careers and leisure time to explain drug decisions made by socially excluded youth. With our mostly conventional cohort, we focus on employment, housing and parenthood. As the cohort matured they began to negotiate these transitions and, in doing so, their priorities changed, and these renewed priorities impacted upon their drug journeys. For some, continuing to take drugs presents a risk to successful accomplishment of these transitions. These transitions became a significant component of the cost-benefit assessment made by young people as they entered adulthood.

Education to work

Many of the cohort continued their education after the school leaving age of 16 at college or university. By the age of 18, 60.7 per cent were in further or higher education and by the age of 22, the majority were employed (68.4 per cent full time, 13.6 per cent part-time) and remained so throughout their twenties. For some, drug use continued to have a function in the context of their developing careers: it provided 'time out', relaxation and stress relief (Williams and Parker, 2001). During adolescence, some discussed drug use as a potential risk to their vocation either due to its illegality or, more usually, its effects on productivity during the working week. In their twenties, many remarked how they were now pursuing their chosen career. Continuing to take drugs was disclosed as posing a risk to their career development and ability to perform at work: 'I say now and then that I might do [take drugs again], but at the same time I'm more concerned about my job' (83x43, female ex-user, age 22).

A female current drug user managed her own business and had recently recommenced taking ecstasy at weekends with friends. However, she was finding it difficult to balance her social life with her work role: 'It's quite addictive actually when you start going out, but it's no good for me cos I've got too much on my head and if I go out on the weekend I just can't function in the week' (53404, female current drug user, age 28). Commitment to a career and concerns about not being able to function at work, particularly when experiencing a 'come down', led some to moderate their drug use or completely desist in adulthood.

What seems crucial to our interviewees is the nature of their work roles and the number of hours worked rather than the transition to work *per se* (Williams, 2007). When drug users had fewer responsibilities at work, for example in manual factory work, or worked part-time, they could choose to take drugs more often. The female current drug user above compares her current employment situation with when she worked part time and took drugs more frequently:

> . . . since I've had the [business] it can't affect it because I've got to be there everyday. [. . .] Last time I was [interviewed] [. . .] I was working half nine to half two so if you're thinking to yourself, 'Oh

you've only got till half two and you can come home and go to sleep' then it didn't really affect it.

(53404, female current drug user, age 28)

Because at 28 this interviewee works full time, when she goes clubbing and taking drugs on a Saturday night she is usually home around 2am whilst her friends continue taking drugs until the following day. Similar to this interviewee, some adopted risk management strategies: they reduced the frequency of their clubbing and drug-taking weekends or their daily smoking of cannabis. Others, however, completely prioritised their jobs in their decision making. A male ex-user decided to stop taking stimulant drugs and smoking cannabis daily when he began working full time:

> The key turning point was me getting a full-time job. [. . .] when I went full-time then it was just like a cut off point then because I'd work, I'd be tired and I'd come home and that was it, didn't want to go out.
>
> (13n16, male ex-user, age 28)

As this interviewee's account illustrates, full-time employment can impinge on leisure choices. Impact on employment is therefore a further factor the sample now includes in their cost-benefit assessment. In adulthood, many began to prioritise their careers and reduce their drug use or completely desist. Nevertheless, others were able to accommodate both their drug use and jobs into their lives. However, this usually involved the daily or regular consumption of cannabis and more occasional stimulant drug use.

Housing transition

By the age of 18, many of the interviewees made the transition from dependent to independent living by leaving home and going to university, or by moving in with friends or a partner. Subsequently, some returned to their family home and have since left again. The survey data revealed that by the age of 27 only a fifth (20.3 per cent) were living with their parents. Initially, after leaving the family home, many reported feeling 'carefree' and were less concerned about the risk their parents might become aware of or concerned about their drug use. A female ex-user recalled that her parents could not imagine that she ever would take drugs, which she believed worked in her favour when she left home: '. . . all of a sudden you go to Uni or, you know, and you think, "What a disgrace", they never think I'm doing anything so I can do what I want' (63534, female ex-user, age 28).

By leaving the parental home and setting up their own home lives, many imagined that they could take illegal drugs as often as they wished without parental suspicion or condemnation. By the age of 28, however, it became apparent that setting up or buying a home alone or with a partner had an effect that was the reverse of what they had anticipated. As more demands are placed on their time and their finances through establishing and running their own homes, some have fewer opportunities for drug use. A female current drug user noted how taking stimulant drugs every weekend affected her ability to maintain her home, and therefore keeps her clubbing to once a month or less: '. . . it's hard to keep a house as well if you go out every weekend cos you can't be arsed ever doing anything, so eating properly and stuff like that' (83820, female current drug user, age 28).

There are signs that, as they near the age of 30, some in the drug-user element of the cohort are beginning to perceive drug use as a problem rather than a pleasure in the context of their transitions to establishing their own homes. Interviewees discussed prioritising the upkeep of their homes and therefore began to reduce the frequency of their drug consumption or completely desist. This was particularly the case for female interviewees, which may reflect traditional gender roles in the home and women's continued greater identification with the home as a projection or representation of their identity.

Parenthood

During their twenties a minority of the cohort made a further key transition to adulthood and became parents. By the age of 27 15.2 per cent were parents. Unsurprisingly, parenthood was predicted by many as a key turning point in their drug journeys: '. . . if I was serious over a girl and she was serious over me, we were getting wed or whatever, or got a kiddie on the way that would be the only thing that would make me stop' (13052, male current drug user, age 22).

Some who became parents prioritised their new role and no longer wanted to risk taking drugs, particularly given the perceived risks that this cohort associated with ecstasy: '. . . having a daughter I thought it's not worth chancing your life on one [ecstasy] tablet' (33262, male current drug user, age 22). Other risks which began to form part of the cost-benefit assessment at this stage of the life course included the difficulty of parenting children whilst experiencing a 'come down' and being too tired from parenting to take stimulant drugs and to go clubbing in particular, and to go out socialising. This led some to reduce the frequency of their drug use or to stop completely.

Although parenthood was cited as a key reason to desist from drug use, some new mothers at the age of 22 had recommenced their drug journeys by their late twenties. When they were new parents they aspired to be 'good' and 'responsible' mothers and continuing to take drugs was perceived to be at odds with this goal (Williams, 2007). Measham (2002) and Gregory (2009) have suggested that for others, their drug use might not be incongruous with good parenting and might even be seen to facilitate better parenting. Over time, however, with trusted support networks available to them to look after their children and acquired drug wisdom, some mothers felt able to conform to responsible notions of parenthood and manage the positive and negative effects such that they started taking drugs again, albeit less frequently. A current drug user in her late twenties describes how her priorities have changed since becoming a parent. Her son places more demands on her time, which has led to a reduction in the frequency of her drug use:

> When I was 18, you know, I was loving life, it was great. You know, I was working hard, plenty of money and I was just having an absolute scream. Where now, you see, my life – like ten years on isn't it? – my life now is about providing. I provide a home now, I'm looking after, you know, I'm looking after my son. Because my priorities have changed, see. And the way that I have fun now is different to what it would be ten years ago.
>
> (23125, female current drug user, age 28)

In late adolescence she started taking cocaine. At times in her life she has done so frequently, even after becoming a parent. However, she now only takes cocaine once or twice a year. As her account demonstrates, becoming a parent is another transition some of the cohort began to consider in their cost-benefit assessments in their twenties and most will probably include in due course.

Summary

As we have discussed before, multiple factors can impact upon drug journeys, and these are different for each individual and in each historical, life transitional period. Drug-active members of our cohort continue to develop their drug wisdom. They know which drugs to take for pleasure and leisure and employ risk management strategies. The cost-benefit approach is still a useful way to understand how decisions to take drugs are made. We concluded from the findings in adolescence that this assessment is not always employed in a way that appears rational to an outsider, or in a way that seems consistent, and sometimes this is still the case. Indeed, some of the sample recalled being subject to serious health effects that they attributed to their drug use, but continued to take drugs. Perhaps in these cases positive effects outweighed the negative effects they experienced. Through their drug experiences many of the cohort now know which individual drugs they would like to take for a specific purpose, how often and to do so in a particular setting.

Both acute and chronic negative physical and psychological effects remain a central part of the cost-benefit assessment for drug users, and are often used to justify current behaviour. In adulthood, however, new issues are now being considered. The interviewees' accounts illustrate the role of both cultural and structural factors in their decision making. Social relationships continue to be important but concerns about parents discovering drug use have largely been replaced by fears about upsetting intimate partners or friends. Social relationships also reduce perceived risks via providing access to drugs from 'trusted' sources. These relationships remain an important feature, therefore, of normalisation. However, as they change, access and accommodation of drug use may be reduced resulting in desistance or reductions in drug use. In these circumstances our respondents have not become drug seekers and rarely turn to alternative unknown sources of drug supply.

By their late twenties, many of the cohort have made the key transitions to adulthood and their priorities have changed. The health risks they perceive are now being assessed alongside their life course position, which brings new risks and responsibilities with it. Some have begun to prioritise their careers or their role as parents and find it more difficult to function effectively in these roles if they have taken drugs. For some, therefore, over time their transitions have led to decisions not to take specific drugs or desistance from drug use. For others, drug use has a specific function and they are still able to continue on their drug journey but at a slower pace.

7 Towards the normalisation of recreational drug use

Overview

This chapter begins with a reproduction of the chapter on normalisation from the first edition of *Illegal Leisure*. We follow this with an update entitled 'Illegal Leisure Revisited: The runaway train of normalisation' that brings our assessment of the normalisation debate up to date.

Introduction

As the 1990s draw to a close the headline figures from the North-West Longitudinal Study seem increasingly unremarkable. Snapshot surveys are routinely returning similar drug-offer or lifetime drug-trying rates. As important as these prevalence surveys have been, they have told us little about how and why young Britons have become, in less than a decade, such determined consumers of 'recreational' drugs to the point that we can begin to talk about the normalisation of *this* type of drug use.

Blessed with a well-resourced, longitudinal investigation which has been able to explore drug use in the context of growing up in 'modern' times, by utilising a whole range of methods, we have purposefully concentrated on these explanatory questions. In this final chapter we turn to the implications of the conclusions reached in the earlier chapters. We begin by drawing together the normalisation thesis. Thus we also offer an answer to the question 'to what extent has mainstream youth culture assimilated and legitimated recreational drug use?' Once we move to this more macro, abstract approach, we must in turn situate any theorising about drug use in the wider context of the social change which has transformed young people's experiences of growing up with 'late modernity' (Giddens, 1991). It is not the nature of adolescence which has changed but the nature of the experience of growing up. Rapid social changes in so many facets of everyday life have conspired to make growing up today 'feel' far less secure and more uncertain and for far longer. The unprecedented increase in recreational drug use is deeply embedded in these social processes since such drug use is both about risk taking but also about using 'time out' to self-medicate in response to the impact of the stresses and strains of both success and failure in 'modern' times.

In the final part of this chapter we challenge the current war-on-drugs discourse developed by consecutive Conservative governments but accepted and maintained by Labour. This whole strategy is based on so many misconceptions and misunderstandings about young people and drugs that it will, in the end, have to be reviewed. By its very nature the process of normalisation demands regulation and *management*. However, the political moment has not yet been reached when the State will accept responsibility for this.

The normalisation of recreational drug use

Although using the term 'recreational' is not without its difficulties, we must begin by emphasising that the normalisation thesis we have developed refers only to the use of certain drugs, primarily cannabis but also nitrates, amphetamines and equivocally LSD and ecstasy. Heroin and cocaine are not included in the thesis. Similarly chaotic combination drug use and dependent 'daily' drug use form no part of our conceptualisation. This is because abstainers, cautious drug users and indeed many of our regular young drug users do not accept or accommodate such approaches to drug taking any more than social drinkers regard violent drunken outbursts or drinking to unconsciousness as an acceptable way to use alcohol. The minority of young people who use 'hard' drugs the hard way are not regarded as recreational drug users by most of their peers.

The concept of normalisation has been used in many contexts but essentially it is concerned with how a 'deviant', often subcultural population or their deviant behaviour is able to be accommodated into a larger grouping or society. For example, the partial assimilation of people with learning difficulties, previously segregated and 'ware-housed', into mainstream communities has often been explained as a process of normalisation (Wolfensberger, 1972).

Normalisation in the context of recreational drug use cannot be reduced to the intuitive phrase 'it's normal for young people to take drugs', that is both to oversimplify and overstate the case. We are concerned only with the spread of deviant activity and associated attitudes from the margins *towards* the centre of youth culture where it joins many other accommodated 'deviant' activities such as excessive drinking, casual sexual encounters and daily cigarette smoking. Although tobacco use is clearly normalised and most young people have tried a cigarette, only a minority are regular smokers and even then their behaviour is only acceptable to their peers in certain settings. So normalisation need not be concerned with absolutes; we are not even considering the possibility that most young Britons will become illicit *drug users*. It is quite extraordinary enough that we have so quickly reached a situation where the majority will have tried an illicit drug by the end of their teens and that in many parts of the UK up to a quarter may be regular recreational drug users.

The key features of our normalisation thesis are as follows.

Drugs availability

We noted in Chapter 4 the incremental rise in drug-offer situations throughout adolescence, so that by the age of 15 a majority of our respondents had been in situations where drugs were available to try or buy and by 18 almost all had been in such situations. In the 'journeys' chapter we showed how behind these figures lie far more potent processes in that drugs are routinely available in school, college, pub and club. Without this ready availability the process of normalisation could not have begun. The commodification of drugs has developed on the back of global processes and it is quite clear that supply cannot be stemmed in free trade, market economies where deregulation, international transport and trade agreements and reductions in frontier controls facilitate drug trafficking as much as legitimate trade (Stares, 1996). Ironically, the rise in drugs seizures, often reported as 'success' in the war-on-drugs discourse, is in fact an indicator of the enormous scale of the movement of undetected illicit drugs.

Drug trying

Although different self-report research techniques produce different rates of drug trying, each approach has plotted sustained upturns during the 1990s. At the beginning of the decade we were finding that one or two in ten of young people, by the age of 18, had ever tried a drug. Prevalence has climbed with each adolescent cohort so that from five to six in ten young Britons are now disclosing drug trying by this age. The trend is quite clear.

The normative nature of drug trying has been further demonstrated by the closure of gender and social-class differences. Traditionally far more young men than women would experiment with drugs. During the 1990s this gender difference has closed rapidly and many studies, like our own, actually record no significant differences by sex. In the same way, being 'middle class' no longer predicts school-aged abstinence and we are now finding that the offspring of 'professional and managerial' parents often have the highest rates of drug trying followed by young people from the lowest socio-economic backgrounds. Given that being black or Asian does not predict higher than average rates of adolescent drug use, the withering of traditional sociological predictor variables is, in political terms, the most challenging aspect of normalisation. If well-behaved, middle-class, sixth-form pupils are trying drugs and higher-education students have voracious drugs appetites (Webb *et al.*, 1996), how can drug trying or use be fundamentally linked to academic failure, delinquency and low self-esteem and thus pathologised. We must also note that drug trying is beginning younger and initiation routinely extends into young adulthood.

Drug use

We have shown how adolescent decision-making journeys have led around a quarter of our samples down the regular-drug-user pathways. Whilst drugs decisions will continue to be dynamic this is a remarkable proportion and a robust measure of normalisation. We have shown in both the pathways and journeys analyses that young people, by and large, make recognisable cost-benefit assessments and the fact that so many broadly settle primarily for cannabis rather than polydrug use is a clear illustration of this. It is important to distinguish at the extremes between the use of cannabis and the use of poly dance drugs in evaluating the scale of normalisation. Whilst many of our regular drug users have moved into combination drug repertoires and look set to continue for some years, as they transfer into the world of nightclubs where dance drug use is endemic (Release, 1997), they remain a discrete minority. Within the dance–nightclub world their behaviour is accepted and indeed celebrated but it is a moot point whether their actual drug taking, which is often judged excessive by more cautious peers, could be easily accommodated outside clubland. On the other hand, the associated dance culture, the style, the music and actual dancing is widely embraced and ecstasy has filtered into more 'everyday' drug taking, for instance at informal parties. On balance, our view is that the young adult dance drug scene of the late 1990s is part of the normalisation process, not in its origins but because it is now sustained by migration from the adolescent drugs pathways we have described (see Measham *et al.*, 1998).

We would want to review this assessment if, in particular, problem drug use becomes prevalent in this population and the dance drug scene becomes the readily identified source. In such circumstances the drugged-up, messed-up clubber might well become a symbol of excess, a techno junkie who has crossed the rubicon beyond the recreational into the problematic and thus beyond wider peer accommodation.

Being drugwise

Although the notion of drugwise youth emerged from our surveys, particularly in the later years, the strongest sense that nearly all young people are drugwise comes from our interview data where abstainers demonstrated their considerable knowledge of the recreational drugs scene simply because they could not escape encounters with drugs and drug users. Whilst a 'soft' incidental measure of normalisation, it is nevertheless an important signal that abstainers have to negotiate and renegotiate their drugs status given that by simply being sociable, studying, training, working and going out at the weekends they regularly receive drug offers and observe drug use. Abstainers, former users and prospective triers were all able and willing to recount drugs stories based on drugs episodes involving siblings, friends, acquaintances and the local pub-club-party scene. Drugs are real to them, they no longer belong to an unknown subcultural world. One result of growing up drugwise was that with intellectual maturity and life experience most abstainers became pragmatic. They drew distinctions between gross misuse of hard drugs on the one hand and 'sensible' recreational use of cannabis and to some extent amphetamines, LSD and ecstasy on the other. This moral accommodation of others' drug use based on a notion of freedom of choice as long as it did not harm anyone else is another essential dimension of the move towards normalisation. For abstainers, drug use remains 'deviant' but it is accommodated and rarely reported to officialdom. There is a growing 'matter of factness' about social drug use amongst contemporary youth. The most potent symbol of this is found in the way drug 'dealing', which carries serious sanctions under the law, is perceived by most young drug users as a sign of trust and friendship. 'Sorting' friends and acquaintances is rarely perceived as a serious criminal offence.

Future intentions

Traditionally, occasional drug trying in adolescence, particularly by well-adjusted young people, was interpreted as an example of 'normal' adolescent experimentation, rule testing and rebelliousness. No doubt these notions still have some explanatory power. However, as our pathways analysis showed, recreational drug use amongst our cohort and samples continues to escalate into young adulthood. The changes in pathways between 17 and 18 years of age were particularly salutary. With over a third of former triers returning to in transition and no less than 37 per cent of those previously in transition becoming current drug users in Year 5, we can see that prospective drug use or future intentions to try or reuse particular drugs remain powerful. This open-mindedness about future drug use often by young adults who went through their adolescence without taking illicit drugs is a further dimension in our particular thesis of normalisation.

Cultural accommodation of the illicit

We have highlighted the fact that developmental 'personality' theories which insist drug use is a sign of abnormality are inappropriate explanatory vehicles. Within sociology and much criminology the other theory most commonly associated with explanations of drug use is subcultural theory. Again, however, because the drug trying we are attempting to explain has moved from being a small minority to majority activity subcultural theory struggles. Indeed, normalisation, because it is about the accommodation of previously 'deviant' activities into mainstream cultural arrangements, sits uncomfortably with subcultural explorations (unless we regard it primarily as a process). In a drugs subculture we find that the purchase, preparation and use of drugs becomes a preoccupation, a central component in users' lives. The armies of young adult, unemployed 'new' heroin users of the 1980s found that because of its physically addictive 'moreish' properties and high price, heroin use soon pulled them into lifestyles which centred on obtaining funds to continue their habit (Parker *et al.*, 1988; Pearson *et al.*, 1986). We find similar subcultural worlds revolving around crack cocaine use at the end of the 1990s (Parker *et al.*, 1998b) and it seems increasingly likely that we will enter the next millenium with regular heroin and combination drug use again becoming prevalent amongst socially excluded youth.

The drug use we have been describing in this study is quite different. It is largely recreational and is centred on less physically addictive drugs. It can be accommodated because most adolescents and young adult users merely fit their leisure into busy lives and then in turn fit their drug use into their leisure and 'time out' to compete alongside sport, holidays, romance, shopping, nights out, drinking and, most important of all, having a laugh with friends. Moreover, as we have seen, such use now belongs as much with females as males and to young people from all social backgrounds.

If anything, the 1950s to 1980s characterised 'subcultural' drug use whilst the 1990s has seen the normalisation of a very different type of 'recreational' drug use. British youth culture has accommodated and perhaps facilitated recreational drug use both in terms of what is acceptable for young people to do and in absorbing and accommodating the language and imagery of drugs via the fashion, media, music and drink industries which thrive on youth markets (Parker *et al.*, 1995). The blurring of the licit and the illicit is an important aspect of normalisation. The close relationship, and pick-and-mix approach to drinking, alcohol and recreational drug use we have identified is a salient example.

These then are the six dimensions of our normalisation thesis. Because the process is incomplete, because the epidemiological drama continues to unfold, we cannot be certain that the current trends will continue indefinitely. They will however travel much further towards normalisation in the short term because such powerful social processes, like the proverbial oil tanker, simply do not suddenly change direction or come to a halt. Epidemiological trends, once set as firmly as these clearly are, always have long lives.

Risk taking as a life skill

Although we side-stepped entanglement with the theoretical debate about modernity, be it 'post', 'late' or 'high', we have throughout the study referred to the implications of growing up in modern times. The transition from childhood through adolescence on towards adulthood and full citizenship is now a longer, more uncertain journey. Whether we call this period between childhood and adulthood 'youth' or adolescence and post-adolescence is unimportant. What we are defining is a far longer period of semi-dependency as young people spend more time in education and training, live at home longer, delay marriage and parenting and so on. Whilst objectively the levels of risk of 'failure' are still differentiated by race, gender, wealth, parental background, educational qualifications and neighbourhood, almost all young people *subjectively* experience this long period of uncertainty when they do not feel confident that the right opportunities, jobs and relationships will fall into place. The hardworking A-level student feels 'stressed out' just as much as the bored, under-trained, young shop assistant or indeed young offenders sitting in their cells for six months.

These subjective experiences, the feeling of negotiating in uncertainty, in a 'risk society', are the result of *individualisation* (Beck, 1992) whereby young people accept success or failure, prosperity or poverty as indicative of their own performance. Structural inequalities once emphasised by political and collective action and certain cultural understandings are no longer so loudly advocated as creating life chances by promoting or prohibiting success. Whether you get on is up to you (Roberts *et al.*, 1994). This type of conceptualising is clearly very different from the developmental and 'subcultural' approaches discussed earlier and indeed post-modernity theory in respect of youth culture reminds us that the processions of 'subcultural' youth formations of the post-war years are no longer so differentiated primarily because of the potency of social change in realigning and redefining class and inter-generational relationships (Furlong and Cartmel, 1997).

The normalisation of recreational drug use, we believe, is consistent with this type of theorising. There is a sense in all this that risk management has become routinised. Because the world owes you no favours and cannot tolerate indecision then perhaps taking no risks is simply too risky. You don't know if the education course, the training programme, the job offer will really deliver. You don't know if the shared flat or the cohabitation will work out, indeed there is evidence all around you that things may not. On the other hand, how else do you move on from the bedroom you've inhabited for 18 years, get on and gain your privacy, your independence, the car, the clothes, the foreign holiday; not by winning the lottery, there's no risk of that. Put in this wider context, drugs decisions seem rather less dramatic. It is those adults unable to comprehend how much more complicated growing up has become who create the drama as the moral panics documented in the first chapter illustrate.

This does not make drug taking safe or the drug user right. We have documented enough ill-conceived, drug-using adventures and self-admissions of poor, often intoxicated, judgements to undermine such a conclusion. On the other hand rational decisions about consumption do lie at the heart of the normalisation thesis as they do with the McDonaldisation of modern societies. Our drug users are essentially extending the same decision-making processes to illicit drugs as others do in respect of cigarette smoking or drinking alcohol or indeed horse riding, hang gliding or mountaineering. It's your decision, you take the risks, you weigh the enjoyment and functional advantages to your life of your social habits against the potential dangers and pitfalls. Significantly, the illegality of drug use and supplying is, as we have seen, rarely perceived as a key risk factor. This, interestingly, is despite the fact that in 1996 40,000 people were cautioned for cannabis possession in England and Wales compared with 4,000 in 1986. The rate of prosecution for possession has doubled to 24,000 over the same period and up to one thousand young people receive custodial sentences each year (Guardian, 1998).

The connections between our longitudinal study of youth and drugs and this type of theoretical approach have emerged gradually, and testing such an approach was certainly not an overt goal at the outset. In this sense we have used a 'grounded' strategy. Our respondents have spoken to us about the importance of leisure and friends and 'time out' as an antidote to struggles at school, college or on the employment market. They have recognised the need to be economical with the truth about their drug use when talking with adults. Parents' conceptions of risk and danger in respect of drugs are, to their mind, so misinformed and exaggerated that they regard lying as an act of concern for their elders' mental health. The cost-benefit risk assessment with which they decide how far to go to 'buzz' and get 'out of it' via alcohol or illicit drugs is an elaborate process. In reaching and reviewing their decisions, abstainers regularly conclude that drug users must make up their own minds. There is no more potent an expression of individualisation than their often-repeated conclusion that the polydrug users they know can be tolerated because 'it's up to them if they want to kill themselves'. In the same way our drug triers and users, certainly once through early adolescence, vehemently refute peer pressure as a key factor in their decision to take drugs. Again they may not always be correct but this is their conclusion. It's how they believe they've got to where they are *vis-à-vis* drugs. They accept individual responsibility.

The followers of the regular drug user pathway, whilst critical of drugs education which is bland or moralistic or unable to mention the positive outcomes of drug use, also readily accept that risk and danger should be emphasised especially to warn off fair-weather experimenters. They are not denying risk nor are most viewing themselves as *invulnerable*. Their judgements may sometimes be poor but they appear to accept occasional bad experiences and negative outcomes as part and parcel of being a drug user. They accept their vulnerability though perhaps deny their mortality.

Rethinking the war on drugs

The misconceptions

In the first chapter we outlined the war-on-drugs discourse showing how it has adapted to different waves of drugs 'problems' from heroin, through ecstasy and raves to young people's drug use. We are now in a better position to highlight the misconceptions and misunderstandings built into this *political* strategy to fight drug 'abuse' in young people.

Firstly the war-on-drugs discourse, as laid out in *Tackling Drugs Together* and reiterated without revision by New Labour, sees a direct link between teenage drug trying and crime. Young drug takers, even users of cannabis it is argued, will quickly become addicted to or disinhibited by their drugs and become young offenders spiralling out of control into a life of drugs and crime. The way to support this argument is to show that persistent young offenders take drugs from an early age, usually beginning with cannabis. This can of course be demonstrated; it is usually true that the small minority of young people who become persistent offenders from early adolescence also use drugs (Graham and Bowling, 1995). In each generation we find a disordered and damaged minority who are delinquents in adolescence and who have a tendency to remain criminogenic into their thirties (Moffitt, 1993). However, we could also say that this group tended to drink alcohol excessively even before their drug use so should we 'blame' alcohol? They also tended to grow up in care, be excluded from school and run away a lot. They often need psychiatric help (Rutter and Smith, 1994). Their drinking, like their drug use, is associated with their disordered and delinquent careers but it does not cause their anti-social behaviour. Their lives would be little different with or without designer drinks or illicit drugs.

We have tracked such young people in this study but again they are a very small minority in any representative normal population. They are the exceptions and for this reason, whilst we need a specific strategy to deal with their problems and those they cause, we should not build an overall approach around them. For most young people recreational drug use, whilst itself illegal, is funded from the legitimate means of pocket money and part-time earnings. Moreover, as we have shown, our sample, including the drug users, mostly have either no or very light delinquent antecedents.

The second misconception is linked to the first but emphasises the addiction rather than crime spiral. However, there are very few signs of dependency in this recreational scene. Obviously we can find examples of this relationship and of course if we interview heroin or crack cocaine users they routinely display early polydrug use in their antecedents (Parker and Bottomley, 1996). However, much like our 'damaged' persistent delinquents, this pathway to problem drug use is rarely taken and again we find that most who take it have atypical social or psychological characteristics and vulnerabilities, many of which they share with the minority of drinkers who become alcoholics.

The next misconception which is widely held is that young people are pressured into drug use. Once again there are fragments of truth here and we too have found cases where, on reflection, older adolescents look back on initiations where they felt pressured. But again this is not usually the case. Our samples have insisted that they have made their own drugs decisions for which they take responsibility. They acknowledge peer influence but cite many other reasons such as curiosity, the need to relax and most of all rational hedonism. Not only is the notion of peer pressure as the central component of drug trying misconceived but it is a source of resentment to many young people when expounded by adults delivering drugs education. Moreover, as we have argued, because adolescents are social, peer-focused beings, almost everything they do can be located in peer effects. This gets us nowhere.

The prevention side of the war-on-drugs industry has developed a number of engaging arguments to defend and succour their position. Faced with the argument that, despite their expensive efforts – well in excess of £100 million a year simply to attempt to prevent young Britons taking drugs (Parker, 1997) – adolescent drug use continues to climb, they sigh with exasperation. There is, they point out, a simple reason for this. So dreadful is the problem that the war must be waged with far more intensity. More money must be spent, more time dedicated to prevention, more shock horror videos made and so on. There is, for them, no other explanation. The suggestion that evaluations of numerous programmes (Dorn and Murji, 1992) are not encouraging is thus ignored. Instead, the warriors reel off the anecdotes: examples of the young person whose death was ecstasy related, the drug-crazed young delinquent who terrorised a neighbourhood and the young woman who said she took drugs because her boyfriend pressured her. All these examples could be true. Their atypicality is ignored, however, because to acknowledge this would be to admit the need to make ideological room for a rational debate. The most extreme of the warriors go further. Non-believers must be suspect. 'You're a legaliser then?', 'You think drugs are good then, do you?', 'You allow your children to take drugs?', 'So you think drugs are safe?'

In short, the resistance to discussing the meaning of young people's drug use and considering how to manage it at a societal level is very strong. It stems from a deep and genuine fear of illicit drug use, a hedonism taboo and a misunderstanding of the distinctions between drugs and types of use. Whilst we have noted signs of the gulf between parents and young people narrowing at a familial level and amongst many of those who work directly with young people, this process has not yet occurred in the highly politicised public-policy debate.

Inconsistent regulation

Because young people's drug use seems unlikely to be a mere fashion or fad and because it has become entangled in the wider moral panic about and blaming of youth described in the first chapter then the last plank of normalisation, a truce between adults and youth about drugs, remains unlaid. Our own view is that strategic pragmatism will prevail but not for several years yet. Whilst no-one knows exactly how the UK will go about managing the normalisation of recreational drug use we do know the shortcomings and dysfunctions of current 'policy' which we should expect any new strategy to address and alleviate.

The ineffective use of resources on primary prevention is minor compared with the resources spent on enforcement. The processing of young people for cannabis possession dominates the policing contact with normalisation as it does all cautioning and prosecuting under the Misuse of Drugs Act. One of the unfortunate consequences of this is that each of the 43 police forces in England and Wales adopt slightly different official and unofficial responses. What happens to a young person found with cannabis is determined more by where he is pro-cessed than by what he has done. Formal responses vary from an on-the-spot warning to an informal caution, to a formal citable caution, to prosecution. Even more worryingly, whilst official policies vary, informal practices are also inconsistent. It is quite acceptable, 'unofficially' for officers simply to drop the offending drug down the drain and finger wag in some police areas, whereas this practice is genuinely discouraged in others. These inconsistencies are perpetrated through the courts. This differential distribution of justice can block educational, occupational and career routes or lead to dismissal in some jobs. 'Enforcement' at school or college is equally a lottery with well over a thousand young people being excluded for drugs incidents from English schools alone each year. These responses not only blight a young person's 'reputation' but make reintegration into the educa-tion system very difficult. Moreover being left at home and 'hanging out' for many months instead of being at school may not be the best way of preventing escalation of drug use if that is a probability in a particular young person. The Home Secretary's son, William Straw, might wish to count himself very lucky that his school took no action against him for supplying cannabis (*Sunday Times*, 28 December 1997).

These diverse and punitive responses are, as we have shown, much talked about by young people through drugs stories. Whilst for abstainers and the cautious ones they may act as a deterrent, they also reinforce the sense of unease with which young people view adult responses to them. Our interviewees often quoted the randomness and inconsistency of official responses as a symptom of the confusion and hypocrisy adults demonstrate in their reactions, particularly to cannabis. The moral authority of 'the law' was seen as badly undermined. This does little to facilitate citizenship and much to further disenchant young people in respect of politics, policing and public services.

The neglect of the public-health dimension

The war-on-drugs approach, because it has difficulty accepting that young people choose to take certain drugs and because it often pathologises those who do, has great difficulty dealing with reducing the harm or risks associated with drug use. To address these issues seriously involves accepting that drug use occurs and treating the user as a citizen – both of which grate with the most committed warriors. We see the hegemony of their approach when we consider how those very risks, dangers and worries, which our young drug users have raised, could be reduced by official intervention.

Again, 'on the ground' we have a growing number of examples of harm-reduction practices but these are barely sanctioned in government strategy. Ideally this situation would be rectified through a holistic strategy supported by legislation and guidance through 'good practice' instructions. Here we merely give a handful of examples of how the public-health imperative is being jeopardised by the 'unreal' drugs debate which dominates public and government thinking.

Currently street drugs are quality unassured. They are not tested or regulated or codified in any official way. Drug dealers at the local level, the 'friends of friends' chain and the users have no idea what they are selling, buying or simply sharing. At present it is only the rules of encounter in the illegal market which maintain quality. We have heard many of our young subjects complain about badly cut amphetamines and unpredictable LSD doses. Many of the bad experiences and acute incidents have been put down to poor quality drugs. We know that a proportion of drugs-related deaths are linked to impurities or indeed exceptional and unexpected purity in the cases of heroin users. There are very few substances consumed by the public which are not regulated and inspected and yet young Britons ingest tens of millions of 'doses' of illicit drugs each week. It is estimated, for instance, that a million ecstasy-like tablets are consumed each week in the UK (Parliamentary Office of Science and Technology, 1996).

We have shown how, through the sharing of information and experiences and recounting of 'drugs stories', young people try to reduce the risks of bad or very bad experiences from drugs adventures. There are undoubtedly harm-reduction messages available, usually through voluntary street agency 'flyers', to help guide young users. However, this information is hard to come by and is generally not delivered to school-aged adolescents even in a targeted way, for instance, to those dance drug users who even at 16 are attending clubs and raves. The mixing of alcohol and drugs, particularly on weekend nights out, was at the source of so many bad experiences and worrying incidents recounted during this study. Here is a harm-reduction message demanding broadcast yet one which cannot be easily sent because of political sensibilities and the Establishment's need to keep alcohol and drugs in separate compartments.

Similarly, because of the generation gulf and distrust of adult reactions, noted in the earlier chapters, young drug users were reluctant to disclose their drug use to relatives or the family doctor even when they felt their drug taking might be causing or triggering ill health. This is an extremely worrying outcome both for young people and health professionals who are likely to misdiagnose and thus inappropriately treat their patients.

A further and related feature of official neglect of the public-health imperative concerns the scientific knowledge deficit about the middle-term and long-term health effects of regular sustained dance drugs–poly drug use. We know that toxicity and neurotoxicity are increased by dose and regularity of use and that multiple drug ingestion tends to increase toxicity over and above the sum of the individual drugs (Parliamentary Office of Science and Technology, 1996). What we do not know is whether today's adolescent and young adult drug users are slowly damaging their health. We are unclear whether or not in 10 or 20 years' time they will be susceptible to physical or more likely mental health problems perhaps related to seretonin transmitter damage in the brain.

Finally, the public-health dimension embraces the wider population. Whilst driving after drinking alcohol is an activity associated with middle-aged and older Britons rather than youth, today's young

Britons are far less fastidious about drug driving. The need to recognise this emerging problem and take responsibility for its management is yet another example of a failure to protect the public.

There is little doubt that the war-on-drugs approach of consecutive Conservative administrations has been responsible for the neglect of the public health dimension. In firstly 'wasting' the early 1990s through neglect and then developing the *Tackling Drugs Together* approach with all its misconceptions, government has been unable to embrace and face the scale of normalisation and in turn has failed to recognise the need to manage and regulate the public-health implications. This contrasts with the multiplicity of public-health initiatives sanctioned when the injecting drug user–HIV connection was made in the mid 1980s. The strategic pragmatism shown then led to major health gains in respect of reducing needle sharing, unsafe sex and the spread of the HIV/AIDS virus. The difference of course was that it was also the health of non-drug users which was at stake. The just-deserts approach – drug users deserve all the problems they endure – had to be temporarily subverted.

Waiting for the truce

We are, unfortunately, some way away from the political moment when the dysfunctions of the war-on-drugs strategy can be addressed. The important public-policy issues – about how we deal with otherwise law-abiding young citizens caught with drugs in their possession, and about how we ensure the health and safety of young people who use drugs – remain unresolved. This is because the complexities of drug use in the 1990s are obscured by ideological and political dogma and most of all by a lack of empathy for young people trying to grow up in modern times. We must wait for a truce before we can face up to the truth.

We turn now to an updated analysis of the normalisation debate, taking into account the experiences of our cohort as they progress through their early adult years.

Illegal Leisure Revisited: the runaway train of normalisation

Looking back over the 12 years since *Illegal Leisure* was first published, no one is more surprised than us by how widely the concept of normalisation came to be discussed, adopted and developed, not just amongst drugs researchers but also within policy circles and amongst practitioners. It is perhaps because normalisation captured something of the zeitgeist of the 1990s, a crossroads in both drug use and drug policy, that it developed as it did. So it is to the historical and cultural context of those early surveys that we first return in our final chapter, before providing our concluding thoughts on how the normalisation thesis has developed in the twenty-first century.

Reflecting back on the early days of the study, perhaps overshadowed by subsequent developments, the primary aim was to explore the relationship between *alcohol* and offending; indeed the first three surveys were funded by the Alcohol Education and Research Council. What was captured in those early years, by chance, was an unexpected and marked upturn in drug use by young people in their early teens. Having documented the 1980s heroin outbreaks (Parker *et al.*, 1988), the first notable feature of our cohort was that they were the 'post-heroin generation' (Measham *et al.*, 1993). Furthermore, not only was a new generation of teenagers using drugs in new ways, we found few statistically significant differences in terms of gender or school class catchment area: the girls in the leafy suburban schools were as likely to be trying cannabis, speed or LSD in those early days as the lads on the estates. Our surveys were the first to capture this increased adolescent drug use that then came to be replicated in both adolescent and adult drug surveys across the decade across the UK. The question raised for the early researchers on the project was why had drug use increased so much and amongst such a diverse group of young people? The point to note here, then, is that the concept of normalisation emerged, very much *grounded* in the trends that we had uncovered and tied in the early days to these unprecedented prevalence levels that took us all by surprise (Measham *et al.*, 1994).

The political context to the early years of this study also seem significant to us. In writing of the new post-heroin generation that emerged in the early 1990s in the UK, our discussions with the young people that we met in schools suggested a stark contrast to public perceptions of drug use at that time. As discussed in Chapter 1, drug use in the 1980s was characterised by a heroin epidemic which took a heavy toll on working-class and socially excluded young people, specifically unemployed young men located in cities, towns and ports with redundant heavy industry. This was very different to the young people who spoke to us in schools about their own, their friends and their families' use of cannabis, amphetamines, perhaps a little ecstasy or LSD at the weekends; to them associated with the pleasures of the weekend, rather than the problems of life. Whilst we wanted to convey our feelings at the magnitude of change in the early 1990s – the 'shock of the new', musically, stylistically and pharmacologically, as the UK emerged out of economic recession – it was also an attempt to challenge both the prevailing discourse of drug users as 'junkies' and the recurrent problematisation of young people and their leisure (Pearson, 1983).

Thus, the underlying political thrust of normalisation was an attempt to cast young people in a more positive light, as reasonable, responsible agents making their drug-taking decisions, weighing up the costs and benefits of their actions, carefully deciding which drugs to take or to avoid. In exploring the increase in weekend, occasional and 'recreational' drug use at this time, it distinguished such usage from the discourse surrounding 'junkies' slave to their daily fix, epitomised by the 'Heroin Screws You Up' public health campaign. This pharmacological shift away from the 1980s required also an appropriate explanatory shift away from the structural, subcultural and psychological explanations, all of which presupposed drug use to be evidence of pathology of one sort or another, and which clearly did not fit our data. Thus we utilised a cost-benefit analysis (Coffield and Gofton, 1994), adapting rational actor theory to the 'sensible' adolescent recreational drug use of the majority (Parker *et al.*, 2002), through a detailed consideration of how young people themselves perceived the individual risks and rewards from drug use in order to make their drug decisions.

We concluded that there were two obvious policy responses to the increased drug use that we had uncovered across the social spectrum in the 1990s. Given the sheer numbers undeterred by illegality, criminalisation and potential consequences in later life for possession of an occasional cannabis joint, this raised the question of how a government should respond to mass, low-level law-breaking. A government can either persist in its attempts to protect young people and deter drug use and cast its net wide(r) or reconsider the aims and efficacy of a particular law. So one possible policy option discussed in our 1998 conclusion was the depenalisation of cannabis, the most widely used drug. This policy option was subsequently (briefly) considered in 2004–9 when cannabis was downgraded from Class B to Class C (and where the government advisory body the ACMD thinks it should have remained), although Class B status was subsequently reapplied. A second policy option we discussed was a commitment to well resourced harm reduction initiatives implemented at the local level through health, education and drugs services, in order to reduce the harm to the individual user, their communities and wider society.

Thus the concept of normalisation was historically and culturally context specific – we attempted to describe what we found at that time in that place. Normalisation made no grander claims in terms of providing an explanatory framework for all drug use. It is therefore with surprise that we note the application, development and even dismissal of the relevance of normalisation as an explanatory model of drug use elsewhere. As the normalisation debate has spread, it has been tested and applied to a wide range of drug users: from Australian clubbers (Duff, 2005) to Scandinavian cannabis smokers (Järvinen and Demant, 2010), and with ongoing projects across Europe, North America and Australasia testing and developing the thesis further. Interesting developments include its expansion from the macro to the micro level, for example, in the work of Pennay and Moore (2010).

Critique of the normalisation thesis and our response

Early critique of the normalisation concept as applied to adolescent drug taking emerged in the late 1990s from Shiner and Newburn (1997, 1999), although the first of these was published before *Illegal Leisure*, in which we first comprehensively described the process of normalisation and the evidence we took to support it. Shiner and Newburn's critique pointed to what were seen to be two fundamental problems with the idea of normalisation. The first charge was that we selectively used evidence that exaggerated young people's drug involvement: the 'big' numbers. For example, we were seen to have made more of 'lifetime' prevalence of drug taking, producing figures suggesting drug-involvement amongst our 16 year olds by the majority (51 per cent), when we ought to have highlighted the much lower levels of past month drug taking (28 per cent for our 16 year olds), a statistic much more likely to include only the regular or 'real' drug users amongst our adolescents. In a similar vein, we were criticised for (ostensibly) not having distinguished more between types of drugs, noting, for example, that adolescent drug use was predominantly the use of cannabis rather than Class As, and between different kinds of drug use (for example, between polydrug use, one-off use, or more sustained use that has stopped).

The early publications on which these critiques were based (Measham *et al.*, 1994; Parker *et al.*, 1995) did, in fact, distinguish between different drugs, as well as between lifetime and more recent use. And the first edition of *Illegal Leisure* (which 'crossed', in publication terms, with these critiques) was the first amongst UK surveys to go beyond the limitations particular to adolescents of using recent drug use as 'proxy' measures for regular use (see Aldridge *et al.*, 1999). Thus, we attempted to disentangle the various drug pathways that adolescents took through their drug-taking decisions, for example differentiating abstainers from ex-users, and current users from those 'in transition'. Nevertheless, this accusation of exaggeration is important, as it points to a perception implicit in the critique that we were painting adolescent drug taking as 'the norm': as normal as a cup of tea (Shiner and New-burn, 1999). To demonstrate, as Shiner and Newburn saw themselves as doing, that far less than a majority of young people were actually regular or committed drug users, was effectively to lay bare the flaw in our argument. But if it was not clear before, the final chapter of *Illegal Leisure* stated plainly that normalisation was never 'concerned with absolutes' or mere prevalence levels; it was enough for us to discover that the majority of our respondents had *tried* an illicit drug by the age of 18. Of the various criteria that we pointed to as evidence of normalisation (availability and use of drugs, drug knowledge, and the cultural accommodation of the illicit), none of these were absolute states that had been reached, finding us at a point where drug taking was 'normal'. Instead, we pointed to *movement* in the perceptions of some kinds of drug taking: from the margins towards the mainstream. Normalisation, for us, was a *process*, and we were certain that this process was a key to understanding the changes underway amongst 1990s adolescents. Parker (2005) came to describe normalisation as a 'barometer of change', ideologically neutral about the rightness or wrongness of drug-taking's social acceptability, but a useful tool in locating the *extent* of social acceptability, and the *direction* of movement away from or towards that point.

The second problem identified with the normalisation thesis in these critiques concerned the extent to which adolescents of the 1990s actually believed drug taking to be acceptable behaviour. Perhaps many more adolescents were taking drugs: but did they really think that doing so was 'normal' and okay? Buried beneath a superficial veneer of approval ('everyone does it', 'it's ok so long as it is only soft drugs') Shiner and Newburn read implicit disapproval. Young drug users, they argued, held the very same values – in common with wider society – that using illegal drugs is wrong. What might appear as approval was instead the attempt by young drug users to neutralise the guilt that resulted from engaging in a behaviour they ultimately felt to be wrong. Far from considering drug taking to be normal and okay, drug-using young people, for example, reacted in a strongly negative fashion to the real or hypothesised drug use of a younger sibling (Shiner and Newburn, 1997).

Shiner and Newburn's critique used neutralisation theory, as formulated by Matza (1964) and Sykes and Matza (1957). Neutralisation theory stood counter to the contention of subcultural theorists that youthful delinquents rebelled by rejecting the dominant social values of wider society, and replaced these instead with their own delinquent values. Matza and Sykes, in contrast, believed that delinquent youth retained broad commitment to wider societal values, and were able to persist in their delinquency by justifying or 'neutralising' their behaviour – in effect, making excuses to allow its continuation. Shiner and Newburn, following Matza and Sykes, suggested that the expression of these kinds of neutralising statements by young drug users was evidence of their underlying opposition to drug taking. Hence, drug taking was not socially accommodated, even by users, as the normalisation thesis would suggest.

We concur with only some of Shiner and Newburn's analysis. The neutralising statements made by young drug users to interviewers ('everyone does it', 'it's ok so long as it is only soft drugs') probably are in fact neutralisations. But it is from here that we part company with Shiner and Newburn, who go on to suggest that if young drug users are in fact making neutralising statements, they must inevitably share the wider consensus values within society *including that drug taking is bad.* There is no question that the members of our cohort are broadly conforming, as evidenced by the fairly conventional choices that characterise the lives of most of them at the age of 27 and indeed our normalisation thesis in part developed out of dissatisfaction with the relevance of subcultural theory to our cohort of young people. In no way would we suggest that the clear implication of the normalisation thesis is that 'youth culture is rebel culture' (Shiner and Newburn, 1999: 151). We suggest, contrary to Shiner and Newburn, however, that it may be possible to conform to societal values generally, but to reject some specifics (e.g. 'it's ok to take drugs so long as it's only soft drugs, and it doesn't interfere with your job/family'). Moreover, the use of neutralising statements need not be interpreted, as Shiner and Newburn have, to mean that drug taking is 'wrong'. Instead, neutralising statements can arise simply in *recognition* of existing social sanction. Thus, rationalisations are made – healthily, appropriately – in order to provide a coherent and acceptable personal narrative to a possibly judgemental observer. These are what Maruna and Copes (2005) refer to as 'good' neutralisations, and what Scott and Lyman (1968) refer to as 'justifications' (accepting responsibility for behaviour but rejecting its pejorative sense), as opposed to 'excuses' (accepting the behaviour is wrong, but denying responsibility for it).

We accept, therefore, that young recreational drug users may make neutralising statements, but disagree with Shiner and Newburn that these are evidence of a deeply held belief that drug taking is 'wrong'. And, what is more, all of this sits comfortably alongside a general acceptance of consensus values. Our young – and now adult – drug takers for the most part live conforming lives. But doing so does not preclude the rejection of particular aspects of broader consensus values. Indeed, herein lies the process of normalisation we observed during the 1990s – the beginnings of the social accommodation of illicit drug taking – moving from the margins (use amongst groups characterised by difference, and a wholesale rejection of mainstream values) towards the mainstream (use amongst groups that are generally conforming).

There are other problems we identify with Shiner and Newburn's critique. One of the more compelling, on first glance, pieces of evidence for their suggestion that even drug takers believe drug taking to be wrong is the negative reaction of their interviewees to the suggestion of a younger sibling's drug use. We concur with Maruna and Copes (2005), commenting in relation to interviewing in neutralisation research generally, who point to the 'demand characteristics' of the interview situation, which make clear who, between the interviewer and interviewee, is the deviant. Interviews like these are highly likely to produce 'artificially created' neutralisations. We suggest that 'cues' in the research context indicating to interviewees what may be socially acceptable replies may have been especially salient to Shiner and Newburn's interviewees. Their teenage research participants were interviewed as part of an evaluation of the peer approach to drugs education, and interviews took place mostly in schools. Even if these adolescents are completely honest in their replies, when faced with an adult interviewer that these adolescents are likely to assume holds anti-drug beliefs, justifications for their engagement in illegal drug taking are highly likely to emerge. Indeed, such justifications for drug taking may be cognitively inevitable for those engaging in behaviour for which there are both legal sanctions and disapproval in certain sections of society. Maruna and Copes refer to this as the 'normality of neutralisations' (2005: 65): ordinary human behaviour in which we all engage.

We do not contend, in our response to Shiner and Newburn's critique, that their respondents were less than truthful in their replies to the interviewer. We simply interpret their responses differently. The justifications of these adolescent drug users, in the form of highly negative reactions to the suggestion of a younger sibling's drug use, are likely to be designed to demonstrate themselves to the interviewer as a certain kind of person: one who 'cares' about a young family member. Adolescent drug users must certainly understand that all substance use – including the use of alcohol and drugs – carries health risks, and some forms of substance use additionally carry risks that result from breaking the law. This recognition of risk need not imply that adolescents believe, for example, that occasional cannabis use is morally 'wrong' in addition to carrying risk. Who amongst us could resist the opportunity to answer a question – about a younger sibling, a son, a daughter – in a way that casts us in a positive light? Demonstrating that one does not wish a loved one to engage in potentially harmful activity does not (inevitably) mean that one believes that activity to be morally wrong or bad. And none of this means that drug-using adolescents themselves are not broadly in agreement with mainstream social values.

A related accusation of exaggeration against the normalisation thesis concerned the extent to which the supposedly sharply rising trends in adolescent drug taking in the early 1990s were as unique as we were making out (see Shiner, 2009; Shiner and Newburn, 1999), or whether, taking a longer historical perspective, there was more continuity with the past than we had been prepared to admit. We concluded in Chapter 1 that, based on national prevalence data, today's generation of adolescents have roughly similar levels of drug taking to that found amongst our cohort's generation – the teenagers of the early 1990s. This in itself suggests a degree of continuity, though we are careful not to overstate this: levels of drug taking found amongst early 1990s adolescents occurred on the back of increasing trends, whereas the opposite is true for today's adolescents. Nevertheless, it is correct that our analysis was not grounded in the long view, historically speaking, and the importance of historical perspective is clear. The consumption of psychoactive substances is documented back to ancient times (see Blackman, 2004) and across almost all societies and tribal groups (Klein, 2008), and it is inevitable that the social acceptability of substances fluctuates around individual substances, around styles of use, and around sanctions and regulations that have come and gone.

In the first edition of *Illegal Leisure*, we stated very precisely that normalisation referred to the use of only certain drugs, and counted primarily cannabis, but also nitrites, amphetamines, and with less certainty, LSD and ecstasy in the list. We debated the question of which drugs the normalisation thesis should be seen to refer to, and never reached complete consensus amongst ourselves on the question. Was normalisation as a concept only to be applied to the drugs most likely to be taken by young people? Or were specific substances not the issue but instead the 'sensible' use of them (see Parker *et al.*, 2002)? It is interesting to return to this question now, in light of having revisited the cohort in adulthood. If our teenagers in the mid 1990s were certain of anything, it was that cocaine powder was in no way acceptable or accommodated by them; it was a drug that went hand-in-hand with heroin (and crack cocaine), and was for them beyond the pale. But before another decade was complete, nationally, and amongst our cohort, cocaine powder had become the second most popular drug after cannabis. Does this mean that normalisation as a concept must be changed as fashions in drugs both come (cocaine) and go (LSD)? Can even excess (as opposed to sensibility) be accommodated so long as it is controlled excess (the 'controlled loss of control', Measham, 2002), in bounded and negotiated times and places, much as many might agree applies to occasional, even rowdy, drunkenness?

Perhaps all along the concept ought to have been attached, in a definitional sense, simply to the use of substances that for the first time in recent history includes the illegal and illicit amongst them. We may then accept that the characteristics of normalisation – how it manifests itself – will change. This kind of approach allows for the popularity of particular drugs to come and go, and for styles of consumption to allow for more or less 'excess' at some times than at others, just as trends in types of alcoholic beverage (from beers to wines and spirits) and styles of alcohol consumption ('binge' drinking or home drinking, for example) fluctuate over time. And of course all of this allows for the process of normalisation to be reversed, as has been occurring for cigarette smoking over recent decades.

Developments in the normalisation debate

There are three key strands of development in the debate since we first described our thesis in 1998 that we wish to highlight here. Firstly, in our emphasis on the rationality of adolescents in their drug-taking decisions, some of the sensuality (Jackson, 2004), the emotionality (Measham, 2004b) and perhaps even irrationality of drug use was overlooked. The work of Griffin and colleagues (2009) has highlighted the allure of altered states of intoxication for young adults in relation to alcohol – the purposeful pursuit of drunken excess to the point of memory loss. In our desire to project the rational cost-benefit analysis and the general reasonableness of young people, some of the compulsions, cravings, passions, pleasures, irrational consumption and simple utter 'caning' was lost.

Secondly, our emphasis on agency – on young people as rational beings making calculated drug-taking decisions – not surprisingly has led researchers more recently to re-emphasise the role of structure. Despite the apparently 'free' choices we make, 'big' variables like gender, poverty, ethnicity and social class continue to function to limit and shape these choices, even as actors often remain unaware of them. For us, in the context of the early 1990s and grounded in our data on adolescent drug use, variables like gender, social class and ethnic considerations seemed less relevant in explaining drug involvement than in previous decades. Indeed: we found evidence of drug trying and use across the socio-economic spectrum, including not only inner-city youth, and not just boys and young men.

The emphasis on agency over structure in our early formulation of the normalisation thesis became a key area for subsequent refinement and reconsideration. The in-depth interviews provided us with the opportunity to look deeper into the lives of our cohort and, in so doing, we uncovered the ways in which structural determinants remain central to young people and to their drug pathways. This reconsideration of structure also became a key feature of recent reconsiderations of the normalisation thesis. Shildrick (2002) and MacDonald and Marsh (2002), for example, developed a notion of 'differentiated normalisation' in order to incorporate the relevance of socio-economic class to our understanding of drug use amongst different groups of young people. Shildrick, in her research on drug use amongst socially excluded young people, found the expression of a range of attitudes towards drug use, ranging from 'cautious and critical' to 'tolerant and accepting' (2002: 44). MacDonald and Marsh (2002) similarly found anti-drug views held by young people who were complete abstainers living in a severely 'excluded' part of north-east England, and even though the area had widespread drug use. This attempt to bridge the divide between research traditions that some have argued downplay the influence of social structures in understanding youth cultures and more mainstream approaches to understanding youth transitions is also apparent in MacDonald and Shildrick's (2007) invoking of the 'leisure career'.

The work of Measham (2002, 2004b) and Østergaard (2007) has explored the continued relevance of gender to our understanding of the meanings, motivations and consequences of alcohol and drug use for young people, reminding us, as Shildrick did for social class, that gender remains one of the important 'big' variables that shapes behaviour in ways that explanations relying on human agency alone do not address. Furthermore, in a recent synthesis of the normalisation thesis and its critique, Measham and Shiner (2009) directly address the application of the agency-structure debate to young people's drug use, arguing for the balance to tip back from its 1990s emphasis on agency through an interplay of social structure and human agency. Drawing on the conceptual developments by Laub and Sampson (2003) on 'situated choice' and Messerschmidt (1997) on 'structured action', they explore how individual decisions or actions are understood within the framework and structural limitations of their social condition, concluding that normalisation is 'a contingent process negotiated by distinct social groups operating in bounded situations' (2009: 502).

Thirdly, in terms of the political impact of our work, whilst we concluded 12 years ago that our empirical data could support decriminalisation and harm reduction (see also Aldridge, 2008), in fact the unprecedented levels of drug use were used to support a decade of drug policy which has instead focused on increased enforcement and prevention, reduced funding for harm reduction and an absence of treatment initiatives for non-offending, non-opiate users. As Blackman argues convincingly (2004, 2007): rather than normalisation potentially being a force for positive change, the increased prevalence and associated debate surrounding drugs being as 'normal' as a cup of tea (Shiner and Newburn, 1999) was used as justification for increased policing and enforcement of the Misuse of Drugs Act as regards young people, leading to an increasingly prohibitionist rather than reforming agenda.

Reflections on revisiting our cohort

We have followed our cohort from their early teens through to their late twenties, so where does that leave our concept of normalisation now, particularly given that not only has our cohort aged but the prevalence of drug taking has fallen across the country? For us, unlike for many of our critics (e.g., Shiner and Newburn, 1997), raw prevalence rates were not the only, nor indeed the central component of the normalisation thesis. Our recognition of social change related as much to understanding how the drug decisions that people make influence how drug taking can fit into ordinary, everyday lives. In short, our thesis rested as much on cultural and attitudinal change amongst drug users and non-users as upon upward trends in prevalence, and for this reason we can identify the threads of normalisation continuing as we follow our cohort into middle adulthood.

This is not to deny that, as one would expect, we are seeing a 'settling down' with lower levels of drug use as our cohort progresses towards their thirties. Past year use of any drug fell from around five or six in ten respondents from age 18 to 22, to around one third at the age of 27, and past month use from about one third to one fifth. This downward trend, however, draws our attention to *relative* levels of use – decline – at the same time as it detracts our attention away from seeing the absolute levels of use, on which we are inclined to focus here. By the age of 27, with most in full-time employment and in long-term relationships, half with mortgages and many with children of their own, our cohort appear to be a fairly conventional and conforming group of young adults. That so many continue to engage in regular drug taking from adolescence well into adulthood speaks to a remarkable stability in drug taking. A wide range of drugs appear to be readily available to them, which sustains diverse weekend polydrug repertoires into middle adulthood (see also Pearson, 2001). Their levels of use at the age of 27 (in 2004) are broadly similar to national levels for their age at around the same time, although we find three times the level of past year cocaine use, and twice the level of ecstasy use, in our cohort compared to national levels. These findings are particularly compelling given that our cohort over the years has become considerably less drug involved than the original sample due to disproportionate attrition of drug users. The fact that they are able to accommodate their drug taking into home, work and family life demonstrates something of a 'commitment' to drug use (Moore, 2004). In spite of reductions in drug taking across the noughties, levels of use amongst our cohort sit not far from historically high levels, as they do for young people nationally (see also Aldridge, 2008).

As social relationships changed from adolescence to adulthood for our cohort, some described how they no longer had easy access to drugs, or how drug use was no longer socially accommodated within their friendship groups, which they offered as an explanation for their total desistance from, or growing moderation in, drug use. Interviewees also spoke about moderating use to deal with the problems that over-indulgence had brought, and explained how their drug use must be fitted in around other life responsibilities such as parenthood, jobs or even mundane house cleaning. Whilst this could be interpreted as counter-normalisation (the discourse of 'settling down'), equally it speaks to us as evidence of normalisation rather than its reverse. What is normalisation in adulthood if not the accommodation of psycho-active experiences into everyday life? Similarly, growing concerns about long-term health effects are also a normal feature of adulthood at this age, for both drug users and non-users. That our adult drug users regularly spoke of moderating or revising their drug consumption in recognition of possible long-term consequences is the normal 'adult' corollary of the short-term consequences that concerned our cohort in their teens, when they, for example, avoided drinking heavily when smoking cannabis to avoid unpleasant 'whiteys'. Far from being fright-ening and out-of-control drug-taking adults, normalisation speaks instead to drug taking that appears mostly well controlled and accom-modated into ordinary daily life, daily life that is probably not all that different to those who seek evening and weekend time-out, relaxation and fun through alcohol consumption.

Our response to the critique seems realised amongst the drug-using adults in our cohort. These adults do not reject mainstream values – their lives, outside of their drug use, sit comfortably amongst these values. And yet, whether we see them as justifying or 'neutralising' their drug taking or not, they appear to accept drug taking as a fairly ordinary, normal activity that is 'okay'. Nowhere is the evidence for normalisation stronger than amongst what we have referred to as the 'opportunistic users' in the cohort. A significant minority of adults are happy to partake when the opportunity arises, but do not vigorously or regularly seek out those opportunities and think little of it whether partaking or not. Indeed, it is this very ordinariness of opportunistic usage that strikes us as evidence of adult normalisation – very similar to the role that alcohol plays in many drinkers' lives. In a world where illicit drugs are not well accommodated, opportunistic users probably would not flourish like this – instead, users would be of the more committed variety, a subcultural and self-identified group united against a hostile society (Becker, 1963).

Normalisation and official responses

An additional dimension that can be employed to assess the evidence for the normalisation thesis is the extent to which normalisation may be evident in government responses to drug use. When we wrote the first edition of *Illegal Leisure*, the policy options that seemed obvious to us in recognising the increasing levels and social acceptability of recreational drug taking included harm reduction initiatives and a ratcheting *down* of criminal justice sanctions. But even policy developments that ratchet *up* enforcement through the criminal justice system (see Reuter and Stevens, 2007) can be seen to reflect an acknowledgement that drug taking is an increasingly common – if dangerous – activity (Huggins, 2007). Writing in 2005, Parker identified a 'welcome, fundamental shift in the official thinking about the need to recognise recreational drug use being widespread but distinctive from problem drug use' (2005: 213). Indeed, some developments over the past ten years in relation to public health information provision targeted at adolescent recreational polydrug users and the first reclassification (downward) of cannabis represented important moves in this direction.

More recently, however, we see policy developments with decidedly contrary implications for normalisation. If there was one drug that we felt confident could be described as normalised in the 1990s, in terms of prevalence, patterns and attitudes to the drug, then it was cannabis. Yet cannabis has changed in terms of assessments of potential harm to users with the advent of the much more potent strain 'skunk', and associated patterns of use which shows signs of being problematic, daily or dependent, particularly amongst young men aged 16–24. Concerns about links between cannabis and mental illness emerged alongside the hydroponic homegrown market in skunk with a high THC content (Murray *et al.*, 2007) leading to a high profile campaign by the media (Daily Mail, 2007a, 2007b). The Daily Mail campaign against skunk continued after its rescheduling, fuelled by research by Murray and colleagues at the London Institute of Psychiatry finding that skunk smokers are seven times more likely to suffer from psychosis (di Forti *et al.*, 2009). In a recent review of the evidence on cannabis, Macleod and Hickman, by contrast, noted that the relationship between cannabis and psychosis may be due to 'residual confounding and measurement error . . . That is not to say they are not causal – they might be, but it is simply impossible to know' (2010: 1338). Amidst the calls for evidence-based policy in respect of cannabis and other drugs, we can see the considerable challenges for both researchers and policy makers where 'evidence' is as hotly disputed amongst the academics as policy is amongst the politicians. In such a climate, there is a greater need than ever for stakeholders to forge an understanding borne of respect rather than expectation or obligation, recognizing the complex and non-linear nature of the relationship between academic findings, political decision making and the democratic process (Black, 2001). The challenge for Britain's coalition government, for academic researchers and for the ACMD is to carry forward a more sophisticated understanding of psychoactive drugs, the positive and negative effects of drug use, as well as of the intended and unintended consequences not just from drug use and supply, but also from drug policy.

As we have noted, current polydrug experimentation continues well into adulthood, with an increased range of drugs in recent years. Whilst we see ebbs and flows in the use of individual drugs like amphetamine, cocaine or ketamine across the years related to availability, price, purity and preferences, overall we can see a robust and continued demand for weekend psychostimulants. Clubbers and party-goers tend to be at the forefront of this experimentation and are amongst the most drug-experienced young adults in the UK (e.g. Measham and Moore, 2009); yet such patterns of use also ripple out to the wider population. However, despite two decades of persistent weekend (and sometimes weekday) recreational drug use evidenced in our longitudinal study, there has been a notable lack of policy responses and resources, aside from 'proactive prohibition' (Measham and Moore, 2008). Rather than decriminalise cannabis as we had speculated in the first edition of

Illegal Leisure, the government has pursued a policy of criminalising the possession and supply of an ever-widening array of psychoactive drugs taken by a small minority of the population, including ketamine, GHB, GBL, BZP, synthetic cannabinoids, substituted cathinones and naphyrone, to which can be added their reconfirmation of the Class A classification of ecstasy and the rescheduling of cannabis to Class B (both despite ACMD recommendations for downgrading: ACMD, 2008, 2009).

In most of the above cases, the recency of uptake, the small numbers involved in their use and in some cases the limited scientific knowledge base surrounding emergent recreational drugs mean that the extent of possible social and medical harms is yet to be fully established. But it is not only in relation to these newer arrivals that the government has used the pre-emptive argument: this has occurred for both cannabis and ecstasy. The pre-emptive argument is significant because it facilitates the cautious and pro-active criminalisation of drugs *before* evidence has emerged and assessment has occurred of significant harm to users or wider society. At the other end of the spectrum, a longstanding knowledge base in relation to a substance (ketamine for example, used for decades in veterinary, paediatric and palliative practice) is no guarantee of its utility where a drug is taken up as a recreational substance, where different patterns of use may lead to harms not previously identified (e.g. Cottrell *et al.*, 2008, where bladder problems are increasingly being linked to chronic recreational ketamine use). Government policy therefore treads a thin line between playing 'catch up' and pre-emptive force.

Concluding remarks

Throughout the 14 years of this longitudinal study, tracking individual drugs careers enabled us to identify the enormous changes which occur from adolescence well into adulthood regarding trying and using drugs. Whilst in their teens, the general trend is towards greater experimentation and in their twenties the general trend is away from drug use; it is notable that beyond this, there is considerable change, including initiation and experimentation well into mid adulthood. Any future study into drug use should not overlook the considerable number of these adult first-time users and the possibilities of diverse drug careers extending into these users' thirties, forties and beyond.

References

Advisory Council on the Misuse of Drugs (2008) *Cannabis: Classification and Public Health*, London: Home Office.

Advisory Council on the Misuse of Drugs (2009) *MDMA ('Ecstasy'): A Review of its Harms and Classification under the Misuse of Drugs Act 1971*, London: Home Office.

Advisory Council on the Misuse of Drugs (2012, forthcoming) *Polysubstance Use*, London: Home Office.

Aitken, P.P. (1978) *Ten-to-Fourteen Year Olds and Alcohol*, Edinburgh: HMSO.

Alcohol Concern (2001) *Alcohol Concern Fact Sheet: Alcopops*. January.

Aldridge, J. (2008) 'Decline but no fall? New millennium trends in young people's use of illegal and illicit drugs in Britain', *Health Education* 108(3): 189–206.

Aldridge, J. and Measham, F. (1997) 'Methodological issues surrounding the measurement of self-reported drinking frequency with youthful respondents', unpublished working paper.

Aldridge, J., Measham, F. and Parker, H. (1996) *Drugs Pathways in the 1990s: Adolescents' Decision Making About Illicit Drug Use*, London: Drugs Prevention Initiative, Home Office.

Aldridge, J., Medina, J. and Ralphs, R. (2010) 'The problem of proliferation: guidelines for improving the security of qualitative data in a digital age', *Research Ethics Review* 6(1): 3–9.

Aldridge, J., Parker, H., *et al.* (1999) *Drug Trying and Drug Use Across Adolescence*, London: Home Office, DPAS Paper 1.

Anderson, P., Bruijn, A., Angus, K., Gordon, R. and Hastings, G. (2009) 'Impact of alcohol advertising and media exposure on adolescent alcohol use: A systematic review of longitudinal studies', *Alcohol and Alcoholism*, 44(3): 229–243.

Aust, R., Sharp, C. and Goulden, C. (2002) *Prevalence of Drug Use: Key Findings from the 2001/2 British Crime Survey*, Findings 182, London: Home Office.

Bachman, J. G., Wadsworth, K. N., O'Malley, P. M., Johnston, L. D. and Schulenberg, J. E. (1997) *Smoking, Drinking and Drug Use in Young*

Adulthood: The Impacts of New Freedoms and Responsibilities, New Jersey: Lawrence Elbaum Associates.

Balding, J. (1997) *Young People in 1996*, University of Exeter: Schools Health Education Unit.

Balding, J. (2000) *Young People and Illegal Drugs into 2000*, University of Exeter: Schools Health Education Unit.

Balding, J. and Regis, J. (1996) 'More alcohol down fewer throats', *Education and Health* 13(4): 61–64.

Bannister, J., Fyfe, N. and Kearns, A. (2006) 'Respectable or respectful? (In)civility and the city', *Urban Studies*, 43(5/6): 919–937.

Barnard, M. and Forsyth, A. (1998) 'Alcopops and under-age drinking: changing trends in drink preference', *Health Education*, 6: 208–212.

Barnard, M., Forsyth, A. and McKeganey, N. (1996) 'Levels of drug use among a sample of Scottish school children', *Drugs: Education, Prevention and Policy*, 3(1): 81–90.

Bauman, A. and Phongsavan, P. (1999) 'Epidemiology of substance use in adolescence: prevalence, trends and policy implications', *Drug and Alcohol Dependence*, 55(3): 187–207.

Beck, U. (1992) *Risk Society: Towards a New Modernity*, London: Sage.

Becker, H. (1963) *Outsiders: Studies in the Sociology of Deviance*, New York: Free Press.

Best, D. (2004) *Delivering Better Treatment: What Works and Why?* NTA National Conference, London.

Black, N. (2001) 'Evidence based policy: proceed with care', *BMJ*, 4 August, 323(7307): 275–279.

Blackman, S. (2004) *Chilling Out: The Cultural Politics of Substance Consumption, Youth and Drug Policy*, Maidenhead: OUP.

Blackman, S. (2007), in M. Simpson, T. Shildrick and R. MacDonald (eds) *Drugs in Britain: Supply, Consumption and Control*, Basingstoke: Palgrave Macmillan.

Boreham, R. and Shaw, A. (eds) (2002) *Drug Use, Smoking and Drinking Among Young People in England in 2001*, London: Department of Health, The Stationery Office.

Brain, K. and Parker, H. (1997) *Drinking with Design: Alcopops, Designer Drinks and Youth Culture*, London: The Portman Group.

Brandt, S., Sumnall, H., Measham, F., and Cole, J. (2010a) 'Second generation mephedrone: The confusing case of NRG-1', *British Medical Journal*, 6 July, 341:c3564 Online. Available: <http://www.bmj.com/cgi/content/full/341/jul06_1/c3564> (accessed 22 July 2010).

Brandt, S., Sumnall, H., Measham, F. and Cole, J. (2010b) 'Analyses of second generation "legal highs" in the UK', *Drug Testing and Analysis*, 2(8): 377–382.

Carnwath, T. and Smith, I. (2002) *Heroin Century*, London: Routledge.

Catalano, R. F. and Hawkins, J. D. (1996) 'The Social Development Model: A theory of antisocial behaviour', in J. D. Hawkins (ed.) *Delinquency and Crime: Current Theories*, New York: Cambridge University Press.

Coffield, F. and Gofton, L. (1994) *Drugs and Young People*, London: Institute for Public Policy Research.

Coles, B. (1995) *Youth and Social Policy: Youth Citizenship and Young Careers*, London: UCL Press.

Collin, M. (1997) *Altered State: The Story of Ecstasy Culture and Acid House*, London: Serpent's Tail.

Collins, L., Graham, J., Hansen, W. and Johnson, C. (1985) 'Agreement between retrospective accounts of substance use and earlier reported substance use', *Applied Psychological Measurement* 9(3): 301–309.

Condon, J. and Smith, N. (2003) *Prevalence of Drug Use: Key Findings from the 2002/3 British Crime Survey*, Findings 229, London: Home Office.

Cottrell, A., Athreeres, R., Weinstock, P., Warren, K. and Gillatt, D. (2008) 'Urinary tract disease associated with chronic ketamine use', *Letters, BMJ*, 336: 973.

Crawford, A. and Flint, J. (2009) 'Urban safety, anti-social behaviour and the night-time economy', *Criminology and Criminal Justice*, 9(4): 403–413.

Critcher, C. (2000) ' "Still raving": Social reaction to Ecstasy', *Leisure Studies*, 19(3): 145–162.

Daily Express (1995) 'You hate drugs? You're a deviant', 25 July, p. 7.

Daily Mail (2007a) 'Boy on skunk cannabis butchered a grandmother', 3 April. Online. Available: <http://www.dailymail.co.uk/news/article-446318/Boy-skunk-cannabis-butchered-grandmother.html> (accessed 22 July 2010).

Daily Mail (2007b) 'Smoking just one cannabis joint raises danger of mental illness by 40 per cent' 26 July. Online. Available: <http://www. dailymail. co.uk/news/article-471106/Smoking-just-cannabis-joint-raises-danger-mental-illness-40.html> (accessed 22 July 2010).

Davies, A. (1992) *Leisure, Gender and Poverty: Working-Class Culture in Salford and Manchester, 1900–1939*, Buckingham: Open University Press.

Denscombe, M. (2001) 'Uncertain identities and health-risking behaviour: The case of young people and smoking in late modernity', *British Journal of Sociology*, 52(1): 157–178.

Department of Health (1995) *Sensible Drinking: The Report of an Inter-Departmental Working Group*, December, London: HMSO.

Di Forti, M., Morgan, C., Dazzan, P., Pariante, C., Mondelli, V., Reis Marques, T., Handley, R., Luzi, S., Russo, M., Paparelli, A., Butt, A., Stilo, S. A., Wiffen, B., Powell, J. and Murray, R. M. (2009) 'High-potency cannabis and the risk of psychosis', *British Journal of Psychiatry*, 195: 488–491.

Dorn, N. and Murji, K. (1992) *Drug Preventions: A Review of the English Language Literature*, London: Institute for the Study of Drug Dependency.

DrugScope (2009) 'DrugScope Street Drug Trends Survey 2009', 11 September. Online. Available: <http://www.drugscope.org.uk/ourwork/pressoffice/press releases/street_drug_trends_2009> (accessed 1 February 2010).

Duff, C. (2005) 'Party drugs and party people: Examining the "normalisation" of recreational drug use in Melbourne, Australia', *International Journal of Drug Policy*, 16: 161–170.

Duff, C. (2008) 'The pleasure in context', *International Journal of Drug Policy*, 19(5): 384–392.

Duffy, D. and Cuddy, K. (2008) *Merseyside DIP Clients: A Comparison of Client Characteristics for Under and Over 25 Year Olds*, Liverpool: Centre for Public Health, JMU.

Duffy, J. (1991) *Trends in Alcohol Consumption Patterns 1978–1989*, Oxon: NTC.

EMCDDA (2009) *Annual report on the state of the drugs problem in Europe*, Lisbon: The European Monitoring Centre for Drugs and Drug Addiction.

Ettorre, E. (1992) *Women and Substance Use*, Basingstoke: Macmillan.

Ettorre, E. (2007) *Revisioning Women and Drug Use: Gender, Power and the Body*, Basingstoke: Palgrave Macmillan.

Fendrich, M. and Rosenbaum, D. P. (2003) 'Recanting of substance use reports in a longitudinal prevention study', *Drug and Alcohol Dependence*, 70: 241–253.

Fillmore, K. (1988) *Alcohol Use Across the Life Course*, Toronto: Addiction Research Foundation.

Forsyth, A. (2001) 'A design for strife: Alcopops, licit drug – familiar scare story', *International Journal of Drug Policy*, 12(1): 59–80.

Fossey, E. (1992) 'Personal communication' (quoted in Plant and Plant, 1992).

Furlong, A. and Cartmel, F. (1997) *Young People and Social Change*, Buckingham: Open University Press.

Giddens, A. (1991) *Modernity and Self Identity*, Oxford: Polity.

Gilman, M. (1998) 'Onion rings to go: social exclusion and addiction', *Druglink*, May/June: 15–18.

Goddard, E. (1996) *Teenage Drinking in 1994*, London: OPCS.

Goddard, E. (2007) *Estimating alcohol consumption from survey data: Updated method of converting volumes to units*, National Statistics Methodological Series No. 37, Newport: ONS.

Goddard, E. (1991) *Drinking in England and Wales in the Late 1980s*, London: HMSO.

Goddard, E. and Ikin, E. (1988) *Drinking in England and Wales in 1987*, London: HMSO.

Graham, H. (1989) 'Women and smoking in the United Kingdom: the implications for health promotion', *Health Promotion*, 3(4): 371–382.

Graham, H. (1994) 'Surviving by smoking', in S. Wilkinson and C. Kitzinger (eds), *Women and Health: Feminist Perspectives*, London: Taylor & Francis.

Graham, H. and Blackburn, C. (1998) 'The socio-economic patterning of health and smoking behaviour among mothers with young children on income support', *Sociology of Health and Illness*, 20(2): 215–240.

Graham, J. and Bowling, B. (1995) *Young People and Crime*, Home Office Research Study 145, London: Home Office.

Gregory, J. (2009) 'Too young to drink, too old to dance: The influences of age and gender on (non) rave participation', *Dancecult*, 1(1).

Griffin, C., Bengry-Howell, A., Hackley, C., Mistral, W. and Szmigin, I. (2009)

' "Every time I do it I absolutely annihilate myself": Loss of (self-) consciousness and loss of memory in young people's drinking narratives', *Sociology*, 43(3): 457–476.

Guardian (1995) 'Drug culture opening new generation gap', 25 July, p. 2.

Guardian (1998) 'Leap in numbers cautioned for having cannabis', *The Guardian* 29 January (based on Commons written reply to Paul Flynn, MP).

HM Government (1994) *Tackling Drugs Together: A Consultation Document on a Strategy for England 1995–1998*, London: HMSO.

HM Government (1998) *Tackling Drugs to Build a Better Britain: The Government's Ten-Year Strategy for Tackling Drugs Misuse*, Cm 3945, London: The Stationery Office.

HM Government (2002) *Updated Drug Strategy*, London: Home Office.

HM Government (2007) *Safe, Sensible, Social: The Next Steps in the National Alcohol Strategy*, London: TSO.

HM Government (2008) *Drugs: Protecting Families and Communities*, London: HMSO.

HM Government (2010) *Drug Strategy 2010 Reducing Demand, Restricting Supply, Building Recovery: Supporting People to Live a Drug Free Life*, London: HMSO.

Hadfield, P. and Measham, F. (2009) 'A review of nightlife and crime in England and Wales', in P. Hadfield (ed.) *Nightlife and Crime*, Oxford: Oxford University Press, pp.17–48.

Hadfield, P., Lister, S. and Traynor, P. (2009) ' "This town's a different town today": Policing and regulating the night-time economy', *Criminology and Criminal Justice*, 9(4): 465–485.

Hales, J., Nevill, C., Pudney, S. and Tipping, S. (2009) *Longitudinal Analysis of the Offending, Crime and Justice Survey 2003–06*, London: Home Office Research Report 17.

Hand, T. and Rishiraj, A. S. (2009) *Seizures of Drugs in England and Wales 2008/09*, London: Home Office Statistical Bulletin 16/09.

Harrison, B. (1971) *Drink and the Victorians*, London: Faber and Faber.

Hawker, A. (1978) *Adolescents and Alcohol*, London: Edsall.

Health Education Authority (1996) *Drug Realities*, London: HEA.

Health Education Authority (1996) *Young People and Alcohol*, London: HEA.

Hellawell, K. (2002) *The Outsider: The Autobiography of One of Britain's Most Controversial Policemen*, London: HarperCollins.

Henderson, S. (1997) *Ecstasy: Case Unsolved*, London: Pandora.

Hibell, B., Andersson, B., Bjarnason, T., Ahlstrom, S., Balakieva, O., and Morgan, M. (2004) *The 2003 ESPAD Report. Alcohol and Other Drug Use Among Students in 35 European Countries*, Stockholm, The Swedish Council for Information on Alcohol and Other Drugs (CAN) and the Pompidou Group at the Council of Europe.

Hibell, B., Guttormsson, U., Shlstrom, S., Balakireva, O., Bjarnason, T., Kokkevi, A., and Kraus, L. (2009) *The 2007 ESPAD Report. Substance Use*

Among Students in 35 European Countries, Stockholm: The Swedish Council for Information on Alcohol and Other Drugs (CAN) and the Pompidou Group at the Council of Europe.

Hoare, J. (2009) *Drug Misuse Declared: Findings from the 2008–09 British Crime Survey*, London: Home Office, Home Office Statistical Bulletin.

Hoare, J. and Moon, D. (2010) *Drug Misuse Declared: Findings from the 2009/10 British Crime Survey*, London: Home Office.

Hobbs, D., Hadfield, P., Lister, S. and Winlow, S. (2003) *Bouncers: Violence and Governance in the Night-time Economy*, Oxford: Oxford University Press.

Hough, M. and Hunter, G. (2008) 'The Licensing Act's impact on crime and disorder: an evaluation', *Criminology and Criminal Justice*, 8(3): 239–260.

Hough, M., Hunter, G., Jacobson, J. and Cossalter, S. (2008) 'The impact of the Licensing Act 2003 on levels of crime and disorder: An evaluation', *Research Report 04*, London: Home Office.

House of Commons Public Accounts Committee (2009) *Reducing Alcohol Harm: Health Services in England for Alcohol Misuse*, London: The Stationery Office Ltd.

Huggins, R. (2007) 'Systematic "normalisation"? – Mapping and interpreting policy responses to illicit drug use', in P. Manning (ed.) *Drugs and Popular Culture: Drugs, Media and Identity in Contemporary Society*, Cullompton: Willan, pp. 260–277.

Hughes, K., MacKintosh, A.M., Hastings, G., Wheeler, C., Watson, J. and Inglis, J. (1997) 'Young people, alcohol and designer drinks: quantitative and qualitative study', *British Medical Journal*, 314.

Humphreys, D. and Eisner, M. (2010) 'Evaluating a natural experiment in alcohol policy: The Licensing Act (2003) and the requirement for attention to implementation', *Criminology and Public Policy*, 9(1): 41–67.

Hunt, N. and Stevens, A. (2004) 'Whose harm? Harm reduction and the shift to coercion in UK drug policy', *Social Policy & Society*, 3(4): 333–342.

Hurst, A., Parker, H., Marr, A., and McVeigh, J.(2009) *AACCE (Non Opiate) Substance Use in the North West of England: The Changing Profile of Substance Users Engaged in Treatment and its Implications for Future Provision*, Liverpool: JMU/Centre for Public Health.

Jackson, P. (2004) *Inside Clubbing: Sensual Experiments in the Art of Being Human*, Oxford: Berg.

Jahoda, G. and Cramond, J. (1972) *Children with Alcohol: A Developmental Study in Glasgow*, London: HMSO.

James, W. H., Kim, G. K. and Moore, D. D. (1997) 'Examining racial and ethnic differences in Asian adolescent drug use: the contributions of culture, background and lifestyle', *Drugs: Education, Prevention and Policy*, 4(1): 39–51.

Jamieson, J. (2009) 'New Labour, youth justice and the question of "respect" ', *Youth Justice*, 5(3): 180–193.

Järvinen, M. and Demant, J. (2010) 'The normalization of cannabis use among young people – symbolic boundary work in focus groups', *Health, Risk and Society*.

Jotangia, D. and J. Thompson (2009) *'Drug use' Smoking, Drinking and Drug Use Among Young People in England in 2008*, E. Fuller, London: NHS Information Centre for Health and Social Care, pp. 125–165.

Kandel, D. B. (1980) 'Drug and drinking behaviour among youth', *Annual Review of Sociology*, 6: 235–285.

Klein, A. (2008) *Drugs and the World*, London: Reaktion.

Kohn, M. (1987) *Narcomania: On Heroin*, London: Faber and Faber

Laub, J. H. and Sampson, R. J. (2003) *Shared beginnings, Divergent Lives: Delinquent boys to age 70*, Cambridge, MA: Harvard University Press.

LeBlanc, M. (1997) 'A generic control theory of the criminal phenomenon: The structural and dynamical statements of an integrative multilayered control theory', *Advances in Criminological Theory*, 8: 215–285.

Leitner, M., Shapland, J., and Wiles, P. (1993) *Drug Usage and Prevention*, London: Home Office.

Lemmens, P. (1994) 'The alcohol content of self-report and "standard" drinks', *Addiction*, 89: 593–601.

Leon, D. A. and McCambridge, J. (2006) 'Liver cirrhosis mortality rates in Britain from 1950 to 2002: an analysis of routine data', *The Lancet*, 367(9504): 52–56.

MacDonald, R. and Marsh, J. (2002) 'Crossing the Rubicon: youth transitions, poverty, drugs and social exclusion', *International Journal of Drug Policy*, 13(1): 27–38.

MacDonald, R. and Shildrick, T. (2007) 'Street corner society: Leisure careers, youth (sub)culture and social exclusion', *Leisure Studies*, 26(3): 339–355.

Macleod, J. and Hickman, M. (2010) 'How ideology shapes the evidence and the policy: what do we know about cannabis use and what should we do', *Addiction*, 105: 1326–1330.

Marsh, A., Dobbs, J. and White, A. (1986) *Adolescent Drinking*, London: HMSO.

Marsh, P. and Fox Kibby, K (1992) *Drinking and Public Disorder*, London: Portman.

Marsh, P., Rosser, E. and Harré, R. (1978) *The Rules of Disorder*, London: Routledge and Kegan Paul.

Maruna, S. and H. Copes (2005) 'Excuses, excuses: what have we learned from five decades of neutralisation research?' *Crime and Justice: A Review of Research*, 32: 221–320.

Matza, D. (1964). *Delinquency and Drift*, New York, John Wiley.

May, C. (1992) 'A burning issue? Adolescent alcohol use in Britain', *Alcohol and Alcoholism* 27(2): 109–115.

McCrystal, P. (2009) 'The Belfast Youth Development Study: A longitudinal study of the onset and development of adolescent drug use', *One Day Symposium: Cohort Studies and Substance Use: Implications for Analysis, Theory and Intervention*, Nuffield College, University of Oxford.

McElrath, K. and McEvoy, K. (2001) 'Heroin as evil: Ecstasy users' perceptions about heroin', *Drugs: Education, Prevention and Policy*, 8(2): 177–189.

McKeganey, N. *et al.* (1996) 'Designer drinks and drunkenness amongst a sample of Scottish school children', *British Medical Journal*, 313, 17 August: 401.

McVie, S. and Bradshaw, P. (2005) *Adolescent Smoking, Drinking and Drug Use. The Edinburgh Study of Youth Transitions and Crime*, Number 7, University of Edinburgh: Centre for Law and Society.

Measham, F. (1996) 'The "big bang" approach to sessional drinking: changing patterns of alcohol consumption amongst young people in north west England', *Addiction Research*, 4(3): 283–299.

Measham, F. (2002) ' "Doing gender" – "doing drugs": Conceptualising the gendering of drugs cultures', *Contemporary Drug Problems*, 29(2): 335–373.

Measham, F. (2004a) 'The decline of ecstasy, the rise of "binge" drinking and the persistence of pleasure', *Probation Journal, Special Edition: Rethinking Drugs and Crime*, 51(4): 309–326.

Measham, F. (2004b) 'Drug and alcohol research: The case for cultural criminology', in J. Ferrell, K. Hayward, W. Morrison and M. Presdee (eds), *Cultural Criminology Unleashed*, London: GlassHouse, pp.207–218.

Measham, F. (2008) 'The turning tides of intoxication: Young people's drinking in Britain in the 2000s', *Health Education*, 108(3): 207–222.

Measham, F. and Brain, K. (2005) ' "Binge" drinking, British alcohol policy and the new culture of intoxication', *Crime, Media, Culture: An International Journal*, 1(3): 263–284.

Measham, F. and Moore, K. (2008) 'The criminalisation of intoxication', in P. Squires (ed.), *ASBO Nation: The Criminalisation of Nuisance*, Bristol: Policy, pp.273–288.

Measham, F. and Moore, K. (2009) 'Repertoires of distinction: exploring patterns of weekend polydrug use within local leisure scenes across the English night time economy', *Criminology and Criminal Justice*, 9(4): 437–464.

Measham, F. and Østergaard, J. (2009) 'The public face of binge drinking: British and Danish young women, recent trends in alcohol consumption and the European binge drinking debate', *Probation Journal, Special Issue*, 56(4): 415–434.

Measham, F. and Shiner, M. (2009) 'The legacy of "normalisation": The role of classical and contemporary criminological theory in understanding young people's drug use', *International Journal of Drug Policy*, 20(6): 502–508.

Measham, F., Aldridge, J. and Parker, H. (2001) *Dancing on Drugs: Risk, Health and Hedonism in the British Club Scene*, London, Free Association Books.

Measham, F., Moore, K., Newcombe, R. and Welch, Z. (2010) 'Tweaking, bombing, dabbing and stockpiling: the emergence of mephedrone and the perversity of prohibition', *Drugs and Alcohol Today*, 10(1): 14–21.

Measham, F., Newcombe, R. and Parker, H. (1993) 'The post-heroin generation', *Druglink*, May/June, 8(3): 16–17.

Measham, F., Newcombe, R. and Parker, H. (1994) 'The normalisation of recreational drug use amongst young people in north west England', *British Journal of Sociology*, 45(2): 287–312.

Measham, F., Parker, H. and Aldridge, J. (1998) 'The teenage transition: From adolescent recreational drug use to the young adult dance culture in Britain in the mid-1990s', *Journal of Drug Issues*, 28(1): 9–33.

Messerschmidt, J. (1997) *Crime as Structured Action: Gender, Race, Class, and Crime in the Making*, London: Sage.

Miller, P. and Plant, M. (1996) 'Drinking, smoking and illicit drug use among 15- and 16-year-olds in the United Kingdom', *British Medical Journal*, 313: 394–397.

Miller, W., Heather, N. and Hall, W. (1991) 'Calculating standard drink units: international comparisons', *British Journal of Addiction*, 86: 43–47.

Miller. P. M. and Plant, M. (1996) 'Drinking, smoking and illicit drug use amongst 15 and 16 year olds in the United Kingdom', *British Medical Journal*, 313: 394–397

Mixmag (2010) 'Mixmag drugs survey', *Mixmag*, London: Development Hell Ltd.

Moffitt, T. (1993) 'Adolescence – limited and lifecourse persistent anti-social behaviour: a developmental taxonomy', *Psychological Review*, 100(4): 674–701.

Moon, D., Walker, A., Murphy, R., Flatley, J., Parfrement-Hopkins, J. and Hall, P. (2009) *Perceptions of Crime and Anti-social Behaviour: Findings from the 2008/9 British Crime Survey*, Home Office Statistical Bulletin 17/09, London: Home Office.

Moore, K. (2004) 'A commitment to clubbing', *Peace Review: A Journal of Social Justice*, 16(4): 459–465.

Moore, K. (2010) 'Exploring symbolic emotional and spiritual expression among "crasher clubbers" ', in S. Collins-Mayo and B. Pink-Dandelion (eds) *Religion and Youth*, Aldershot: Ashgate, pp. 89–96.

Moore, K. and Measham, F. (2006) 'Ketamine use: Minimising problems and maximising pleasure', *Drugs and Alcohol Today*, 6(3): 29–32.

Moore, K. and Measham, F. (2008) ' "It's the most fun you can have for twenty quid": motivations, consequences and meanings of British ketamine use', *Addiction Research and Theory*, 16(3): 231–244.

Mott, J. and Mirrlees-Black, C. (1995) *Self-Reported Drug Misuse in England and Wales: Findings from the 1992 British Crime Survey*, London: Home Office Research and Planning Unit Paper 89.

Murji, K. (1998) 'The agony and the ecstasy: drugs, media and mortality', in R. Coomber (ed.) *The Control of Drugs and Drug Users: Reason or Reaction?* Amsterdam: Harwood Academic Publishers, pp.69–85.

Murray, R., Morrison, P., Henquet, C. and DiForti, M. (2007) 'Cannabis, the mind and society: The hash realities', *Nature Reviews Neuroscience*, 8: 885–895.

National Treatment Agency (2009) *Getting to Grips with Substance Misuse amongst Young People*, London: National Treatment Agency for Substance Misuse.

Newbury-Birch, D., White, M. and Kamali, F. (2000) 'Factors influencing alcohol and illicit drug use amongst medical students', *Drug and Alcohol Dependence*, 59(2): 125–130.

Newcombe, R. (1995) *Summary of UK drugs prevalence surveys 1964–94*, Liverpool: 3D Research Bureau.

Newcombe, R., Measham, F. and Parker, H. (1994) 'A survey of drinking and deviant behaviour among 14/15 year olds in north-west England', *Addiction Research*, 2(4): 319–341.

Newton, A. and Hirschfield, A. (2009), 'Violence and the night-time economy: A multi-professional perspective', *Crime Prevention and Community Safety*, 11(3): 147–152.

O'Malley, P. and Valverde, M. (2004) 'Pleasure, freedom and drugs: The uses of "pleasure" in liberal governance of drug and alcohol consumption', *Sociology*, 38(1): 25–42.

Østergaard, J. (2007) 'Mind the gender gap? When boys and girls get drunk at a party', *Nordic Studies on Alcohol and Drugs*, 24(2): 127–148.

Parker, H. (1997) *Managing the Normalisation of Recreational Drug Use Amongst Young Britons*, Leicestershire: Association of Chief Police Officers Drugs Conference.

Parker, H. (2005) 'Normalization as a barometer: recreational drug use and the consumption of leisure by younger Britons', *Addiction Research and Theory*, 13(3): 205.

Parker, H. (2009) 'Drugs Strategy loses its way', *Drink and Drug News*, 4–7 May, London.

Parker, H. and Bottomley, T. (1996) *Crack Cocaine and Drugs Crime Careers*, London: Home Office Publications Unit.

Parker, H. and Egginton, R. (2002) 'Adolescent recreational alcohol and drugs careers gone wrong: Developing a strategy for reducing risks and harms', *International Journal of Drugs Policy*, 13: 419–432.

Parker, H. and Measham, F. (1994) 'Pick 'n' mix: changing patterns of illicit drug use amongst 1990s adolescents', *Drugs: Education, Prevention and Policy*, 1(1): 5–13.

Parker, H. and Williams, L. (2003) 'Intoxicated weekends: Young adults' work hard-play hard lifestyles, public health and public disorder', *Drugs: Education, Prevention and Policy*, 40(4): 345–368.

Parker, H. J., Aldridge, J. and Measham, F. (1998a) *Illegal leisure: The Normalization of Adolescent Recreational Drug Use*, London, New York: Routledge.

Parker, H., Bakx, K. and Newcombe, R. (1988) *Living with Heroin: The Impact of a Drugs 'Epidemic' on an English Community*, Milton Keynes: OUP.

Parker, H., Brain, K. and Bottomley, T. (1998b) *Evolving Crack Cocaine Careers: New Users, Quitters and Long Term Combination Drug Users in N.W. England*, London: Home Office Research and Statistics Directorate.

Parker, H., Egginton, R. and Bury, C. (1998c) *Heroin Outbreaks Amongst Young People in England and Wales at the end of the 1990s*, London: Report to the Police Research Group, Home Office.

Parker, H., Measham, F. and Aldridge, J. (1995) *Drugs Futures: Changing Patterns of Drug Use Amongst English Youth*, London: Institute for Study of Drug Dependency (reprinted 1996).

Parker, H., Williams, L. and Aldridge, J. (2002) 'The normalization of "sensible" recreational drug use: Further evidence from the North West England Longitudinal Study', *Sociology*, 36(4): 941–964.

Parliamentary Office of Science and Technology (1996) *Common Illegal Drugs and their Effects: Cannabis, ecstasy, amphetamines and LSD*, London: Post.

Pearson, G. (1983) *Hooligan. A History of Respectable Fears*, London: Macmillan.

Pearson, G. (1987) *The New Heroin Users*, Oxford: Basil Blackwell.

Pearson, G. (2001) 'Normal drug use: Ethnographic fieldwork among an adult network of recreational drug users in inner London', *Substance Use and Misuse*, 36(1): 167–199.

Pearson, G., Gilman, M. and McIver, S. (1986) *Young People and Heroin: An Examination of Heroin Use in the North of England*, London: Health Education Council.

Pennay, A. and Moore, D. (2010) 'Exploring the micro-politics of normalisation: Narratives of pleasure, self-control and desire in a sample of young Australian "party drug" users', *Addiction Research and Theory*, 18(5): 557–571.

Perri 6, Jupp, B., Perry, H. and Lasky, K. (1997) *The Substance of Youth*, York: Joseph Rowntree Foundation.

Pilkington, H. (2007) 'Beyond "peer pressure": rethinking drug use and "youth culture" ', *International Journal of Drug Policy*, 18(3): 213–224.

Plant, M. and Miller, P. (2000) 'Drug use has declined among teenagers in United Kingdom', *British Medical Journal*, 320: 1536.

Plant, M. and Plant, M. (1992) *Risk-Takers: Alcohol, Drugs, Sex and Youth*, London: Tavistock/Routledge.

Plant, M., Bagnall, G., Foster, J. and Sales, J. (1990) 'Young people and drinking: results of an English national survey', *Alcohol and Alcoholism* 25(6): 685–690.

Plant, M., Peck, D. and Samuel, E. (1985) *Alcohol, Drugs and School Leavers*, London: Tavistock/Routledge.

Prime Minister's Strategy Unit (2004) *Alcohol Harm Reduction Strategy for England*, London: HMSO.

Ramsay, M. and Percy, A. (1996) *Drug Misuse Declared: Results of the 1994 British Crime Survey*, London: Home Office Research Study 151.

Ramsay, M. and Spiller, A. (1997) *Drug Misuse Declared: Results of the 1996 British Crime Survey*. London: Home Office Research Study 172.

Ramsay, M., Baker, P., Goulden, C., Sharp, C. and Sondhi, A. (2001) *Drug Misuse Declared in 2000: Results from the British Crime Survey*, Home Office Research Study No. 224, London: Home Office Research, Development and Statistics Directorate.

Reith, G. (2004) 'On the edge: Drugs and the consumption of risk in late modernity?' in S. Lyng (ed.) *Edgework: The Sociology of Risk-Taking*, New York: Routledge.

Release (1997) *Release Drugs and Dance Survey*, London: Release.

Reuter, P. and Stevens, A. (2007) *An Analysis of UK Drug Policy: A Monograph Prepared for the UK Drug Policy Commission*, London: UK Drug Policy Commission.

Roberts, K. (1995) *Youth and Employment in Modern Britain*, Oxford: Oxford University Press.

Roberts, C., Kingdom, A., Frith, C. and Tudor-Smith, C. (1997) *Young People in Wales: Lifestyle Changes 1986–96*, Cardiff: Heath Promotion Wales.

Roberts, K., Clark, S. and Wallace, C. (1994) 'Flexibility and individualisation: a comparison of transitions into employment in England and Germany', *Sociology*, 28(1): 31–54.

Rowlands, O., Singleton, N., Maher, J. and Higgins, V. (1997) *Living in Britain: Results from the 1995 General Household Survey*, London: Office for National Statistics Social Survey Division.

Royal College of Psychiatrists (1986) *Alcohol our Favourite Drug*, London: Tavistock.

Rutter, M. and Smith, D. (1994) (eds) *Psycho-social Disorders in Young People*, Chichester: John Wiley.

Sampson, R. J. and Laub, J. H. (1993) *Crime in the Making: Pathways and turning points through life*, Cambridge, MA: Harvard University Press.

Saunders, N. (1997) *Ecstasy Reconsidered*, London: Nicholas Saunders.

Scott, M. B. and Lyman, S. M. (1968) 'Accounts', *American Sociological Review*, 33(1): 46–62.

Scottish Council on Alcohol (1996) *Young People and Alcohol in Scotland: A Survey of Branded Preferences of 15–17-year-olds*, Glasgow: SCA.

Seddon, T. (2000) 'Explaining the drug-crime link: theoretical, policy and research issues', *Journal of Social Policy*, 29(1): 95–107.

Seddon, T. (2006) 'Drugs, crime and social exclusion: Social context and social theory in British drugs-crime research', *British Journal of Criminology*, 46(4): 680–703.

Shapiro, H. (1999) 'Dances with drugs: Pop music, drugs and youth culture', in N. South (ed.) *Drugs: Cultures, Controls and Everyday Life*, London: Sage, pp.17–35.

Shildrick, T. (2002) 'Young people, illicit drug use and the question of normalization', *Journal of Youth Studies*, 5(1): 35–48.

Shiner, M. (2009) *Drug Use and Social Change: The Distortion of History*, Basingstoke: Palgrave Macmillan.

Shiner, M. and Newburn, T. (1996) *The Youth Awareness Programme: An Evaluation of a Peer Education Drugs Project*, London: Drugs Prevention Initiative, Home Office.

Shiner, M. and Newburn, T. (1997) 'Definitely, maybe not? The normalisation of recreational drug use amongst young people', *Sociology*, 31(3): 511–529.

Shiner, M. and Newburn, T. (1999) 'Taking tea with Noel: The place and meaning of drug use in everyday life', in N. South (ed.) *Drugs: Cultures, Controls & Everyday Life*, London: Sage, pp.139–159.

Simpson, M. (2003) 'The relationship between drug use and crime: a puzzle inside an enigma', *International Journal of Drug Policy*, 14: 307–319.

Stares, P. (1996) *Global Habit: The Drug Problem in a Borderless World*, Washington: Brookings Institute.

Stockwell, T. (2006) 'Alcohol supply, demand and harm reduction: What is the strongest cocktail?' *International Journal of Drug Policy*, Special Edition: Harm reduction and alcohol policy, 17(4): 269–277.

Sykes, G. M. and Matza, D. (1957) 'Techniques of neutralization: A theory of delinquency', *American Sociological Review*: 664–670.

Thornberry, T. P. (1987) 'Toward an interactional theory of delinquency', *Criminology*, 25: 863–891.

Thornton, S. (1995) *Club Cultures: Music, Media and Subcultural Capital*, Cambridge: Polity Press.

Tuck, M. (1989) *Drinking and Disorder: A Study of Non-Metropolitan Violence*, HORPU Research Report 108, London: HMSO.

Turner, C. (1990) 'How much alcohol is in a "standard drink"? An analysis of 125 studies', *British Journal of Addiction*, 85(1) 171–175.

UK Focal Point on Drugs (2008) *United Kingdom Drug Situation*, London: Department of Health.

Vervaeke, H. K. E. and Korf, D. J. (2006) 'Long-term ecstasy use and the management of work and relationships', *International Journal of Drug Policy*, 17: 484–493.

Wearing, B. *et al.* (1994) 'Adolescent women, identity and smoking: leisure experience as resistance', *Sociology of Health and Illness*, 16(5): 626–643.

Webb, E. *et al.* (1996) 'Alcohol and drug use in UK university students', *Lancet*, 348: 922–925.

Wibberley, C. (1997) 'Young people's feelings about drugs', *Drugs: Education, Prevention and Policy*, 4(1): 65–79.

Williams, L. (2007) *A Lifecourse Perspective on Drug Use from Adolescence to Adulthood: Onset, Continuity, Turning Points and Desistance*, School of Law. Manchester: University of Manchester, Doctor of Philosophy. Online. Available: <http//www.law.manchester.ac.uk/staff/lisa_williams> (accessed 22 July 2010).

Williams, L. and Parker, H. (2001) 'Alcohol, cannabis, ecstasy and cocaine: drugs of reasoned choice amongst young adult recreational drug users in England', *International Journal of Drug Policy*, 12: 397–413.

Williams, L. (forthcoming) *Bridling the Horse: Drug Journeys from Adolescence to Young Adulthood*, London: Willan/Routledge.

Wolfensberger, W. (1972) *The Principal of Normalization in Human Services*, Toronto: National Institute on Mental Retardation.

Wright, J. and Pearl, L. (1990) 'Knowledge and experience of young people regarding drug abuse 1969–1989', *British Medical Journal*, 300: 99–103.

Index

drinks industry 15, 58–9
drinks product choices 55, 57, 58–9,
   67–9, 90–1, 94
Drug Action Teams 18
drug dealing 159–61, 184, 205
drug driving 73, 214
drug offers within cohort 103, 113;
   availability 95–6, 104–6, 114; drug
   pathways analysis 131–2; in-
   transition users 120; via social
   networks 159–61, 191–5
drug pathways analysis 43, 115–55;
   adulthood transitions 135–55;
   alcohol use 133–4, 149–50;
   construction of drug status
   variables 116–18, 141–3; drug
   offers and drug trying 131–2; drugs
   attitude scale 120–2, 144; initial
   developments 115–16; risk-taking
   indicators 134–5; smoking 132–3,
   148–9; validation of drug-user
   categories 118–20, 143
drug purity levels 12, 21, 214
drug strategies (UK) 16–18, 22,
   210–15; *see also* policy responses
drug trying by cohort 96–103;
   adulthood transitions 106–14;
   drug pathways analysis 131–2;
   experiences of 101–3, 111–13;
   former triers 106; impact of
   gender, social class and race
   99–100, 110–11, 112, 114;
   initiation 98, 142–3, 162–4;
   normalisation thesis 203–4, 218;
   reasons for trying drugs 164–8;
   recency of use 98–9, 103, 106,
   107–10, 114
drug use trends 1, 4–25; alcohol use
   13–15; normalisation thesis 222;
   'peak' of the 1990s 5–6; post 2000
   trends 7–13
Drugs Act (2005) 107
drugs attitude scale (DAS) 120–2,
   144
Drugs Futures (1995) 46
Drugs Interventions Programme 18,
   23
*Drugs: Protecting Families and
   Communities* (2008) 18
DrugScope 12

drugwise concept 123, 126, 156, 184,
   185, 189–90, 199, 205
drunkenness 13, 71, 72, 78–9; adult
   alcohol use 85, 86–7, 94;
   'determined' 14, 88; normalisation
   of 88, 223

E *see* ecstasy
Economic and Social Research
   Council (ESRC) 27, 28, 47
ecstasy: access to 191; adulthood
   transitions 105–10, 114, 155, 226;
   alcohol combined with 74;
   availability 158; Class A
   classification 229; 'come down'
   from 190; cost-benefit assessment
   168, 184, 198; dance drug scene 4,
   21, 58, 89; dealing 160; drug offers
   within cohort 96, 104, 105, 113;
   drug use trends 6; early surveys on
   drug use 216; experiences of
   trying 101–2; as 'favourite' drug
   73; former triers 146; friendships
   174–5; initiation 98, 164; in-
   transition users 120, 129; lifetime
   prevalence 97, 106, 107; national
   consumption levels 214; negative
   effects of 178, 181–3;
   normalisation thesis 202, 205, 222;
   past year prevalence 9, 10, 11,
   108–9; policy responses 17, 18;
   polydrug repertoires 21, 22, 190;
   positive effects of 171; risk of
   death 189; social relationships 195
*Edinburgh Study of Youth Transitions
   and Crime* 45
education on drugs 18, 21, 209
education to work transition 195,
   196–7
enforcement 225, 227
enjoyment 87, 169, 170–1, 185, 187
ESPAD *see* European Schools Survey
   Project on Alcohol and Other
   Drugs
ESRC *see* Economic and Social
   Research Council
ethical dilemmas 30–1
European Schools Survey Project on
   Alcohol and Other Drugs
   (ESPAD) 9, 13, 14n11